Language, Authority and Criticism

Language, Authority and Criticism

Readings on the School Textbook

Edited by

Suzanne de Castell
Allan Luke
and
Carmen Luke

The Falmer Press

London . New York . Philadelphia

UK   The Falmer Press, Falmer House, Barcombe, Lewes, East Sussex, BN8 5DL

USA   The Falmer Press, Taylor & Francis Inc., 242 Cherry Street, Philadelphia, PA 19106-1906

First published in 1989

British Library Cataloguing in Publication Data

Language, authority and criticism: readings on the school textbook.
  1. School texts.
  I. de Castell, Suzanne.   II. Luke, Allan.   III. Luke, Carmen.
  371.3'2.

ISBN 1-85000-365-3
ISBN 1-85000-366-1 (Pbk.)

Library of Congress Cataloging-in-Publication Data

Language, authority and criticism.
  Bibliography: p.
  Includes indexes.
  1. Textbooks. I. de Castell, Suzanne.   II. Luke, Allan.
  III. Luke, Carmen.
LB3045.L36   1989   371.3'2   89-3919
ISBN 1-85000-365-3
ISBN 1-85000-366-1 (Pbk.)

Typeset in 10/12 Bembo by
Alresford Typesetting & Design, New Farm Road, Alresford, Hants.

Printed in Great Britain by
Redwood Burn Limited, Trowbridge, Wiltshire.

Contents

Editorial Introduction: Language, Authority and Criticism

Since the advent of the printing press, the literate public has had increasing access to a wide range of texts: religious tracts, broadsheets, novels, newspapers and, more recently, texts for the 'functionally literate', government pamphlets, packages, advertising brochures and application forms. Each historical and contemporary genre of text has served particular social and cultural purposes, and correspondingly has generated varying literary conventions, discursive and linguistic forms and, for targeted audiences, interpretive strategies.

Of the many kinds of text available to the modern reader, the school textbook holds a unique and significant social function: to represent to each generation of students an officially sanctioned, authorized version of human knowledge and culture. Within the context of compulsory public schooling in industrial and post-industrial cultures, textbooks form shared cultural experiences, at times memorable and edifying, while at others eminently forgettable and uneducational.

The appropriate content and form of the school curriculum have always been contested terrain both for the public and for educators. Since the time of Luther and Melanchthon, the design and selection of authorized school texts have reflected educators' and public officials' sense of what, for children, is of moral and educational value. From Spencer's (1890) classic inquiry into *What Knowledge Is of Most Worth?* through Durkheim's (c.1900) sociological analysis of the role of education in cultural preservation, to the linking of curriculum and ideology in the work of Young (1971) and Apple (1979) up to recent work such as Inglis's (1985) critique of the currently selected curricular 'narratives' which today dominate school subject-matter in Britain, or Hirsch's (1987) brutishly conservative proposal for a common culture and a core 'cultural literacy', the central curriculum questions have always concerned the selection of school knowledge and its justification.

What should children read? How should the stories, scientific and historical knowledge — the central expressions of a culture — be taught? Key to these questions is the assumption that in pluralistic, advanced capitalist societies some kind of consensus can or should be reached about what will count as a 'common culture'. For while school promoters in previous centuries could forward an ethos of God and empire as unquestionably virtuous curricular content, claims on what should count as authorized cultural knowledge now must reflect the diversity of social formations, groups and communities in contemporary nation-states.

The institutions and groups involved in the development, adoption and implementation of textbooks comprise a very broad field indeed, and, of course, vary nationally and regionally. In general, the design and selection of textbooks fall to various groups of university trained professional 'experts': curriculum designers, implementers and evaluators, subject-area authors/specialists, publishers' editorial and marketing personnel, and those administrators charged with responsibility for the screening and adoption of texts on a local, regional and national basis. The curriculum field extends wider still. Virtually everyone involved in mass education is implicated in the process of cultural selection: educational psychologists, applied linguists and literary critics are consulted; parents and special interest groups monitor texts for objectionable moral, religious and political content; and, of course, teachers and students on a daily basis include, omit and emphasize.

It is particularly to those who work directly with school texts — educators, administrators and researchers — that this volume is directed. Throughout their university training, teachers and researchers are taught how to evaluate and teach specific texts. They might be introduced to any one of a number of scales for assessing grade-level readability; they might learn to evaluate textual cohesion; or they might be instructed to identify sexist, racist or social class bias in textbooks. More practically, teachers are taught how to decipher and enact the instructions provided in publishers' 'teachers' guides'. For their part, educational researchers acquaint themselves with models of curricular design and evaluation, so that they can assess 'objectively' the worth and efficiency of particular textbooks in transmitting identifiable skills, knowledge and competences. For all this specialized training, however, rarely are future teachers or researchers given pause to consider the unique status of the textbook as the primary medium of formal education, nor to consider the variety of theoretical and practical questions to which that status gives rise.

This collection, then, is an attempt to draw from the diverse range of cross-disciplinary inquiry on the school textbook a set of essays which identifies the kinds of issues teachers, curriculum developers, subject-area specialists, educational psychologists and sociologists need to confront in order to make informed conscientious decisions regarding textbook content, form, selection and use. We have restricted our coverage to include only those subject-matters whose codification systems are primarily linguistic; this has meant the exclusion of discussions on mathematics, many aspects of the sciences, art, music and the 'televisual' text. Our purpose is not to provide yet another taxonomy or system for assessing which texts to adopt, but rather to render problematic the very process of textbook construction, selection and use. We have tried throughout to represent a broad range of themes and approaches to the study of textbooks and have drawn on the current work of scholars from North America, Europe and Australia.

The essays in this anthology are organized into four main themes: textbook knowledge, textbook form, textbook production, and textbook language, authority and criticism. First and most clearly evident are questions about the *content* of a text: its semantic structures, formulae or illustrations. At this initial level of inquiry into textbook content, then, the first set of questions is concerned with selection, omission and censorship. Why present *this* knowledge, *this* literature, *these* ideas, *these* particular approaches? Why not others? As curriculum theorist Dennis Lawton (1975) reminds us, the school curriculum represents a '*selection* from culture.' Raymond Williams's discussion (Chapter 5) of the selective tradition invites us to explore questions about *whose* culture is selected at a given point in a culture's history, and why some knowledge appears to be essential or 'canonical' for the demarcation of a discipline, while other knowledge appears to be marginalized, disregarded, even intentionally excluded or censored. Many of the essays in Part I draw central concepts and a general analytical direction from Williams's work.

Part II, on textbook form, moves from the analysis of curricular content, the overt messages conveyed by the curriculum, to a consideration of form. This set of concerns encompasses rhetorical, literary, graphic and material aspects of textbooks. The presupposition of 'content analysis' in the past has been that what a text (literally) says is what it (figuratively) means; and this is at best a dubious assumption, increasingly so with the emerging corpus of scholarship from literary theorists, semioticians, linguists and rhetorical theorists on the character of textual discourse. What is called for at this level is exploration of the ideational and figurative structuring of textual knowledge.

The 'formal cause' of the curriculum is the level of analysis represented in Part III of this anthology. This is the background of text production and selection, of which neither students nor teachers are generally made explicitly aware. Thus it has not been an area which typically has been given great thought. In trying to provide readers with some sense of the social and economic forces which mediate the development, publication and adoption of textbooks and which ultimately influence what will count as school knowledge for children, the third section of the book includes discussions of the textbook publishing industry, the prospects and pitfalls of local publishing as an alternative to the multinational corporations' production of learning materials, and the legal and political constraints which influence textbook adoption and censorship.

This level of inquiry matters because the way textbooks are designed and produced, selected and finally authorized for use in public schools appears to have a significant impact on the *criticizability* of texts — something which is obviously of central interest and importance to educators.

Scholarship in the field of literacy studies has contributed to understanding how the separation of writer, reader, text, message and context — made possible through the material and symbolic representation of human understanding in the form of the written word — enables and encourages both orthodoxy on the one hand and heresy on the other; both dogmatism on the one hand and critical analysis and reflection on the other. The idea that it is the medium of the written word which simultaneously gives textbooks their authority and their criticizeability brings us to the fourth and final section of the book, which deals with how textual knowledge may be differently constructed and reconstructed in the context of institutional use.

The central question in Part IV is how students, teachers and textbooks contribute to the production of 'the curriculum'. As Heath (1982) has noted, social interaction centring on a text can best be viewed as a 'literacy event'. Reading and writing practices are socially constructed, culture-specific, and rule-governed. Across different classroom contexts, and even within the same classroom, teachers may structure literacy events quite differently for different individuals and groups of learners, who may, despite use of identical textbooks, emerge from instruction with differing versions of the same textual 'content'. The concern with the instructional mediation of textbook knowledge encompasses questions of who defines 'the curriculum', of whether the curriculum can be 'preserved' and 'transmitted' in textual form, and of how literary and material form *itself* can pre-figure meanings and interpretations for both students and teachers.

This leads us to the question of potentially diverse rhetorical and interpretive communities, and to a recognition that debate and controversy over what should be taught may stem not only from epistemological questions about the nature and justification of educational knowledge, but also from social, ethical and political questions about the vastly unequal conditions under which people live within what is often only in name the 'same' society, a 'common' culture. What makes school knowledge worthwhile and meaningful depends upon the life it has after and outside the school. Clearly, different social lives make quite different the meaning and worth of the same school knowledge.

Inviting readers to explore at increasingly covert and complex levels the epistemological presuppositions of presenting curriculum content in textbook form will, we hope, sharpen the perception and inform the practice of educators who today, as in the past, are responsible for the educational well-being of students from a diversity of interpretive communities — for whom, by whom and with whom the meanings and values of textual knowledge can and must be differently made.

We should like to acknowledge the assistance of the Social Science and Humanities Research Council of Canada, of Christine Cox at Falmer Press, and to thank the many contributors and colleagues who worked with us on this project, especially our co-workers, Eileen Mallory, Devi Pabla, Surjeet Siddoo and Shirley Heap, to whom this book is dedicated.

Acknowledgement

Raymond Williams passed away while this volume was in final stages of completion. The editors would like to acknowledge his continuing influence on their work and that of others in the fields of educational and cultural studies.

References

APPLE, M.W. (1979) *Ideology and Curriculum*. London: Routledge and Kegan Paul.

DURKHEIM, E. (1956) *Education and Sociology*. (Trans.) S.D. Fox. New York: The Free Press.

HEATH, S.B. (1982) 'Protean shapes in literacy events: Ever-shifting oral and literate traditions,' in TANNER, D. (Ed.), *Spoken and Written Language; Exploring Orality and Literacy*. Norwood, N.J.: Ablex.

HIRSCH, E.D. (1987) *Cultural Literacy*. Boston, Mass.: Houghton Mifflin.

INGLIS, F. (1985) *The Management of Ignorance: A Political Economy of the Curriculum*. Oxford: Basil Blackwell.

LAWTON, D. (1975) *Class, Culture and the Curriculum*. London: Routledge and Kegan Paul.

SPENCER, H. (1890/1966) *Education: Intellectual, Moral, and Physical*. Osnabrück: Otto Zeller.

YOUNG, M.F.D. (Ed.) (1971) *Knowledge and Control*. London: Collier-Macmillan.

Part I
Textbook Knowledge

Chapter 1

Hegemony and Literary Tradition in the United States

Alan Wald
University of Michigan

The issue of hegemony and literary tradition in the United States is one that urgently requires extensive and highly detailed investigation. In order to provide a precise focus and to allow room for the analysis of several texts, I shall confine myself in this essay to only one aspect of the larger issue: the treatment of racial minorities in college literary anthologies. Obviously such texts play a major role in shaping the preconceptions of future teachers as well as others who are regarded as authoritative spokespersons for critical interpretation and evaluation in a society.

My contention is that what is usually referred to as the United States (or, even worse, 'American') 'literary tradition' or 'canon' of major works, as codified in classroom texts and anthologies as well as in conventional literary histories, is neither a scientifically determined nor an arbitrary phenomenon. Regardless of the subjective intentions and rationalizations of the literary historians and anthologists themselves, the dominant tradition objectively serves dominant class interests and thus contributes to the maintenance of a class society.

This means that the United States literary 'tradition' is actually a *selective* tradition that ratifies certain works as important and excludes others, not according to any measurable standard of quality but in response to the national self-consciousness as registered among, and interpreted by, privileged social layers, within the limitations of a certain world view at different historical junctures. This analysis of the underlying function of tradition does not mean that theories of aesthetic quality are irrelevant to its making, or that market considerations are beside the point, or that the canonizers and anthologists are without autonomy. But it does suggest that these and many other mediating factors in the process of canon formation are subordinate to deep-rooted cultural prejudices and prevailing social trends.

Here one might adapt a famous statement by Karl Marx: 'Literary scholars and anthologists make their own literary canon, but they do not make it just as they please; they do not make it under circumstances chosen by themselves, but under circumstances directly encountered, given, and transmitted from the past.' A cogent elaboration of this theoretical perspective is offered by Raymond Williams (see Chapter 5, this volume):

> From a whole possible area of past and present, certain meanings and practices are selected for emphasis and certain other meanings and practices are neglected or excluded. Yet, within a particular hegemony, and as one of its decisive processes, this selection is presented and usually successfully passed off as 'the tradition', 'the significant past'. What has then to be said about any tradition is that it is in this sense an aspect of contemporary social and cultural organization, in the interest of the dominance of a specific class. It is a version of the past which is intended to connect with and ratify the present. What if offers in practice is a sense of predisposed continuity (p. 58).

Thus it seems fair to conclude that literary tradition *is* largely *an ideology*; that is, an expression of what Marx called 'definite forms of social consciousness', expressing the interests of groups and classes. As ideology, literary tradition serves, among other things, to organize, monitor and transform power in society (Eagleton, 1975, p. 6; see also Therborn, 1980). This is why, according to Table I of United States literature anthologies used in undergraduate and graduate courses during the past decades, there were few works by women and Blacks in the standard texts until those particular sectors of the population revolted anew in the 1960s and 1970s. Then, retrospectively, certain writers and books (although far too few) became partially integrated into the canon. The belated inclusion of Kate Chopin and Charles W. Chestnutt in many of these anthologies is an example of the revision of the canon under social pressure.

Moreover, the preface to the 1979 edition of the *Norton Anthology of American Literature* reports that the editors decided to make the changes that appear in the new version, including the addition of more female and Black writers, after polling 1700 teachers (Gottesman *et al.*, 1979, p. xxiii). In other words, these 1700 teachers suddenly voted the culture of women and Afro-Americans into existence, as far as this canon-making textbook is concerned. What will it take before these same teachers or their counterparts decide to vote Chicano, Native American Indian, Puerto Rican, Asian American, gay, working-class, and other non-dominant cultures into existence as well?

A further point I wish to argue in this essay, and to demonstrate by example, is that cultural hegemony — that is, in Antonio Gramsci's conception, rule by consent, with which the ideology of literary tradition is ultimately bound up — operates so subtly that even the *terms* in which we learn to evaluate culture are biased in favour of Euro-American patriarchal culture, in which Shakespeare is the paradigm for great literature while oral and folk cultures are often regarded as inferior.[1]

Table 1. *American Literature Anthologies Currently in Use*

Title of text	Total number of contributors	White females	Black males	Black females	American Indians	Chicanos	Puerto Ricans	Asian Americans
Major Writers of America (Harcourt, Brace and World, 1962)	28	1	0	0	0	0	0	0
American Literature (Washington Square, 1966), 3 vols, 18th and 19th centuries only	108	7	0	0	0	0	0	0
American Poetry and Prose (Houghton Mifflin, 1970), 5th ed.	102	8	9	2	0	0	0	0
Anthology of American Literature (Macmillan, 1974), 2 vols.	124	10	7	2	0	0	0	0
Literature of America (Wiley, 1978)	127	17	23	3	19[a]	0	0	0
The Norton Anthology of American Literature (1979), 2 vols.	131	25	12	2	0	0	0	0
Major American Short Stories (Oxford, 1980)	34	8	2	0	0	0	0	0
American Literary Survey (Viking, 1980), 3rd expanded ed.	119	15	10	2	0	0	0	0
Magill Surveys in American Literature (Salem, 1980), 4 vols.	147	28	9	2	0	0	0	0
The American Tradition in Literature (Random House, 1981)	164	28	8	1	14[b]	0	0	0

Notes:
[a] All the contributions are anonymous except for one by N. Scott Momaday and four speeches.
[b] All the contributions are anonymous.

United States Culture

The mechanism of bourgeois hegemony is very visibly at work in the conventional notions of 'American literature' or 'American culture' that most students in the United States receive. Merely to talk as if there exists in the United States a single, only moderately differentiated, clearly identifiable literature or culture is a dangerously misleading simplification that misrepresents the entire history of the formation of the United States as a modern nation.

This one-sided history is dispensed in the introduction to many of the anthologies listed in Table 1, as well as in standard literary histories such as *The Literature of the United States* by Marcus Cunliffe, who writes: 'America is, of course, an extension of Europe in Europe's expansionist phase. It has been peopled mainly by Europeans. The "involuntary immigrants" — Negro slaves — from Africa are an exception, and their presence has modified American society . . . . Culturally speaking, America might be called a European colony' (Cunliffe, 1968, pp. 14). More popularized versions of this history from the point of view of the victors are dispensed in television shows, movies, comic books and patriotic ceremonies on national holidays, in which there is usually a great deal of talk about 'our Pilgrim forefathers', 'the winning of the West' and, of course, George Washington as 'the father of our country'.

Unfortunately, such symbols of national history hardly explain the reality of North American historical and cultural development. It is true, of course, that *one aspect* of the historical formation of our nation involves European expansionism, Puritan pilgrims, settlers moving westward and the leading role of a wealthy slave-holder named George Washington in fighting the British and serving as president. But this history has only to do with the trans-Atlantic immigrants to the North American continent; that is, it has only to do with the history of those Europeans who crossed the ocean to improve their life circumstances. Some of these immigrants were explorers serving in the name of their kings and queens; others were mercantile capitalists trying to get rich; others were victims of religious persecution in Europe; and still others were masses of poor people from Italy, Ireland, Jewish shtetls in Eastern Europe and elsewhere, driven from their home-lands by poverty or intolerance and looking for work in the 'New World'.

Of course, a good deal of the cultural legacy of this last group — the poor immigrant masses — has been neglected, obscured or distorted. That is, we are much more likely to read and know about the diaries of British explorers such as Captain John Smith or the political documents of a famous slaveholder names Thomas Jefferson than we are to study the letters, memoirs, poems and songs of the impoverished working people who came here from various parts of Europe, especially in the great waves around the turn of the century. Much of this material has not even been preserved, let alone published in classroom texts.

Nevertheless, keeping these qualifications in mind, I think we can still say that it is mainly the culture of males from European immigrant groups that is taught in United States educational institutions as supposedly representing all 'American culture'. What the cultures of these groups have in common — and what makes them seem to cohere as a unified entity — is that they are all based upon the Judeo-Christian tradition (expressed in the Bible, which contains a group of myths about which almost everyone in the United States is taught) and they are all derived from literature of the European tradition that goes from Homer and the Greek dramatists through Dante and Shakespeare and then up to the novel, which became, after the rise of capitalism, *the* generalized literary form throughout all of Europe.

Thus, a selected patriarchal Euro-American literature and culture, based upon and adapted from parts of the immigrant population of Europe, are commonly mistaken for what is known as 'American' culture; hence, what is purported to be 'our' canon is centred on Cooper, Hawthorne, Melville, James and so on, with a sequence of literary themes centred on Puritanism, Independence, Westward Expansion, the Gilded Age, Expatriatism and so on. But this is only part of the story, for there is an entirely different sector of the population living on the section of the North American continent that falls within the borders of the United States for whom the notion of racist slaveholders, such as Washington and Jefferson, as the founders and fathers of 'their' country and 'their' culture is not only absurd — it is probably insulting and repugnant. First and foremost among them are the non-whites: Afro-Americans, Chicanos, Native American Indians, Asian Americans and Puerto Ricans.

The Legacy of the 1960s

Consciousness of the discrepancy between the myth and reality of 'American culture' grew considerably during the 1960s. This was a decade of tumult in which literature by and about racially oppressed groups erupted on the scene in a manner somewehat analogous to the way in which literature about the working class, immigrant and 'bottom dog' life burst into the pages of United States literature during the Great Depression. The thrust of much of the widespread politico-nationalist thought in the 1960s was to argue for the existence of a unique cultural achievement by Blacks and certain other groups whose incorporation into United States society bore a greater resemblance to a colonization process than to an immigration process. Thus, Chicano culture was no longer viewed as an adaptation of Mexican culture to the Euro-American environment, but was said to be a unique blend — Chicano; Black American culture was defined by Black writers as neither African nor a 'damaged' variety of Euro-American culture, but as something new and positive — Afro-American; and so on.

Unfortunately, the complexity of this argument is often missed even by critics sympathetic to cultural pluralism. For example, William J. Harris in his 1981 essay called '*The Yardbird Reader* and the Multi-Ethnic Spirit' states that the 1960s and 1970s were dominated by forms of 'black nationalism which assumed that race was the most significant factor in a black person's life . . . .' But, to document this claim, he quotes Amiri Baraka that 'Black people are a race, a culture, a Nation', a formulation that clearly tells us that discussions of race consciousness took place in a much broader context than is ever disclosed in Harris's (1981, pp. 10–15) critique. Although Harris sees the achievements of the 1960s as preparatory to a new and higher stage that he identifies with the 'multi-ethnic spirit' of *The Yardbird Reader* in the mid-1970s, the exigencies of his thesis cause him to caricature Black nationalism by reducing a complex politico-cultural development to a sort of mirror image of white nationalism, which he then indicts for extolling one culture at the expense of another.

This approach to nationalism, in which Harris more or less equates Black and white cultural nationalism, is quite the reverse of the far more fruitful Marxist understanding of nationalist movements. Lenin made a famous differentiation between the nationalism of an oppressed group (one that has been deprived of control of land, language, economy and culture) and the nationalism of an oppressor group (one that rules land, language, economy and culture through force and hegemony). Most contemporary Marxists use this differentiation as the starting point for the evaluation of precise nationalist movements in terms of existing class forces and relationships in a particular society at a particular time.

Harris also makes the inaccurate claim that the major thrust of the politico-nationalist movements of the oppressed in the 1960s was one that was opposed to any kind of unity with other oppressed and non-dominant groups; actually, the question was — and remains to this day — '*How* and *on what basis* should unity be achieved?' However sympathetic Harris may be to a revision of the canon, he in no way resolves the difficult issue of the relationship between immigrant and colonized minorities by writing as if, prior to the 1970s, the necessity for alliances and cultural diversity was unrecognized or even opposed by the rebellious politico-cultural movements of the day.

In fact, the single most influential theoretical work of the earlier period was Frantz Fanon's *The Wretched of the Earth* (English translation, 1966), which unambiguously argues that the re-establishment and valorization of the culture of the oppressed is only a preliminary step to the achievement of a truly international culture. In his conclusion to 'Reciprocal Bases of National Culture and the Fight for Freedom', the most frequently discussed section of his book, Fanon (1966) affirms that the correct orientation toward promoting the nationalist consciousness of a colonized group

> is of necessity accompanied by the discovery and encouragement of universalizing values. Far from keeping aloof from other nations, therefore, it is national liberation which leads the nation to play its part on the stage of history. It is at the heart of national consciousness that international consciousness lives and grows. And this two-fold emerging is ultimately the only source of all culture (p. 199).

There is no doubt that in the ferment and heat of the 1960s many ambiguous, poorly thought out and even foolish statements were however made. What is really needed is a thorough book that scrupulously examines the decade in a way that distinguishes what was central from what was epiphenomenal, and that puts individualized spokespersons such as cultural nationalist Ron Karenga in a proper perspective. Because Harris's essay is typical in its emphasis on the more limited aspects of the legacy of the 1960s, it is necessary to provide a balance by extracting those elements from the 1960s that provide more useful concepts for analyzing and overcoming cultural hegemony.

For example, part of the declaration of cultural independence that occurred in the 1960s on the part of racially oppressed minorities involved a crucial polemic against liberal notions of assimilation and integration. Harold Cruse and others demonstrated that such notions could simply be euphemisms for advocating that racial minorities should have the 'freedom' to acculturate to Euro-American values — a doomed effort that could only bring humiliation and failure to the majority of the oppressed. After all, one of the hallmarks of Euro-American culture is its deep-rooted racism, and a society based on such a culture — and which needs divisions among races for economic reasons — will never grant true equality to the majority of its darker-skinned members. *does it nec. have to be a race divis.?*

Another part of the politico-nationalist argument of the 1960s was that Blacks and certain other groups had some features of an 'internal colony' within the larger context of United States capitalist society. There was never any agreement as to whether 'internal colonialism' was primarily a metaphor, a description of real economic relations today, or a legacy of past experience that persists in spite of the major economic changes that have occurred in twentieth century United States capitalism.

The main point — stated clearly by Robert Blauner in *Racial Oppression in America* (1972) and recently theorized in a more comprehensive fashion by Mario Barrera in *Race and Class in the Southwest* (1979) — is that colonized minorities differ from the European immigrant ethnic minorities in at least three respects: historically, the colonized minorities were incorporated into the nation by force and violence (for example, as slaves kidnapped from Africa, or as the population of a territory that was invaded by outsiders); economically, the colonized minorities became special segments of the work force (for example, as chattel or as migrant labourers); and culturally, the colonized minorities were subject to repression and misrepresentation on a scale surpassing the experience of any European ethnic immigrant group in the United States (for example, the campaign to extirpate African languages and religions, and the banning of certain Native American Indian religions).

The point of the 'internal colonialism' argument was never that colonized minorities suffered cultural discrimination while immigrant European ethnic groups did not. There is evidence that even blond and blue-eyed Scandinavian-Americans have grown up with feelings of self-hatred and a belief that their own culture is inferior. Moreover, there is substantial documentation showing that the cultural achievements of women and workers within these immigrant groups have also been unfairly disparaged. So the difference between the cultural discrimination suffered by immigrant minorities and colonized minorities must be understood partly in terms of the degree of intensity of the discrimination, and partly in terms of the historical context in which the particular discriminatory acts occurred. (For example, the denial of the legitimacy of bilingualism to the Chicano population is qualitatively different than it is to the Franco-American population, because the Chicanos are still inhabiting what is historically their own land.)

In emphasizing the centrality of this 'internal colonialism' analysis, my purpose is not at all to discourage comparative analysis of, for example, Afro-American and Jewish-American writing; it is to deny any simplistic and sentimental analogies between colonized groups and immigrant groups to the effect that 'we are all hyphenated Americans', or 'we are all minorities of one kind or another against whom there has been discrimination', etc. This is a pseudo-universalism that can serve to obscure important differences in cultural formation and in degrees of oppression. What is needed instead is a forceful clarification of the differences in the cultural patterns of immigrant and colonized groups — for one of the crucial needs of the 1980s is a theoretical framework for explaining why racial minorities still confront special forms of oppression in the United States. This point will have to be cogently defended against school administrators who are arguing that students must go 'back to basics' (often a code term for the exclusive study of Euro-American culture from the Euro-American perspective) and against politicians who are advocating the old racist doctrine that 'anyone who really wants to make it in our egalitarian society can do so', as they eliminate the minimal Federal assistance that has been given to oppressed groups under previous administrations.

Of course, one must be in sympathy with Black, Chicano and other scholars from racially oppressed minorities who resent the depiction of their cultures as exotic or narrow; and I can understand why many artists from these groups feel that they ought to be recognized as artists first and not immediately pigeon-holed as a special type of 'minority' artist. But it must also be understood that, regardless of our personal yearnings to step beyond the hypocritical terms of Euro-America's prejudice and stereotyping, there can be no genuine cultural equality achieved in this society without a complementary struggle for social equality. The truth of the matter is that the facile conflation of colonized and immigrant groups into the same ambiguous category of 'ethnic studies', in addition to being historically inaccurate has played into the hands of those who, in the conservative 1980s, have been dedicated to the abolition of affirmative action programmes in regard to university hiring, the establishment and maintenance of special institutes, and the inclusion of the culture and history of racially oppressed groups in the curriculum. We must not forget that the entire basis of the affirmative action argument is that certain groups have historically experienced *special* oppression and currently face *special* obstacles to equal treatment. I believe that in the 1980s writers, scholars and students working in the culture of 'internal colonialism' must play a vanguard role in defending the need for such programmes and for increasing available resources.

In order to carry out the counter-hegemonic task described above, it is necessary for us to rely on the best theoretical acquisitions and examples of cultural practice in the 1960s and 1970s. For example, in that time there was a considerable influence wielded by Third World activists in the colonial revolution. Some writers and critics found themselves spontaneously taking up Amilcar Cabral's (1973) call to 'return to the source' — to revitalize and learn the hidden and distorted and almost erased cultures that the colonizers have tried to wipe out as part of their struggle to dominate colonies in the Third World as well as 'internal colonies' in the United States.

What is important in Cabral's work, as well as in the work of Fanon and others, is that he gave expression to the thesis that, for a colonized people, the cultural struggle is inherently political; even an activity as basic as the accurate reconstruction of the history of an oppressed group can threaten the hegemony of the ruling class. Thus, in contrast to the experience of the American left during the 1930s, when politics and literature often existed in awkward and contradictory relationships, the 1960s and 1970s produced works of imaginative literature that are truly remarkable in their harmonious blending of cultural affirmation and undoctrinaire but politically challenging concepts.

Non-dominant Cultures

It is crucial to recognize that for each of the colonized cultures excluded from the Euro-American canon and tradition, there are alternative traditions — traditions that are wholly apart from, or else engaged in a complicated interaction with, the dominant tradition. The point is that the ideology of the Euro-American literary tradition does not operate merely to shut out the specific literary achievements of the colonized minorities and other groups; it is that these groups have diverse and internally complex cultural traditions of their own that are suppressed or not understood. We must recognize that the very terms with which we have been trained to discuss and evaluate Euro-American literature — 'Romanticism', 'Frontier Epic', 'Alienation', 'National Consciousness' — are inadequate or must be radically redefined for the non-dominant cultures.

This general proposition can be made concrete by contrasting two examples of writing. The first is an excerpt from T.S. Eliot's (1922, p. 31–2) *The Waste Land*:

Unreal City,
Under the brown fog of a winter dawn,
A crowd flowed over London Bridge, so many,
I had not thought death had undone so many.
Sighs, short and infrequent, were exhaled,
And each man fixed his eyes before his feet.
Flowed up the hill and down King William Street,
To where Saint Mary Woolnoth kept the hours
With a dead sound on the final stroke of nine.
There I saw one I knew, and stopped him crying: "Stetson!
"You who were with me in the ships at Mylae!
"That corpse you planted last year in your garden,
"Has it begun to sprout? Will it bloom this year?
"Or has the sudden frost disturbed its bed?
"O keep the Dog far hence, that's friend to men,
"Or with his nails he'll dig it up again!
"You! hypocrite lecteur! — mon semblable, — mon frere!"

This is a segment of what is possibly the most important and influential poem in the English language, written by a poet born and educated in the United States. Eliot later moved to England, but usually insisted on a single, undifferentiated literacy tradition. I am citing it to demonstrate, perhaps with an extreme example, just how dependent a piece of literature generally taught in the United States as 'American literature' can be on what is really a distinctive Euro-American culture. As we can see even the location or setting of the poem is Europe — as evidenced by the references to London Bridge and the Church of St Mary Woolnoth. Moreover, all the literary allusions in the poem came from European predecessor poets. The phrase 'Unreal City' is borrowed from the French poet Charles Baudelaire, while the line 'death had undone so many' and the passage about people flowing 'with eyes fixed before their feet' are borrowed from Dante's *Inferno*, to suggest that life is comparable to a living hell.

The poem depends also on a knowledge of London geography and the Europeans' Christian Bible when it says that St Mary Woolnoth 'makes a dead sound on the final stroke of nine.' St Mary Woolnoth overlooks the financial district of the city, so it can reasonably be assumed that the crowds depicted in this poem are largely made up of bankers, businessmen and stockbrokers. Moreover, there is a special significance in the hour that the church clock strikes because, as the Gospel of Matthew records, Christ died on the cross at the ninth hour. So there is an association here between the financial district clock's striking nine to announce the new working day and the murder of Christ and those values for which Christ stood. In other words, when the business day starts, authentic Christianity dies.

The point is that most of the social, historical and cultural substance of this portion of the poem is *Euro*-American. The difficulty of the poem is caused not only by its being an intellectual poems that requires a wide range of knowledge before the reader can fully appreciate its complexity; the difficulty is also that this intellectual content is almost exclusively European-derived. One has to know something about European haberdashery to see the significance of naming a man 'Stetson' (which is a special kind of hat); one has to know something about the Roman naval victory over the Carthaginians at Mylae to understand the reference to the battle in the poem; and one would have to know the work of other European writers — not only Baudelaire and Dante but also the playwright John Webster — to appreciate the other literary allusions at work. Finally, one would have to know French in order to interpret the last line.

Now let's examine a second poem, 'Plainview: 2', by N. Scott Momaday (1974, pp. 6–8):

I saw an old Indian,
at Saddle mountain.
He drank and dreamed of drinking
and a blue-black horse.

Remember my horse running.
Remember my horse.

Remember my horse running.
Remember my horse.
Remember my horse wheeling.
Remember my horse.
Remember my horse wheeling.
Remember my horse.
Remember my horse blowing.
Remember my horse.
Remember my horse blowing.
Remember my horse.
Remember my horse standing.
Remember my horse.
Remember my horse standing.
Remember my horse.

Remember my horse hurting.
Remember my horse.
Remember my horse hurting.
Remember my horse.
Remember my horse falling.
Remember my horse.
Remember my horse falling.
Remember my horse.

Remember my horse dying.
Remember my horse.
Remember my horse dying.
Remember my horse.

A horse is one thing.
An Indian another
An old horse is old
An old Indian is sad.
I saw an old Indian at Saddle Mountain
He drank and dreamed of drinking
And a blue-black horse.

Remember my horse running.
Remember my horse.
Remember my horse wheeling.
Remember my horse.
Remember my horse blowing.
Remember my horse.
Remember my horse falling.
Remember my horse.
Remember my horse dying.
Remember my horse.

Chapter 21, this volume) and by analyzing the books' content. Accordingly, I draw on the findings of a comprehensive textual analysis of thirty-four American romance novels (Christian-Smith, 1987) and discuss the preliminary findings of an ethnography of teenage girls' romance novel reading in schools.

The Materiality of the Text: Educational and Tradebook Publishing

Elsewhere I have discussed the importance of grounding gender discourses constructed in popular fiction within their social, economic and political conditions of production (Christian-Smith, 1986, 1987). In the present volume, Apple's and Lorimer and Keeney's chapters (Chapters 12 and 13) carefully explore the sets of market relations surrounding the production of school texts. Much of what they observe is also apparent in young adult publishing.

Once widely read in the 1940s and 1950s, teen romance novels have experienced a resurgence in popularity largely through sophisticated marketing techniques so that these romances are now the third most widely read books by teenage girls (Market Facts, 1984). Romance novels are defined as those books focusing on the first love experiences of girls (Christian, 1984 a). These books have reappeared in the midst of several large-scale mergers within educational and trade publishing that have had the effect of endowing profit and loss sheets with a new importance (Coser, Kadushin and Powell, 1982; Whiteside, 1981). Adult romance novels comprise the most lucrative segment of publishing today, accounting for at least half of all mass-market paperbacks sold in 1985 (Wainger, Personal Communication, 1985). Strong sales of teen romance novels have provided a substantial infusion of capital into juvenile divisions, transforming them from barely profitable to highly lucrative (Smith, 1981).

In 1980, Scholastic, a leader in providing educational materials and the world's largest publisher of young adult paperbacks, conducted market research within its TAB teenage book club and ascertained that novels featuring first love experiences were most popular with girls (Lanes, 1981). Accordingly, Scholastic developed the first teen romance series, 'Wildfire', whose tremendous initial success of 1.8 million books sold in the first year prompted other publishers such as Bantam, Simon and Schuster and Dell to develop their own teen romance series. To date there are more than a dozen series romances and many individual books with romantic motifs. While the new teen romances have been hailed as the 'publishing phenomenon of the decade' (Lanes, 1981, p. 5), they have simultaneously fuelled debates regarding the kinds of tradebooks available to young readers as instructional texts within classrooms.

The controversy has centred on some parents' and librarians' concerns over the romances' limited representations of femininity and these texts' perceived status as instructional materials (Keresey, 1984). In the aftermath of this continuing controversy, Scholastic's reputation for supplying quality books through its book clubs has been called into question in the professional literature (Harvey, 1982; Pollack, 1981). Less discussed is the resemblance of Scholastic's books to the 'Hi-Low' format characteristic of books used in reading instruction for reluctant readers and the related social implications of using such books with girls. Hi-Low refers to a specific category of print materials characterized by short sentences and paragraphs, controlled vocabulary and concept load and containing elements that are of supposed interest to readers of specific age groups.[2] Although Scholastic disavows any links between their romance novels and materials for reluctant readers, Christian-Smith's (1987) comprehensive textual analysis of these and other romance novels has found an uncanny resemblance between Scholastic's romances and other Hi-Low materials.

Romance novels are components of the highly profitable Hi-Low materials for reluctant readers (Christian-Smith, 1987). Since the 1970s, paperbacks have been specifically written and marketed for the reluctant reader under the rubric of 'classroom libraries' which claim to capture students' interests as well as facilitating their growth in reading. Much of the literature on reading instruction argues that reluctant readers can best be taught to read through such Hi-Low materials (Estes and Vaugh, 1973; Fader and McNeil, 1968). The use of romance novels as instructional texts with female reluctant readers is in part an expression of this thinking. Scholastic's Hi-Low libraries *Action, Double Action* and *Sprint* clearly differentiate content based on gender assumptions. As noted, boys' books feature adventures and mystery while girls' books involve romance, dating and choices involving early marriage or remaining in school. Recently, romances have become important components of Scholastic's popular Tab book club and the classroom libraries offered by other suppliers of Hi-Low materials such as Sundance and Quercus. Teen romance series can thus be regarded as parts of a larger variety of instructional materials that have historically been part of Scholastic's and other educational publishers' offerings to schools. Along with other Hi-Low materials, these texts contain implicit gender themes.

Methodology

During an eight-month period in 1985–1986, I conducted an ethnography of teen romance fiction readers in three schools in Lakeview, a large US mid-western metropolitan area, to determine who reads teen romance novels, the extent of their use in classrooms and what meanings female readers make in their interactions with these books. In this section I present the preliminary findings regarding the first two areas of inquiry. The sites were two suburban middle schools, grades 7–8 Jefferson and Sherwood Park, which contained about 300 students each, mostly white, and Kominsky, an urban, racially mixed 7–9 junior high school. Both Jefferson and Sherwood Park tracked their students (low, medium and high) for reading instruction based on the results of district-wide and individual school standardized reading test scores, teacher recommendation and students' previous grades. Kominsky and Sherwood Park also have reading support service through the federally funded Chapter 1 programme.[3]

Five related methods were used to collect data: a Reading Interest Survey, a Reading Survey, participant observation, interviews with all significant subjects (teachers, students, counsellors and librarians), and examinations of library and classroom reading checkout cards, reading summaries, examples of curricular materials and other related documents. A sample of seventy-five girls who were heavy romance novel readers was assembled through the latter methods. The findings reported here are the result of observing, interviewing and surveying twenty-nine of the seventy-five heaviest romance novel readers and their five teachers.

Romance Novels as Instructional Texts in Classrooms

Teen romance novels are overwhelmingly read by middle-class suburban White girls aged 12–15 and, to a lesser degree, by Black and Hispanic adolescent girls. Since girls themselves do not constitute an undifferentiated group of students, I was interested in determining how the heavy romance novel readers were grouped instructionally. In each school a majority of them were identified by teachers, counsellors and librarians as less than 'able' readers and were tracked into remedial or low ability reading classes with some also receiving reading instruction through Chapter 1 programmes.

Since there is a continuing controversy regarding the status of teen romance novels in schools, I interviewed the girls' five reading teachers, all women, regarding their attitudes towards romance novels. Three were aware of the controversy and all felt some degree of apprehension regarding their use. The contradictory position of teachers is nicely illustrated by the observations of two teachers:

> I feel guilty about letting the girls order these books through TAB. I read a couple of them once. They are so simple and the characters in the novels are stereotypes. You know, mom at home in her apron, dad reading the paper with his feet up. But the girls seem to like the books and the class-room sure is quiet when they're reading them. (Mrs M)

> The girls just love them (romances). I see them reading their books in study hall and even in lunch. Can you believe that! I'm just happy that they are reading, period. (Mrs K)

Most romance novel reading occurred during independent study which was in great abundance since instruction itself was mostly organized around individual learning models to provide, in the teachers' estimation, for the specific needs of each student. Student and teacher interactions were mostly limited to the correcting of skill sheets, updating reading folders, giving directions or answering procedural questions. Occasionally teachers would present a group lesson. However, students mostly read privately and rarely shared their reading with their teachers.

The romance novels in these classrooms occupied a highly contradictory position both in teachers' minds and in their practices. In the ensuing sections, I offer a reading of selected teen romance novels and conclude by discussing how the novels address tennage girls and from where their power and authority to speak is derived.

Becoming a Woman: Romance, Beauty and Sexuality

This reading of a sample of thirty-four adolescent romance novels (Christian, 1984 a, 1984 b) is grounded in a close textual analysis using semiotic methodology developed by Barthes (1967, 1974) and McRobbie (1978) in her study of the teenage girls' magazine, *Jackie*, and in Foucault's (1980) work on discourse formation. My aim here is to specify how power relations work in and through these romance novels to form a discourse on femininity. Following Foucault, I will view power both as an assemblage of force relations within a particular discursive field and as a process through which resistance and confrontation transform and strengthen these same power relations.

Semiotics proceeds by locating sets of codes through which meaning is created (Belsey, 1980; Culler, 1982). In the following analysis I shall focus on the ways that the code of *romance* structures the feminine discourse constructed in the thirty-four novels. This code has a long tradition in women's fiction from the Brontes to today's romances as a primary structuring mechanism of books focusing on feminine experience (Radway, 1984).

This sample is representative of those books that have been highly recommended by major selection instruments such as *Booklist*, *School Library Journal* and *Hornbook* that are commonly used by librarians and teachers when selecting books for young readers. The sample also contains many of those romance novels that were most popular with the teenage female readers I studied. A list of these books can be found at the conclusion of this chapter.

This analysis was also concerned to trace the historical evolution of the feminine discourse. Williams (1977; Chapter 5, this volume) notes that cultural forms are far from being homogeneous assemblages of meanings. Rather, they are composed of *residual* meanings and practices formed in the past which continue to structure the present and *emergent* or current cultural practices that co-exist with residual practices. The use of residual and emergent as categories enabled the location of changes in the books so that they could be grouped into three periods according to changes in the code of *romance*.

Period I   1942–1959
Period II   1963–1979
Period III 1980–1982

The code of romance organized the discourse on adolescent femininity in all periods. It involves not only emotion and caring, but is also about the negotiation of relations of power and control between girls and boys. That love is central in facilitating and completing girls' development is seen in the remarks of Aunt Cordelia in *Up a Road Slowly* (Hunt, 1986, p. 103): 'A woman is never completely developed until she has loved a man; when that happens in the right way she is happy in other people's love as well as her own; . . . You might say she knows completeness.' Although the code of romance did not significantly change over the forty-year period, the active resistances of heroines in the novels of Period II (1960s and 1970s) to practices that were not commensurate with their understanding of 'proper' romantic and sexual conduct were also important in their becoming women. These are the common threads in all the novels which form the code of romance:

1 Romance is a transforming experience endowing girls' lives with meaning and structure.
2 Romance is about male power and control.
3 Romance is an assemblage of feelings and emotions.
4 Romance is personal private experience.
5 Romance manages sexuality by privileging heterosexuality.
6 Romance is a way for girls to manage gender relations.
7 A precondition to romance is beauty which develops physical presence as a characteristic of femininity.
8 Romance and beautification develop early gender relationships to work and commodities.

Romance is credited with being the experience that brings girls to womanhood by virtue of its ability to single out girls, bestowing on them special status and recognition at the moment of becoming a girlfriend. Becoming popular with peers is but a part of this 'individual specialness' which only girlfriends experience in the novels. The very practical side of this 'specialness' is evident in Jean Burnaby's observation that her boyfriend, Tom Kitchell, 'had brought her to a pinnacle of repute; she had become known as one of the popular girls who . . . was seen everywhere that mattered' (Emery, 1952, p. 143). In *Seventeenth Summer* (Daly, 1942, p. 60) Angie Morrow's romance with Jack Duluth is presented as the turning point in her life where '(g)oing with a boy gives you a new identity.'

However, implicit in this moment of specialness are dynamics of power and control which circumscribe the form and expression of girls' authority and power, all the while celebrating male prerogative. In becoming 'his girl' the girlfriend takes up a position where she is literally his. That boyfriends do consider girlfriends their property underlies the many references to ownership ranging from the expression 'my girl' (Quin-Harkin, 1981) to the cold and often abusive treatment of any girl who refuses to become a form of male property (Mazer, 1979). Furthermore, in becoming the girlfriend feminine power becomes confined to an informal system of persuasion, fragility and helplessness rather than assertiveness. While this informal system was not textually recognized as a legitimate form of power, analysis of individual novels revealed that several heroines did try to secure a role in shaping the power structure of romance. For example, Victoria Martin (Pascal, 1979) is assertive with boys. However, the consequence of this is that she ultimately loses her boyfriend. This textual device serves to foreclose the possibility of gender struggle as usual within relationships and to define such struggles as essentially negative. In this manner, social relations of dominance and subordination are maintained in the texts. Hence, romance at its deepest level is concerned with power: who has it and who may legitimately exercise it.

The novels render romance as a personal private experience existing out of time and isolated from the larger social structure. As Angie Morrow notes, 'people can't tell you about things like that, you have to find them out for yourself' (Daly, 1942, p. 3). Since romance is situated in personal life, whatever problems girls have in the novels with negotiating the terms of intimacy are considered to be individual and personal, rather than characteristic of romance per se. The rendering of these struggles as private and idiosyncratic renders the power relations of romance very resistant to change due to their removal from public scrutiny. Hence, romance is both a mechanism through which experience is parcelled out into the 'public' and the 'private', and one by which those divisions are maintained.[4]

Within the novels, girls interpret their sexuality in terms of romance which establishes love, feelings and emotions as its proper content. Sexuality refers to the array of statements and practices regarding the construction of sites of pleasure, and the designation of objects of desire which reside within a network of power and control characterized by prohibitions and constraints (Foucault, 1980).

Each period contributes to establishing the linkages between romance and sexuality by privileging romance as the only legitimate context for sexual expression. In Periods I and III sexual expression is mostly limited to chaste kissing and hugging within steady relationships. Jane Howard of *The Boy Next Door* (Cavanna, 1956) demands that Ken Sanderson go through the rituals of romance before he can kiss her. In the Period III *Princess Amy* (Pollowitz, 1981) Amy Painter's outrage at Guy Wetherington's kiss can be only understood within the larger context that links sexuality with romance. The kiss as a signifier for love is evident in all three periods where romances are, as the song goes, 'sealed with a kiss.'

In several novels of Periods II–III (1963–1979; 1980–1982), where there are genital relationships, these are also formed and legitimated through the tethering of sexuality to romance. For example, in *My First Love and Other Disasters* (Pascal, 1979) Jim's attempts to go beyond kissing during early dating constitute improper conduct, as far as heroine Victoria Martin is concerned, once she realizes that Jim has no intention of becoming romantically involved (pp. 98–102). Where the kiss signified love in previous novels, genitality in a steady relationship also becomes a signifier for love. In *I'll Always Remember You ... Maybe* (Pevsner, 1981) the relationship of Paul and Darien has all the characteristics of a trial marriage before it is interrupted by Paul's departure for college. After several months Paul visits Darien. Darien interprets the occurrence of intercourse as a sign of Paul's renewed love for her (pp. 116–18) despite the lack of letters and phone calls from Paul which signal a breach in their relationship. Genital relationships only occur in four novels of the thirty-four and these are clustered in Periods II and III. Although there is no direct endorsement of genital relationships involving girls, the novels imply that this alone will constitute adult female sexuality. The fact that Paul and Darien have had a steady relationship legitimates genitality. Hence, the 'really useful' sexual knowledge that girls learn through romance forwards sexuality as an expression of love and commitment, and the notion that romance is the only 'proper' context for sexuality.

In the novels boys are presented as the only legitimate objects of girls' desire. In *Wait for Marcy* (Du Jardin, 1950) 15-year-old Marcy's initial lack of interest in boys and preference for the companionship of her female friends prompt parents' concern that she is developing in the 'normal direction' (p. 14). Heterosexuality is constructed as the natural and unquestioned form of sexual desire in the novels of Periods I and III and is endorsed unconditionally in Period II despite the presence of two novels about love relationships between girls, *Ruby* (Guy, 1976) and *Hey, Dollface* (Hautzig, 1978).

The potential critical power of this emerging sexual discourse is undercut at several points because the girls' relationships are already foregrounded in hetero-sexuality. Their relationships are constantly measured against the former and found lacking. On one occasion Val (*Hey, Dollface*) seeks the advice of her mother and teacher, Miss Udry, concerning her feelings for Chloe. Her mother believes that lesbian relationships are substitutes for some inability to attract men (Hautzig, 1978, p. 64), while Miss Udry views lesbian desire as a phase in 'normal' sexual develop-ment (pp. 86–7). The strong homophobia in both novels is most pronounced in *Ruby* when Ed Brooks, a school mate of Ruby and Daphne, confronts Ruby: 'I knew something was wrong with you. Dykes is your thing. He put his hand to his forever swollen crotch. You want to feel the real thing? Here, I'll let you feel it' (Guy, 1976, p. 58). Here the 'real thing', symbolized by the penis, becomes a larger signifier for 'proper' desire and male control over girls' sexuality. The subsequent attempts of Daphne's mother to compel her 'to go straight', as well as Ruby's father's reconsideration of his ban on dating boys, help to establish heterosexuality as the prevailing sexual discourse.

In the novels, girls also used romance as a way of managing sexual expression in order to control male aggressiveness. In *Up in Seth's Room* (Mazer, 1979) the conflict between Seth and Finn concerns Finn's exercise of her right to control her body and to define the nature of her sexual pleasure. For Finn this involves kissing and caressing while Seth exerts constant pressure towards intercourse. Seth's desire to 'wear [Finn] down one way or another' (Mazer, 1979, p. 190) exposes the relations of power and control that underpin sexuality. Finn summons up romance and compels Seth to assume proper romantic conduct in an attempt to avert the worst consequences of his sexual demands.

That girls understand the connections between romance and beautification is seen in the many examples of their immersion in beauty routines once they meet a potential boyfriend. A look in the mirror is enough to convince Maddy Kemper (Conford, 1981) that she is 'Drab Person of the Year' from face to personality. This 'recognition' and her interest in Adam Holmquist are what prompts her to cultivate a 'new look'. While it is true that heroines often protest what Julie Connors (Stolz, 1956) calls feminine 'glossing and burnishing', an unqualified endorsement of the value of beautification remains because pretty girls get boyfriends.

Beautification is one of the ways through which the feminine consciousness becomes centred in the body. Julie Connors once again notes that all this beauty activity is natural, 'as much a part of a girl as her heartbeat' (Stolz, 1956, p. 159). Feminine consciousness is constructed with every stroke of the hair brush and twist of the curl. Girls' femininity and their positions within larger discourses on the female body are constructed during moments of 'recognition'. Such a moment is crystallized in *Wait for Marcy* when Marcy debuts in party dress in front of her family and boyfriend, Steve. Steve conveys his reaction through an appreciative 'WOW' while her parents are described as 'dazed'. This moment of recognition involves dynamics which culminate in the body as a symbol of femininity. Heroines' sense of worth evolves from the recognition that their beauty produces. So while a girl is singled out for her beauty, this recognition is articulated through relations of power and control that render femininity synonymous with ornamentation and spectacle while mitigating against regarding the girl as a total person.

Beautification and romance are important for situating girls within the discourses of work and consumption and are crucial textual means through which the sexual division of labour is reproduced. Consumption not only involves girls' use and transformation of commodities and services, but also entails learning how to maintain their future families. Interacting with beauty products in the home, girls engage in activities that are primarily regarded as feminine and personal. The shopping trip for clothes, cosmetics and household goods cements girls' relationships to commodities in novels such as *Going on Sixteen, Sorority Girl* and *Drop-Out*. Furthermore, girls and adult women are the only ones who do housework and care for children in the novels. These activities augur girls' future unpaid domestic work. By continually situating the novels in the home, and presenting it as the setting for becoming beautiful and being recognized for beauty efforts, the novels offer domestic activities as the only modes of feminine activity worthy of recognition.

Textual representations of plans for college or a career are not abundant in the novels or are rendered as '[I'll] get a job somewhere and work for a while until I get married' (Cavanna, 1949, p. 23). The incompatibility of marriage and career is directly expressed in the novels of the 1960s and 1970s where girls like Natalie Fields must choose between romance and their desires for careers (Le Guin, 1976).

Creating Femininity

Radway (1984) contends that cultural products such as romance fiction present imaginative resolutions to gender relations and are productive of certain subject positions for readers. Romance novel reading occurs mainly during adolescence, a crucial period in girls' developing gender identity when decisions regarding their futures are made (Christian-Smith, 1987). Adolescent female readers are offered certain discursive positions and practices as girlfriends, consumers, future wives and mothers. This is in part accomplished through an implied community of interest existing between the fictional narrative subject and the reader. Heroines such as Angie Morrow (*Seventeenth Summer*) directly address the reader, offering her a position of identification with the heroine as sister or friend, one who shares the experience of being in love, as the girl belonging to a boy.

The adolescent female reader is further constituted as the consumer of society's goods, but never as worker and acknowledged producer of those goods. Through a girl's desire to get and keep a boyfriend her gender identity is consolidated around the consumption of goods of the personal and domestic nature. The reader is ultimately offered romance as a way of protecting feminine interests and of managing male assertiveness. While romance provides her an avenue for exploring patriarchal relations, the reader is never offered ways of effectively challenging what is oppressive about them. She sees that challenges to dominant gender relations in the novels momentarily disturb but never fundamentally alter these relations. The novels finally hold out to her the traditional position of keeper of heart and hearth for her future family. These discursive positions are highly problematic in view of the larger experiences of women and girls in today's economy.

Women must do paid work to support themselves and families as wages deteriorate. More and more women are heading families and are constituting an economically disadvantaged underclass (Scott, 1984). The general notion covered throughout forty years of adolescent romance fiction, that domesticity and child-care will be girls' primary adult vocations, is contradicted by these realities. And it is precisely through this residual view of adult femininity that the romances work as conservers of the social structure and are powerful modes of forestalling and rearranging the ongoing struggles of women around fair wages and domestic arrangements. This positioning of adolescent female readers within this feminine discourse is all the more contradictory when it is recalled precisely who these readers are. They are often girls like the twenty-nine in my ethnography who are on the brink of choosing courses that will prepare them not for lives of full-time housekeeping, but for lives of waged work with limited pay and advancement all the while juggling their domestic and childcare responsibilities. It is to these girls that the novels speak.

Authority, Power and Knowledge

Baker and Freebody (Chapter 21, this volume) maintain that much of the authority of texts comes from the practices within the social and political contexts of schooling. The ethnographic data I report show that there is indeed considerable tension surrounding the educative practices that eventually endow texts such as romance novels with authority.

Much of the power and authority of these texts is constituted through the prevailing discursive construct of the reluctant student. The overriding ideology that 'whatever interests students' is therefore appropriate reading mollified many teachers' apprehensions regarding the value of romance novels as instructional materials. Furthermore, the romances' characteristics of high interest and low readability perfectly fit part of the requirement of instructional materials for reluctant readers. These textual features of the romances, when interfaced with the dominant instructional practices and arrangements, further legitimated romances as acceptable instructional materials.

The larger institutional context in which teachers were pressured to demonstrate students' growth in reading as measured by test scores compelled them to seek materials that would motivate reading. This was another legitimation for romances as instructional materials. The reputation of school publishers like Scholastic further provided teachers with an additional stamp of approval. Although that reputation is being questioned, the teachers were largely unaware of this. Teachers acknowledged that intensification of their work load, the increasing numbers of students and the immense paper work for those teaching in federally funded programmes made it difficult to select materials carefully. They strongly relied on the reputation of publishers (see Lorimer and Keeney, Chapter 13, this volume).

Gender specifically intersects with this reluctant reader discourse in the form of the assumed differential reading interests of adolescent girls and boys. Although much of the independent classroom reading was self-selected, staff invariably suggested books with romantic and family themes to female readers. Teachers and librarians summoned up traditional beliefs about 'girls' books and boys' books' to support their authority to recommend books, assuming that girls would be naturally interested in romance novels. Part of the authority of these romance novels emanates therefore from the power of teachers to speak for their students from a knowledgeable position (see Luke, de Castell and Luke, Chapter 19, this volume).

Teachers' positions of power and authority were reinforced by the emphasis upon strict classroom discipline. A 'good' classroom was one where students were quiet and working. In some classrooms teachers regarded the romances as a solution to the growing discipline problems of female students because the romances secured girls' interests and held them for long periods of time. The overall ideology of 'whatever interests students' is therefore appropriate reading mollified many teachers' apprehensions regarding the value of romances as instructional texts. However, this view is ultimately not defensible because it was reading without meaningful communication between students and teachers regarding students' reflections on their reading. This practice mitigated against what is perhaps the most important aspect of learning from reading, that of making sense of books through engaging with others.

The case of Mrs B and her students at Kominsky shows how textual authority is often the outcome of the complex dynamic existing between students and teachers regarding who has the authority to define what is a legitimate school text. As a strong advocate of 'quality' teen literature, Mrs B's initial assessment of the romances as 'trash' gave way to some tolerance.[5] Mrs B accommodated the romances within her ideology of 'quality' literature by striking this bargain with the girls: for every romance read, other types of book had also to be read. The reality was that Mrs B wanted to disinterest the girls in the romances so that they would read books she recommended. When students inquired into the reasons behind her dislike of romances, Mrs B did not offer any substantive explanations.

However, romance novel reading proliferated in Mrs B's class. This reading was the outcome of five students' questioning the notion of the 'trashy' romance by their vehement championing of their romance reading. Girls defended their reading by throwing back to Mrs B her exhortations to read something of interest to them. They also legitimated their choices of romances by citing their own mothers' examples of romance reading, as well as the real and imagined support of their mothers for their own right to choose their reading. The five girls further challenged Mrs B's position of authority to choose texts by languishing over teacher selected books, mutilating the pages and covers, all the while complaining how boring the books were. Or the girls would retire to the book nook to covertly read favourite romances they had hidden among the floor cushions. The latter exemplifies the ways that female students actively reinterpreted school ideologies regarding their own reading instruction to wrest authority and control within the classroom. In so doing, of course, they provided yet another legitimation for the romance novel as instructional text.

Finally, the placement of many of these girls in other low-tracked classes like maths and science interfaced with teachers', counsellors' and the girls' own expectations regarding their futures, thus providing an important context for romance novel reading. Over half of the twenty-nine girls expected to marry before 20 and work a few years before childbearing. Towards this end, the girls dated with the hopes of establishing a long-term relationship with a single boy. Teachers' and counsellors' perceptions coincided with those of the girls' with one teacher volunteering that in the end the romances which girls 'devoured' would prepare them well for their future lives as good wives and mothers. Hence these larger instructional arrangements linked with the girls' expectations and content of the romance novels to provide a similar set of gender meanings across the curriculum.

Conclusion

The phenomenon of young adult tradebooks as textbooks is increasing as teachers continue to seek print texts that will engage their students and publishers continue to cultivate that lucrative market, the schools. It is as commodity and cultural artifact that the textbook, whatever its form, must be the continued object of study and research to determine how it constructs students and teachers as gendered subjects. The present chapter is a contribution towards understanding this complex process. While texts may offer readers certain discursive positions around gender, these positions by no means comprise a unitary identity as the text would imply, but are a multiplicity of shifting positions. So while texts like romance novels claim to speak with a degree of authority the truth about girls, their hopes and dreams, that authority is not eternal but a mere moment to be dislodged by readers and teachers.[6]

Notes

1 The analysis of books will be confined solely to gender and romance due to space limitations. For an analysis of how the codes of sexuality and beautification shaped femininity see Christian-Smith (1987). Discussions of generation, class and race are contained in Christian (1984 a).

2 Readability, or the difficulty of reading text, is most often estimated through counting sentence length and word length. A number of the Hi-Lows that I have analyzed using readability measures are written at the fourth to fifth grade level. Publishers routinely estimate readability and print it in terms of grade level on the copyright page.
3 In 1965 Congress passed the Elementary and Secondary Education Act known as Title I (now Chapter 1) as a part of its 'War on Poverty'. Chapter 1's focus was improving the reading and mathematics knowledge of the poor and educationally disadvantaged. Although Chapter 1 funding has been severely curtailed of late, it still remains the major form of compensatory education within many American school districts.
4 This is not to argue that the public and the private are in reality separate realms. That they often appear to be is the result of the work of ideology which creates the impression of separate spheres.
5 Some of the major adolescent book awards in the United States are the American Library Association's Notable Books, the Newbery Award and the National Book Award.
6 Preliminary ethnographic analysis indicates that romance reading is very contradictory. Marge, one of the most assertive and street-wise girls in the sample, contended that the romances do not accurately portray female-male relationships in that 'real life' romance is often very violent. Her experiences with enormous male sexual violence belie the almost total lack of this in the romances. However, Marge wistfully commented that she wished boys she knew were like the boys in the novels: 'treatin' you good. Not bossin' you round and tryin' to hit on you all the time.'

References

BARTHES, R. (1967) Elements of Semiology. London: Jonathan Cape.
BARTHES, R. (1974) S/Z. New York: Hill and Wang.
BELSEY, C. (1980) Critical Practice. London: Methuen.
CHRISTIAN, L.K. (1984 a) Becoming a Woman through Romance: Adolescent Novels and the Ideology of Femininity. Unpublished doctoral dissertation, University of Wisconsin, Madison.
CHRISTIAN, L.K. (1984 b) 'The new romances: Selling jeans on the outside and femininity inside,' The Advocate, 3, 82–90.
CHRISTIAN-SMITH, L.K. (1986) 'English curriculum and current trends in publishing,' English Journal, 75, 55–7.
CHRISTIAN-SMITH, L.K. (1987) 'Gender, popular culture and curriculum: Adolescent romance novels as gender text,' Curriculum Inquiry, 17, 365–406.
COSER, L.A., KADUSHIN, C. and POWELL, W. (1982) Books. New York: Basic Books.
CULLER, J. (1982) Theory and Criticism after Structuralism. Ithaca, N.Y.: Cornell University Press.
ESTES, T. and VAUGH, J. (1973) 'Reading interests and comprehension: Implications,' The Reading Teacher, 27, 149–53.
FADER, D. and McNEIL, D. (1968) Hooked on Books: Program and Proof. New York: Berkley Books.
FLESCH, R. (1981) Why Johnny Still Can't Read. New York: Harper and Row.
FOUCAULT, M. (1980) The History of Sexuality. New York: Vintage Books.
HARVEY, B. (1982) 'How far can you go in a teen romance?' Village Voice, 27, 48–9.
KERESEY, G. (1984) 'School bookclub expurgation practices,' Top of the News, 40, 131–8.
LANES, S. (1981) 'Here come the blockbusters — teen books go big time,' Interracial Books for Children Bulletin, 12, 5–7.
McROBBIE, A. (1978) Jackie: An Ideology of Adolescent Femininity. Occasional Paper. Birmingham: Centre for Contemporary Cultural Studies.

Market Facts. (1984) *1983 Consumer Study on Reading and Book Purchasing: Focus on Juveniles.* New York: Book Industry Study Group.

National Assessment of Educational Progress (1976, October) *Reading in America: A Perspective on Two Assessments* (Reading Report No. 06–R–01). Denver, Color.: NAEP.

National Commission on Excellence in Education (1983) *A Nation at Risk.* Washington, D.C.: US Government Printing Office.

OTTO, W., PETERS, C.W. and PETERS, N. (1977) *Reading Problems.* Reading, Mass.: Addison-Wesley.

POLLACK, P. (1981) 'The business of popularity,' *School Library Journal,* 28, 25–8.

RADWAY, J. (1984) *Reading the Romance.* Chapel Hill, N.C.: University of North Carolina Press.

RETAN, W. (1982) 'The changing economics of book publishing,' *Top of the News,* 38, 233–5.

SCOTT, H. (1984) *Working Your Way to the Bottom.* London: Pandora Press.

SHATZKIN, L. (1982) *In Cold Type.* Boston, Mass.: Houghton-Mifflin.

SMITH, W. (1981) 'An earlier start on romance,' *Publishers Weekly,* 220, 56–61.

SULEIMAN, S.R. and CROSMAN, I. (1980) *The Reader in the Text.* Princeton, N.J.: Princeton University Press.

TOMPKINS, J.P. (1980) *Reader-Response Criticism.* Baltimore, Md.: Johns Hopkins University Press.

WHITESIDE, T. (1981) *The Blockbuster Complex.* Middletown, Conn.: Wesleyan University Press.

WILLIAMS, R. (1977) *Marxism and Literature.* Oxford: Oxford University Press.

Books Used in This Study

Sally Benson (1969 ed.) *Junior Miss.* New York: Pocket Books.

Betty Cavanna (1946) *Going on Sixteen.* New York: Scholastic Book Services.

Betty Cavanna (1949) *Paintbox Summer.* New York: Westminster Press.

Betty Cavanna (1956) *The Boy Next Door.* New York: William Morrow and Company.

Beverly Cleary (1959) *Jean and Johnny.* New York: Dell Publishing.

Beverly Cleary (1963) *Sister of the Bride.* New York: Dell.

Ellen Conford (1981) *Seven Days to a Brand New Me.* New York: Atlantic, Little, Brown.

Maureen Daly (1968 ed.) *Seventeenth Summer.* New York: Simon and Schuster.

Rosamond Du Jardin (1943) *Practically Seventeen.* New York: Scholastic Book Service.

Rosamond Du Jardin (1950) *Wait for Marcy.* New York: Scholastic Books.

Ann Emery (1952) *Sorority Girl.* Philadelphia, Penn.: Westminster Press.

Jeanette Eyerly (1963) *Drop-Out.* New York: Berkley Books.

Benedict and Nancy Freedman (1947) *Mrs. Mike.* New York: Berkley Books.

Patricia L. Gauch (1979) *Fridays.* New York: Pocket Books.

Rosa Guy (1973) *The Friends.* New York: Holt.

Rosa Guy (1976) *Ruby.* New York: Viking.

Deborah Hautzig (1978) *Hey, Dollface.* New York: William Morrow.

Ann Head (1967) *Mr. and Mrs. Bo Jo Jones.* New York: New American Library.

Irene Hunt (1966) *Up a Road Slowly.* New York: Grosset and Dunlap.

Madeline l'Engle (1965) *Camilla.* New York: Delacorte.

Ursula Le Guin (1976) *Very Far Away from Anywhere Else.* New York: Bantam.

Katie L. Lyle (1973) *I Will Go Barefoot All Summer for You.* New York: Dell.

Norma Fox Mazer (1979) *Up in Seth's Room.* New York: Dell.

Elizabeth Ogilvie (1956) *Blueberry Summer.* New York: Scholastic Books.

Francine Pascal (1979) *My First Love and Other Disasters.* New York: Viking.

Stella Pevsner (1980) *Cute Is a Four-letter Word*. New York: Archway Books.
Stella Pevsner (1981) *I'll Always Remember You . . . Maybe*. New York: Pocket Books.
Melinda Pollowitz (1981) *Princess Amy*. New York: Bantam.
Janet Quin-Harkin (1981) *California Girl*. New York: Bantam.
Mary Stolz (1956) *The Day and the Way We Met*. New York: Harper and Row.
James L. Summers (1953) *Girl Trouble*. New York: Scholastic Books.
Brenda Wilkinson (1981) *Ludell and Willie*. New York: Bantam Books.
Paul Zindel (1969) *My Darling, My Hamburger*. New York: Bantam.

Chapter 3

Children's Literature: A Research Proposal from the Perspective of the Sociology of School Knowledge[1]

Joel Taxel
University of Georgia

The past several decades have witnessed an explosive growth in research in children's literature. This scholarship is noteworthy both for its varied focuses and for its diverse authorship. Despite these differences, much of the interest in literature for children derives from the belief that 'what is read does indeed influence the reader' (Zimet, 1976, p. 14). That is, people are arguing about literature for children because they believe that books affect children's attitudes and behaviour.

Despite differences in affiliation, orientation and research emphasis, it is possible to identify two basic thrusts in research in children's literature. The first is textual and includes analysis of the individual texts or groups of texts written for children (e.g., Christian-Smith, Chapter 2, this volume; Deluca, 1984; Kuznets, 1985; Taxel, 1984, 1986; Tremper, 1980). The authors of these varied studies all tacitly grant objective status to the text and, in effect, claim that their textual interpretation is the 'preferred' one. Implicit in this approach is the assumption that meaning is determined by the text itself. This orientation manifests itself in the overwhelming majority of literature classes when teachers assist students in discovering the meaning of a literary work, be it *Charlotte's Web* or *Hamlet*.

The second and sharply contrasting thrust of research in children's literature focuses on the reader rather than on the text. Here the claim is that no literary work exists without reference to a specific reader. In fact, literary works are seen as coming into being in the 'transaction' that occurs when reader meets text (Rosenblatt, 1938/1976; 1978). Following Rosenblatt's lead, other response theorists and researchers (e.g., Agee and Galda, 1983; Applebee, 1978; Bleich, 1978; Holland, 1968; Iser, 1978) have sought to outline the broad array of developmental, psychological and social factors which contribute to the creation and realization of literary works by adult and child readers.

Clearly, these two approaches have quite different conceptual, philosophical, epistemological, methodological bases, and quite different implications for pedagogy. As Kelly-Byrne (1984–85, p. 196) has noted, 'the difference between a critic simply reading a text or instead trying to find out how people actually respond to a text, is a light year difference.' In this chapter I shall elaborate on this dichotomy and suggest a cycle of research which I believe has the potential to lend a measure of coherence to a field of study which at present is divided over issues of fundamental significance. The conceptual framework for this presentation derives from the sociology of school knowledge. It should be noted that few of those who study children's literature actually subscribe to this perspective. One of my basic contentions, however, is that literature constitutes an important source of children's knowledge about and orientation to the social world. Because children's literature historically has been biased in favour of, and against, readily identifiable social groups and because the sociology of school knowledge perspective is vitally concerned with the very particular ways that children's subjective views of the world are formulated, I believe that this perspective promises to infuse the discussion of children's literature with a greater concern with the issues of justice and equity than is generally the case. In addition, since those adopting this framework seek to understand the many complex and interrelated relationships so vital to the creation of social phenomena, the sociology of school knowledge should prove helpful in unifying the diverse strands of inquiry into children's literature referred to above.

The Sociology of School Knowledge

Curriculum researchers and sociologists of education have begun to apply the insights of critical social theorists to the study of schooling with increasing frequency. Central to this research is an interest in establishing the connections between schools and society. More precisely, researchers are seeking to better understand the relations between schools and the array of socioeconomic and political institutions which both give rise to and are influenced by them. Of special concern is the role played by the process of schooling in the reproduction of a social order divided by class, race and gender (e.g., Apple, 1979, 1982). This concern has led to investigations which have sought to understand how the formal and informal knowledge presented in schools contribute to the formation of values, world views and beliefs supportive of an inequitable social system.

Studies by Anyon (1979, 1981), Beyer (1983), Carlson (Chapter 4, this volume), Gilbert (Chapter 6, this volume), Taxel (1981, 1984), Wald (Chapter 1, this volume) and others have documented the extent to which textbooks, literature for children, commonly utilized approaches to instruction and the social relations of the classroom (i.e., the hidden curriculum) are dominated by the world views and ideological perspectives of those occupying positions of socioeconomic pre-eminence in society. Williams (Chapter 5, this volume) refers to this dominating set of world views and perspectives as a 'selective tradition'. He argues that the intentionally selective transmission of the knowledge, history and culture of only certain groups from the larger universe of possible knowledge, history and culture is central to the process of social and cultural definition and identification. The selective tradition provides historical and cultural ratification of the social order and is an important element of the 'hegemonic culture' which constitutes the sense of reality for most people in a society.

The concept of a hegemonic selective tradition provides a powerful lens through which to view the numerous content analyses which point to the existence and persistence of racism, sexism and anti-union sentiment in a wide range of instructional materials, including literature for children (Taxel, 1981). More concretely, the argument is that when children are repeatedly exposed to messages which, for example, denigrate women or an ethnic group, they are likely to develop negative attitudes toward women and these groups. Similarly, if children's literature and textbooks exclude or underrepresent women or members of certain ethnic or social groups, readers may conclude that these groups, and the individuals in them, are not important members of the society. The historic dominance of Anglo men (and boys) in literature and textbooks thus is said to provide an important source of legitimacy for the power and dominant position which Anglo men have long held in society. Wexler (1982, p. 279) touches on some of these points in his summary and critique of extant research in the sociology of school knowledge:

> This new sociology of school knowledge and curriculum demonstrates that social power is culturally represented, and that knowledge and culture are essential moments in the process of social domination . . . . The selective transmission of class culture as common culture silences the cultures of the oppressed, and legitimates the present order as natural and eternal.

It is essential that the existence of the selective tradition not be construed as the result of a centralized conspiracy to control the hearts and minds of nations like the United States, Great Britain, Australia and Canada. Williams argues that selective traditions are continuously being constituted, reconstituted and contested and that the 'struggle against selective traditions . . . is a major part of all contemporary cultural activity.' Thus, while research has documented the pervasive racism and sexism in children's literature, it is also the case that contradictory, oppositional tendencies — those that run counter to, and directly challenge, the selective tradition — are present in almost every historical period (Sims, 1982; Taxel, 1986). Harris's (1986) study of the lamentably short-lived *Brownies Book Magazine* is a dramatic case in point. Founded in 1920 by the Black sociologist and activist W.E.B. DuBois, the *Brownies Book* was an explicit attempt to provide a positive alternative to the selective tradition of this era which either excluded Black people, their history and their culture from children's literature or presented Blacks in a grotesquely pejorative manner.

In addition to developing a more subtle, nuanced analysis of the selective tradition in textbooks and literature, critically-oriented researchers more recently have become vitally concerned with understanding the ways that students react or respond to the messages contained in these materials. Increasingly, this research has focused on student resistance to these messages. This dual focus of research in the sociology of school knowledge on the analysis of the various school curricula and observation and analysis of students' response and resistance to them parallels the dual thrust of research in children's literature.

Resistance theories are a direct challenge to the claims of those like Bowles and Gintis (1976) who would have us believe that students passively accept the values, world views and ideological perspectives contained in both the formal and hidden curricula of schools. Their assumption was that students uncritically accept and internalize, for example, the racist and sexist messages contained in children's literature and textbooks. Observational studies by Anyon (1981) and Willis (1977), however, indicate that this explanation is simplistic and often false. Moreover, these studies have shown the many creative, often contradictory, and at times self-defeating ways in which students accept, reject, modify and transform the various dimensions of the school curriculum. It is here that the parallels between resistance and reader response theories are evident. Both theories reject the assumption of a passive individual who simply absorbs the values, world views, perspectives, etc., contained in the school curriculum or literary text. Instead, both resistance and response theorists posit an active, creative and dynamic individual engaged in a process of meaning-making on the basis of a complex variety of factors.

Consequently, just as those investigating the culture of schooling cannot assume that such study need entail only an analysis of the various curriculum materials, neither can those interested in literature for children assume that an understanding of that literature can be gained solely through analyses, however rigorous, of the literary works themselves. Therefore, it is increasingly apparent to those who have sought to document the existence of a selective tradition in literature for children that research must seek to determine whether the meanings researchers attribute to literary works 'superimpose themselves automatically and finally into the consciousness and behavior of all audiences at all times' (Gitlin, 1979, p. 253). Put simply, the issues are: do readers actually derive the same meanings from literary works as the critics; does what is read really influence the reader as critics are apt to believe?

My suggestion is that inquiries into the responses of readers and the analyses of texts be joined into a broadly conceived cycle of research which would account for the creation of the text itself by an author and its subsequent production and distribution by the publishing industry. The ultimate objective of the research cycle would be a description of the ways in which individuals and/or groups (e.g., authors, editors, publishers and readers) at the various stages of cultural creation, production and consumption contribute to the 'making of meaning' at particular moments in history. The remainder of this chapter is devoted to a more detailed explication of this research proposal.[2]

Analysis of the Creation of Literary Works

Basic to the perspective being presented is the belief that the creation of a literary work cannot be viewed as the result of a process in which a writer, moved solely by his or her artistic impulses, simply creates. It is assumed that writers are social agents who both respond to and help create socioeconomic, historical and political conditions. Consequently, far more needs to be known about how the biographical experiences of individual authors, and groups of authors, contribute to the creation of literature. This would entail investigations of how, and in what fashion, specific historical, regional, ethnic, social class and other more idiosyncratic factors predispose authors to write in particular ways.

Kelly (1970), for example, focuses on the fascinating interrelations between certain persistent, formulaic qualities of late nineteenth century magazines such as *St. Nicholas* and the 'Gentry' authors who created them. Coming primarily from well-to-do homes in the Northeast, these writers watched with horror as the values they believed America was built on (e.g., family, individual responsibility and initiative) were undermined by the vulgar materialism of the so-called Gilded Age. Kelly explains how the conjunction of biography and a specific socioeconomic and historical setting contributed to the creation of fictional formulas designed to present children with 'strategies for order' at a time when the world appeared to have lost its moral compass. Erisman (1966) and Zipes (1983) take a similar approach in their analyses of the work of L. Frank Baum, author of the still popular Oz books.

Relatively little has been written about developments within corporations which publish literature for children. Turow's (1978) now dated volume deals with the crucial question of how publisher-market relations affect which books get to children. Sims's (1982) study of recent fiction about the Afro-American experience points out that the groundwork for the development of an authentic Black literature was paved not only by the heightened consciousness concomitant to the Civil Rights Movement, but also by the Elementary and Secondary Education Act of 1965 which provided Federal funds for school and public libraries. This legislation, in effect, created a market for books about Black children. Unfortunately, as Sims (1982) and Myers (1979) have noted, the disappearance of these funds, at least in part, has been responsible for the current lean period in the publishing of books about Afro-Americans.

Perhaps the most significant, and insufficiently appreciated, development in the publishing industry today is the steady absorption of previously independent publishing houses by multinational conglomerates (Glazer, 1981). According to Chaikin (1982), among the many effects of this phenomenon is an unwillingness on the part of the publishers to take chances on new authors or to publish books without an assured market. One of the more ominous harbingers of a future under the sway of this multinational corporatist control are the seemingly innumerable 'teen romance series'. Called the 'publishing phenomenon of the decade' (Lanes, 1981), these formula-written novels are born of market research which indicated a conservative backlash to the women's movement and what many saw as the lack of restraint evident in literature for children and young adults published in the late 1960s and 1970s under the guise of the 'new realism'. These 'Harlequins for Teens' have already sold millions of copies, are being aggressively promoted by mass-marketing campaigns that are without precedent in the history of children's book publishing[3] and, as Christian-Smith's chapter in this volume indicates, are increasingly being utilized as instructional materials in American classrooms.

Analysis of Literary Works

Christian-Smith's (Chapter 2, this volume) semiotic analysis of teen romances reveals that feminine identity in her sample of novels published over a forty-year period is constructed around the anachronistically defined codes of romance, beauty and sexuality. Her study reflects both the desire of researchers to understand the literary and value structure of children's literature and their interest in bringing greater theoretical and methodological sophistication to research. Unquestionably, the many analyses of the content of children's literature have helped to establish the extent to which children's literature omits girls and women or portrays them in a stereotypic fashion (e.g., Dixon, 1977; Knodel, 1982; Lieberman, 1972; Schubert, 1980; Stewig and Knopfel, 1975; Weitzman *et al.*, 1973), either excludes or stereotypes various minority groups (e.g., Broderick, 1973; Dixon, 1977; Klein, 1985; MacCann and Woodward, 1972; Zimet, 1976), presents other 'anti-human values' (e.g., Council on Interracial Books for Children, 1976), or fosters political ideas and messages which are biased in favour of the dominant social groups (e.g., Dixon, 1977). Nevertheless, most of this research lacks a theoretical framework which explains the remarkable consistency of the findings over time. Also lacking is a theory which would explicate the social functions of children's literature.

Kelly (1970, 1974) provides the foundations for such a theory and also urges that analyses of children's literature consider the complex social, political, historical and ideological forces which influence authors to write as they do. Arguing that writing for children is part of a process whereby particular values, assumptions, principles and patterns for maintaining social order are legitimated, Kelly suggests that the social function of nineteenth century periodical fiction for children was to ratify a vision of the world and a model of behaviour consistent with the authors' perceptions of a desirable social order.

I, like Kelly, have assumed that children's literature is an important source for children to draw upon as they construct their conceptions of reality. I have argued that reality in children's literature is largely defined by the perspectives, values and world views of those who wield economic and political power in society. Despite some significant, if uneven, progress in the past decade and a half, the canon of children's literature continues to be dominated by a selective tradition which both reflects and contributes to the reproduction of the present, inequitable social order (Taxel, 1981).

In a study of Revolutionary War fiction (Taxel, 1984), I extended Kelly's (1970, p. 91) notion that fictional form, or narrative structure, is 'informed and sustained by a particular definition of social experience.' My analysis revealed quite different value and ideological commitments implicit in the different 'models of social action' contained in a sample of novels that spanned more than three-quarters of a century. Characters in books written between 1899 and 1930 were encouraged to adhere to values and follow courses of action which were quite different from those of characters in novels written between 1967 and 1976. Moreover, I discovered that certain major historical events appear to have tremendous influence on the fictionalized accounts of the Revolution written around the time of their occurrence. Novels like *Johnny Tremain* (Forbes, 1943), written during World War II, were said to be reflective of American attitudes toward that world-wide conflagration. In contrast, the bitterly divisive nature of the Vietnam War was apparent in novels like *My Brother Sam is Dead* (Collier and Collier, 1974), where the justice of the American cause was called into question, and in *Freelon Starbird* (Snow, 1976), where the cause was explicitly debunked. Despite important changes in novel content and structure, the sample was dominated by a simplistic interpretation of this pivotal event in American history. The sample as a whole was also described as conservative because, with the exception of Edwards's (1972) *When the World's on Fire*, the novels ignored the terrible plight of Black people during the Revolution while giving the false impression that it resulted in the creation of a near-perfect form of government.

More recently (Taxel, 1986), I compared the markedly different models of social action contained in two novels which chronicle the painful, growing awareness of young Black girls to the bitter realities of race relations in the United States during the first third of the twentieth century. At first glance the novels are seen to share many important structural elements. However, Cassie Logan of *Roll of Thunder, Hear My Cry* (Taylor, 1977 a) is taught by her parents that racism must be confronted with the cautious, yet insistent demand that the dignity and worth of all people be respected. The Logans engage in a variety of courageous actions which are reflective of this philosophy (e.g., they organize a boycott of a store owned by an especially belligerent 'redneck'). In contrast, Ben Sills, in Ouida Sebestyen's *Words by Heart* (1979), instructs her daughter, Lena, to turn the other cheek and wait on the Lord in the face of racist provocations, thus suggesting that social change will occur when racism's victims show sufficient faith and patience. Although the study did not include detailed biographies of the authors, it was clear that the quite different background experiences of Taylor, who is Black, and Sebestyen, who is white (Mercier, 1979; Taylor, 1977 b), go a long way in explaining their novels' radically different models of social action.

Zipes's (1979, 1983, 1985) studies of folk and fairy tales are the final body of work to be treated in this section. In his efforts to develop a social history of the fairy tale, Zipes (1979, p. 317) argues that the genre emerged in Europe when writers like Charles Perrault and Wilhelm and Jacob Grimm 'appropriated the oral folktale and converted it into a type of literary discourse about mores, values, and manners so that children would become civilized according to the social code of the time.' According to this view, the bourgeois and aristocratic writers of the sixteenth through eighteenth centuries transformed the folk tale into a new literary genre, the fairy tale, which reflected a change in values that resulted from the breakdown of feudalism and the rise of capitalism.

Central to Zipes's work is his explanation of how the changes in the tales led to a radical shift in the 'discourse on socialization' implicit in them. He argues that the tales most often printed and read for the last two centuries (e.g., *Cinderella, Snow White, Sleeping Beauty* and *Little Red Riding Hood*) emphasize male adventure and power and female domesticity and passivity. By the late nineteenth century the two dominant variants in America and Western Europe of *Cinderella*, for example, were those of Perrault and the Brothers Grimm. Zipes (1985) suggests that their variants, which are based on an oral tale celebrating the ritualistic initiation of a young girl into a matrilineal society, transformed the tale into one which outlined the domestic requirements necessary for a young girl to make herself acceptable for marriage. Significantly, Zipes's focus on the relations between historically specific 'discourses on socialization' parallels that of Kelly (1970) on 'strategies for order' Taxel's (1984, 1986) concern with 'models of social action', and Christian-Smith's (Chapter 2, this volume) interest in 'codes of romance'.

Analysis of Response to Literary Works

Culminating the cycle of research is the analysis of precisely what occurs when readers, especially child readers, actually read books. What is sought is an understanding of the dynamics of the transaction which takes place when individuals interact with literary works, and the nature of the many factors which give each 'realization' (Iser, 1978) opr 'evocation' (Rosenblatt, (1978) of a text its particular characteristics. In contrast to the research just discussed, which effectively grants objective status to the literary text (and to the researcher's reading of it), response theorists emphasize, to varying degrees, the importance of the reader in the 'creation' of a literary text. Indeed, in some models of the act of reading (e.g., Bleich, 1978) the text is not even granted the status of 'object' outside of an individual reader's perception of it. Clearly, the key to the response process lies in Rosenblatt's notion of a 'transaction' between reader and text. As Galda (1983, p. 2) explains, there is 'a consensus across theoretical perspectives that a dialectic between reader and text constitutes reading and responding to a literary work.'

A primary focus of the research on response has been the delineation of the specific variables which give a particular evocation of a text its distinctive characteristics. Factors such as the experiential background and psychological make-up of the reader are believed to account for readers' particular styles of response (e.g., Holland, 1968). Thus to give what may perhaps be an extreme example, a southern woman who can trace her lineage back to early eighteenth century Virginia planter class, and who is an avid reader of romances, is likely to have a radically different response to books like *Gone With the Wind* and *Roots* than would a southern Black woman who is the descendant of slaves.

Cognitive development, often explained with reference to Piagetian theory, is another factor which has attracted considerable attention. Primary grade children, for example, are believed to be developmentally unable to draw inferences or comprehend the symbolic dimension of texts (e.g., Galda, 1982). Favat (1977), also drawing on Piagetian theory, argues that the fascination which children aged 6–8 have with folk and fairy tales is the result of the correspondence between the cognitive and mental outlook of children that age and the structure of the tales themselves (e.g., the belief in magic, animism). Additional factors such as a child's developing sense of story, certain aspects of the texts themselves and the context in which the reading occurs are also said to prescribe the way a reader responds (Galda, 1983).

Despite the richness and diversity of this research, there are significant gaps in it which the proposed cycle of research would fill. Little attention thus far has been given to how such crucial factors as gender, ethnicity and socioeconomic status influence response. How, for example, would the responses of a middle-class Black child differ from those of a white child from a fundamentalist family to books like *Roll of Thunder, Hear My Cry* and *Words by Heart*?

Very few studies have investigated response in the course of regular day-to-day classroom interactions. While studies by Hickman (1981) and Kiefer (1983) point to the vital importance of peer pressure and interaction and the crucial influence of the teacher in shaping response, these studies do not even begin to approach the multifaceted, multilayered 'phenomenology' or 'ethnography of audiences' called for by Gitlin (1979). A final gap in the research is the conspicuous absence of studies on the response of readers to the sociopolitical dimensions of texts. Particularly in need of investigation is the question of whether the meanings ascribed to literary works, such as those cited in the previous section, are in fact those apprehended by different audiences in different settings. Both Kelly and I have subscribed to the view that children's literature has the social function of legitimating particular values, assumptions and principles reflective of particular, historically rooted social interests. Implicit in this perspective is the assumption that the reader does, in fact, derive essentially the same meanings from a text as does the researcher. Clearly, these positions are at variance with the reader response research, with its insistence on the diverse, idiosyncratic nature of response, as well as resistance theory, which conceives of social actors as active, dynamic makers of their own meaning. The work of several key response theorists does appear to offer the means to begin resolving this apparent theoretical contradiction.

Iser (1978) and Rosenblatt (1978) see the literary experience as potentially enabling readers to 'transcend the limitations of their experiences; to formulate themselves; and to assess cultural norms and values.' This occurs by virtue of the complementary function of the literary experience to join past experience of life and a text to present some new slice of experience (Whalen-Levitt, 1980, p. 12). Iser (1978) concludes that during the act of reading 'the old conditions the form of the new and then selectively restructures the old' (quoted by Whalen-Levitt, 1980, p. 12). Literary experiences thus are viewed as important to a reader's conceptual-ization of reality because they provide a unique opportunity for readers to formulate and reformulate 'symbolic reservoirs' (Whalen-Levitt, 1980, p. 12). In contrast to the theory of the social functions of children's literature, the Iser/Rosenblatt formulation allows for the possibility that, despite the documented presence of dominant and dominating ideas in texts, there can be no certainty that readers will perceive or accept them as such. Indeed, readers may ignore, reject, modify, transform, or accept these ideas on the basis of previous experience, their stage of cognitive development, mental set, or any number of other factors. In rejecting the assumption that readers passively internalize a text's messages, this formulation effectively asserts or reclaims the agency of the reader.

Iser's (1978) assertion that the 'work' is located somewhere between the text itself and the reader, and is actualized as a result of the interaction between the two, clarifies this complex point. The reader perceives the message by composing it and consequently the 'division between subject and object no longer applies, and it follows that meaning is no longer an object to be defined, but is an effect to be experienced' (quoted by Weaver, 1985, p. 308). This formulation also allows us to fuse reader response theory with the resistance theories of Apple (1982) and Giroux (1983). This fusion has significant implications not only for theory and research, but for pedagogy as well.

Viewing children as active and dynamic makers of meaning, rather than as the passive recipients of the ideas contained in literary works, necessitates that both researchers and teachers seek a more precise understanding of how individual children, and groups of children, in diverse instructional settings at specific socio-historical moments, construct meaning from particular literary works. Basic to this approach is the recognition of the vital role of ethnic and social class background, past experiences, level of cognitive and social development, etc. in the process of making meaning.

For the teacher, the view of the child as an active participant in the 'creation' of literary texts requires that literary study and analysis be undertaken in ways that are significantly different from those practised in the past. The role of the teacher of literature, in essence, is transformed from one who leads readers to the 'correct' meaning of a literary work, to one who seeks to create the conditions which will permit children, under guidance of the text, to construct 'their own' literary work. Development of a 'community of readers' who exchange ideas, share insights and perceptions, deliberate over areas of agreement and disagreement, etc. is an essential prerequisite to the development of the emancipatory, transformative pedagogy advocated by curriculum theorists such as Apple (1982) and Giroux (1983).

Although particular meanings or interpretations are never imposed, it is still possible to develop strategies that will assist children in demystification of hegemonic selective traditions which, as we have seen, are the foundation of the sense of reality held by most people in our society (Taxel, 1982, 1986, 1987). Students, for example, are encouraged to react freely and openly to literary texts perceived to be racist and sexist and to compare these texts to others containing more fully realized and realistic characters. Critical scrutiny of Taylor's *Roll of Thunder, Hear My Cry* (1977) makes it possible to lay bare the glaring contradiction between the United States' cherished ideology of liberty and justice for all and the relentless denial of these rights to its Black citizens. Likewise, students can examine novels about historical events like the American Revolution or the Vietnam War and consider the implications of the varying historical interpretations implicit in them (Taxel, 1984; Saul, 1985). The point that this approach to pedagogy does not merely substitute the imposition of one set of meanings for another deemed 'more progressive' is crucial. Indeed, at the very heart of the approach is a faith in children and a firm belief that a fundamental goal of education must be to empower them to read, write and think critically and to make difficult decisions after weighing available in the light of varying conceptions of what is right and just.

It is firmly believed that such a cycle of research can lead to the development of a true sociology of children's literature. By adapting the suggestions contained in this chapter to the needs of studies of particular children, child audiences and literary texts written for them, we can perhaps begin to cut through what Whalen-Levitt (1980) refers to as the 'longstanding impasse' or 'dualism' between reader and text which has long plagued scholars in the field. In so doing we can take a giant step toward an understanding of how children came to understand their world. Such understanding is indispensable to any attempt to transform it.

Notes

1. The author wishes to thank Susan Cox for her assistance in the preparation of this chapter.
2. Janice Radway's (1984) ethnography of a community of adult romance readers deals with many of the issues and concerns addressed in this chapter. Although there is much to be learned from Radway's study, the fact that her 'subjects' were adults makes for considerable differences between her project and the one proposed.
3. This is not to suggest that the teen romances are the first mass-market, formula-written books for children. Edward Stratemeyer, for example, built an organization that published many enormously popular series and, according to Taylor (1985, p. 355), 'still sells about 6,000,000 books each year.'

References

AGEE, H. and GALDA, L. (Eds) (1983) 'Response to literature: Empirical and theoretical studies,' *Journal of Research and Development in Education*. 16, 3, 1–75.

ANYON, J.M. (1979) 'Ideology and United States history textbooks,' *Harvard Educational Review*, 49, 361–86.

ANYON, J.M. (1981) 'Social class and school knowledge,' *Curriculum Inquiry*, 11, 3–42.

APPLE, M.W. (1979) *Ideology and Curriculum*. London: Routledge and Kegan Paul.

APPLE, M.W. (1982) *Education and Power*. Boston, Mass.: Routledge and Kegan Paul.

APPLEBEE, A. (1978) *The Child's Concept of Story: Ages Two to Seventeen*. Chicago, Ill.: University of Chicago Press.

BEYER, L. (1983) 'Aesthetic curriculum and cultural reproduction,' in APPLE, M. and WEIS, L. (Eds), *Ideology and Practice in Schooling*, Philadelphia, Penn.: Temple University Press.

BLEICH, D. (1978) *Subjective Criticism*. Baltimore, Md.: Johns Hopkins University Press.

BOWLES, S. and GINTIS, H. (1976) *Schooling in Capitalist America: Educational Reform and the*

Contradictions of Economic Life. New York: Basic Books.

BRODERICK, D. (1973) *Image of the Black in Children's Literature*. New York: Bowker.

CHAIKIN, M. (1982) 'What's going on in publishing,' *The Advocate*, 1, 144–8.

COLLIER, J.L. and COLLIER, C. (1974) *My Brother Sam Is Dead*. New York: Scholastic Books.

Council on Interracial Books for Children (1976) *Human and Anti-Human Values in Children's Books*. New York: Racism and Sexism Resource Center for Educators.

DELUCA, G. (1984) 'Exploring the levels of childhood: The allegorical sensibility of Maurice Sendak,' *Children's Literature*, Vol. 12. New Haven, Conn.: Yale University Press.

DIXON, B. (1977) *Catching Them Young: Political Ideas in Children's Fiction*. London: Pluto Press.

EDWARDS, S. (1972) *When the World's on Fire*. New York: Coward, McCann and Geoghegan.

ERISMAN, F.R. (1966) *There Was a Child Went Forth: A Study of St. Nicholas Magazine and Selected Children's Authors, 1890–1915*. Doctoral dissertation, University of Minnesota.

FAVAT, A. (1977) *Child and Tale: The Origins of Interest*. Urbana, Ill.: NCTE.

FORBES, E. (1943) *Johnny Tremain*. New York: Dell.

GALDA, L. (1982) 'Assuming the spectator stance: An examination of the responses of three young readers,' *Research in the Teaching of English*, 16, 1–20.

GALDA, L. (1983) 'Research in response to literature,' *Journal of Research and Development in Education*, 16, 1–7.

GIROUX, H. (1983) *Theory and Resistance in Education: A Pedagogy for the Opposition*. South Hadey, Mass.: Bergin and Garvey Publishers.

GITLIN, T. (1979) 'Prime time ideology: The hegemonic process in television entertainment,' *Social Problems*, 26, 251–66.

GLAZER, S. (1981) 'The merry-go-around: Who owns whom; or ain't nothing sacred anymore? *Texas Library Journal*, 57, 7–9.

HARRIS, V. (1986) *The Brownies Book: Challenge to the Selective Tradition in Children's Literature*. Doctoral dissertation, University of Georgia.

HICKMAN, J. (1981) 'A new perspective on response to literature: Research in an elementary school setting,' *Research in the Teaching of English*, 15, 343–54.

HOLLAND, N.H. (1968) *The Dynamics of Literary Response*. New York: W.W. Norton.

ISER, W. (1978) *The Art of Reading: A Theory of Aesthetic Response*. Baltimore, Md.: Johns Hopkins University Press.

KELLY, R.G. (1970) *Mother Was a Lady: Strategy and Order in Selected American Children's Periodicals, 1865–1890*. Doctoral dissertation, University of Iowa.

KELLY, R.G. (1974) 'Literature and the historian,' *American Quarterly*, 26, 141–59.

KELLY-BYRNE, D. (1984–85) 'The 1984 conference of the Children's Literature Association, Charlotte, North Carolina, May 24–27: A participant's response,' *Children's Literature Association Quarterly*, 9, 195–8.

KIEFER, B. (1983) 'The responses of children in a combination first/second grade classroom to picture books in a variety of artistic styles,' *Journal of Research and Development in Education*, 16, 3, 14–20.

KLEIN, G. (1985) *Reading into Racism: Bias in Children's Literature and Learning Materials*. London: Routledge and Kegan Paul.

KNODEL, B. (1982) 'Still far from equal: Young women in literature adolescents,' Paper presented to annual meeting of National Council of Teachers of English Spring Conference, 15–17 April 1982. ERIC No. 217 425.

KUZNETS, L. (1985) '"High fantasy" in America: A study of Lloyd Alexander, Ursula Le Guin and Susan Cooper,' *The Lion and Unicorn*, 9, 19–35.

LANES, S. (1981) 'Here come the block busters — Teen books go big time,' *Interracial Books for Children Bulletin*, 12, 2, 5–7.

LIEBERMAN, M. (1972) 'Some day my prince will come: Female acculturation through the fairy tale,' *College English*, 34, 383–95.

MacCANN, D. and WOODWARD, G. (Eds). (1972) *The Black American in Books for Children: Readings in Racism*. 2nd ed. Methuen, N.J.: Scarecrow Press.

MERCIER, J.F. (1979) 'Story behind the book, *Words By Heart*,' *Publisher's Weekly*, 215, 40.

MYERS, W.D. (1979) 'The black experience in children's books: One step forward, two steps back,' *Interracial Books for Children Bulletin*, 10, 6, 14–15.

RADWAY, J. (1984) *Reading the Romance: Women, Patriarchy and Popular Literature*. Chapel Hill, N.C.: University of North Carolina Press.

ROSENBLATT, L.M. (1938/1976) *Literature as Exploration*. New York: Noble and Noble.

ROSENBLATT, L.M. (1978) *The Reader, the Text, the Poem: The Transactional Theory of the Literary Work*. Carbondale, Ill.: Southern Illinois University Press.

SAUL, E.W. (1985) 'Witness for the innocent: Children's literature and the Vietnam War,' *Issues in Education*, 3, 185–97.

SCHUBERT, N. (1980) 'Sex-role stereotyping in Caldecott Award Books,' ERIC No. 220 870.

SEBESTYEN, O. (1979) *Words by Heart*. New York: Bantam.

SIMS, R. (1982) *Shadow and Substance: Afro-American Experience in Contemporary Children's Books*. Urbana, Ill.: NCTE.

SIMS, R. (1983) 'Strong, black girls: A ten year old responds to fiction about Afro-Americans,' *Journal of Research and Development in Education*, 16, 3, 21–8.

SNOW, R. (1976) *Freelon Starbird*. Boston, Mass.: Houghton Mifflin.

STEWIG, J.S. and KNOPFEL, M.L. (1975) 'Sexism in picture books: What progress?' *The Elementary School Journal*, 76, 151–5.

TAXEL, J. (1981) 'The outsiders of the American revolution: The selective tradition in children's fiction,' *Interchange*, 12, 206–28.

TAXEL, J. (1982) 'Sensitizing students to the selective tradition in children's literature,' Paper presented to the American Educational Research Association Convention, 19 March, 1982. ERIC No. 213 647.

TAXEL, J. (1983) 'Historical fiction and historical interpretation,' *The ALAN Review*, 10, 32–6.

TAXEL, J. (1984) 'The American revolution in children's fiction: An analysis of historical meaning and narrative structure,' *Curriculum Inquiry*, 14, 7–55.

TAXEL, J. (1986) 'The black experience in children's fiction: Controversies surrounding award winning books,' *Curriculum Inquiry*, 16, 3, 245–81.

TAXEL, J. (1987) 'Teaching children's literature,' *Teaching Education*, 1, 1, 12–15.

TAYLOR, M. (1977 a) *Roll of Thunder, Hear My Cry*. New York: Avon Press.

TAYLOR, M. (1977 b) 'Newbery acceptance speech,' *The Hornbook*, 55, 401–9.

TAYLOR, M.A. (1985) 'Edward Stratemeyer,' in G. ESTES (Ed.), *American Writers for Children before 1900*. Detroit, Mich.: Gale Research Co.

TREMPER, E. (1980) 'Black English in children's literature,' *The Lion and the Unicorn*, 3, 2, 105–24.

TUROW, J. (1978) *Getting Books to Children: An Exploration of Publisher-Market Relations*. Chicago, Ill.: American Library Association.

WEAVER, C. (1985) 'Parallels between new paradigms in science and in reading and literacy theories: An essay review,' *Research in the Teaching of English*, 19, 298–316.

WEITZMAN, L., EIFLER, D., HOKADA, E. and ROSS, C. (1972) 'Sex-role socialization in picture books for pre-school children,' *American Journal of Sociology*, 77, 1125–50.

WEXLER, P. (1982) 'Structure, text, and subject: A critical sociology of school knowledge,' in M. APPLE (Ed.), *Cultural and Economic Reproduction in Education: Essays on Class, Ideology and the State*. London: Routledge and Kegan Paul.

WHALEN-LEVITT, P. (1980) 'Literature and child readers,' *Children's Literature Association Quarterly*, 4, 4, 9–13.

WILLIAMS, R. (1977) *Marxism and Literature*. London: Oxford University Press.

WILLIS, P. (1977) *Learning to Labor: How Working Class Kids Get Working Class Jobs.* Lexington, Mass.: D.C. Heath.

ZIMET, S.G. (1976) *Print and Prejudice.* London: Hodder and Stoughton.

ZIPES, J. (1979) *Breaking the Magic Spell: Radical Theories of Folk and Fairy Tales:* Austin, Tex.: University of Texas Press.

ZIPES, J. (1983) *Fairy Tales and the Art of Subversion: The Classical Genre for Children and the Process of Civilization.* New York: Wildman Press.

ZIPES, J. (1985) 'Semantic shifts of power in folk and fairy tales,' *The Advocate,* 4, 181–8.

Chapter 4

Legitimation and Delegitimation: American History Textbooks and the Cold War

Dennis L. Carlson
Rutgers University

The prevalence in American political and cultural discourse of a Cold War interpretation of the world situation has come under increasing criticism and public scepticism as the Reagan era ends and as the Soviet Union undergoes changes that are not easily reconcilable within the framework of the Cold War ideology. Nevertheless, we should not expect to see Cold War interpretations abandoned by all, since such a view of the world has been deeply ingrained in the public and it serves the interests of powerful social and economic groups. Instead, the coming years are likely to witness growing conflicts among interpretive frameworks, with supporters of a Cold War ideology attempting to rekindle a sense of 'them' versus 'us', of 'freedom', 'democracy' and 'the American way' pitted against 'the evil empire'. Teachers and students will inevitably have to deal with conflicts among various interpretive frameworks in social studies classes. With this in mind, I want to raise in this chapter the issues of how history textbooks portray US-Soviet relations in the post-World War II era, and how they either simplify these relations consistent with a Cold War ideology or, conversely, 'open up' discourse on US-Soviet relations by challenging Cold War interpretations and presenting alternative interpretive frameworks. I also want to speculate on how teachers might help students use their history texts in ways that reveal their ideological sub-texts and promote reconstructive thinking. Finally, I want to locate this discussion within a critical theoretical framework by posing the issues in terms of legitimation and delegitimation in advanced capitalist society.

Legitimation of the Cold War Ideology

Legitimation, at least as it has been understood within the critical tradition, may be defined as the capacity of the state to engender and maintain the belief that existing institutions, structures and state policies are the most just and appropriate ones for the society generally when in fact they facilitate the power of dominant social groups.[1] This critical theory of legitimation is grounded in a Marxist understanding of class conflicts and dynamics as primary driving forces in social and cultural development. The state is seen to protect and subsidize the interests of élite groups in the economy within this class dynamic. How, then, does legitimation of a Cold War ideology by the state fit within this picture of class interests and dynamics? While I do not mean to imply that there is a unilateral determinacy between the pragmatic interests of élite economic groups and the promotion of a Cold War ideology by the state, it is clear that these two factors *are* related in significant ways that need to be explored. The subsidization of a vast military industry, for example, is one of the ways the state helps 'prop up' the declining rate of profits in the economy generally. Furthermore, as Davis (1984) argues, while the US share of world industrial production has begun to decline in the late twentieth century, America continues to perform an essential maintenance role for the reproduction of the general conditions of world capitalism, and this partially accounts for its preponderance of military power. That the Nicaraguan or Chilean people should democratically choose to follow a socialist road to development, for example, represents no real threat to the great majority of Americans. But it does represent a threat to the hegemony of capitalist 'freedoms' to exploit markets and resources around the world with little if any restriction. Davis observes that 'those sections of capital outside the lush gardens of the defense industry have gained from the innumerable spin-offs and multiplier-effects of the military budget, including the vast state subsidization of research and development' (pp. 9–10). Continuation of current or higher levels of spending in the military budget are therefore likely in the near future, even if this subsidization proves unproductive socially (leading among other things to a fiscal crisis of the state in support of basic human services) and potentially catastrophic if it leads to nuclear war. Finally, the continuation of a Cold War mentality has served to stigmatize all forms of socialist political thinking in America — even the democratic socialist perspectives typically represented in Western European politics. According to the Cold War ideology, socialism is merely a code word for or variant of world communism and is therefore a threat to the 'American way of life'. The ending of the Cold War, consequently, may serve to relegitimate the democratic socialist tradition in America — a situation which élite social groups would find most disturbing.

How, then, does the state manage to perpetuate the legitimation of this situation? That is, what are the particular elements of a Cold War ideology that serve to validate claims by the state that it acts in the interests of the democratic majority? Let me suggest several elements of a Cold War ideology and indicate how each is manifested in the textbooks surveyed.[2] The first element is central to the legitimation of all state policy in advanced capitalism, but certainly applies to military policy in particular. Issues are depoliticized in these textbooks through use of a narrowly instrumental, means-ends way of thinking: what Habermas (1973) calls 'purposive-rational' thinking. That is, issues tend to be treated merely as technical matters, and the only debate normally recognized is over the most effective means of achieving an unquestioned national foreign policy. This also

47

in an ongoing fashion, then at any given point it is difficult to say who is initiating and who is reacting. Obviously, both sides are cast in both roles at the same time. By failing to represent the dialectic or interactive quality of superpower relations, and by maintaining the entrenched distinction between Soviet initiation and American reaction, the textbooks resist the charge that America might also be guilty of 'meddling' around the world.

Delegitimation of the Cold War Ideology

So far I have suggested how the general discursive form as well as specific discursive content of American history textbooks serve to legitimate a dominant Cold War ideological interpretation of the world consistent with the assumptions and interests of élite economic groups. This is the most significant and overriding conclusion of my own research, and it is in line with what other critical theorists in education have had to say about the so-called 'hidden curriculum' of the social studies curriculum.[4] Let me now turn to the oppositional or countervailing notion of delegitimation as it applies to the analysis of history textbooks.

Habermas (1973) argues that the expanded role of the state in advanced capitalism creates an increased need for legitimation; yet, 'it [the state] can no longer rely on residues of tradition that have been undermined and worn out during the development of capitalism' (p. 36). Legitimation can be disassociated from national consensus and 'the will of the people' only temporarily and at great cost. The existence of an independent or 'free' press is an essential component of this general system of legitimation, since codes of journalistic neutrality and objectivity in the press, along with the range of opinion typically represented in the press, validate the notion that what is reported is the 'truth' and politically disinterested. The problem with this system of legitimation is that simultaneous tendencies exist towards the 'unmasking' or delegitimation of state policy when the press assumes an independent, free market form. For example, state policy and its consequences may be held up to revealing scrutiny in press exposés and investigative reporting; or policy consequences and mistakes may be sensationalized in ways that undermine public confidence in the state. Habermas (1973, p. 72) observes that the policy of the state in advanced capitalism cannot help but produce 'unintended, unsettling and publicizing effects' which lead to the forced politicization of a whole range of issues the state would prefer were kept depoliticized (see also Clark and Dear, 1984, pp. 153–74). Furthermore, the state cannot take effective action against this 'stirring up' of issues in the press, since as Clark and Dear (1984) observe in their study of legitimation in American policital culture: 'Inevitably, if avenues for free expression are curtailed then, according to this model, legitimacy itself collapses' (p. 162). The state thus finds itself in a dilemma, facing a crisis of legitimation which can be overcome only through the transformation of the state and the interests it serves.

The continued legitimation of huge military budgets and periodic incursions or threats of incursions around the world to defend American corporate interests consequently remains problematic in the late twentieth century. Most importantly, the ultimate absurdity of a military-oriented state policy in a nuclear age cannot be effectively defended, especially when television movies such as 'The Day After' openly explore the possibility of something going wrong. The nuclear freeze movement, for example, has done much to politicize issues revolving around American defence policy in general. There has also been rising criticism of the sacrosanct treatment of the military budget. Reports of huge cost overruns, kickbacks and profit-gouging in the defense industry help reveal the close partnership between that industry and the state and some of the social costs of that partnership.

To what extent do social studies textbooks reflect these tendencies towards the delegitimation of state policy that exist in the popular press and culture? Evidence of some legitimation 'problem' is to be found, first of all, in the reaction of politically conservative and rightist groups in America to what they perceive to be an anti-American bias in history textbooks. As one example, Herbert London, who heads a pro-business 'Visions of the Future Education Program' for the Hudson Institute, argues in his recent book, *Why Are They Lying to Our Children?* (1985), that some textbooks are unrealistically grim about the future of 'the American way of life' and that they deliberately adhere to an ideology that blames America for many of the world's problems. He cites examples of textbooks which warn ominously of a possible nuclear holocaust, famine in the Third World and environmental expansionism. While critics such as London overlook much (as I have already shown) and exaggerate what they do find to reach these conclusions about an anti-American, anti-business and anti-'progress' slant in textbooks, we need to make sense of their reactions in some way without totally dismissing them.

First of all, as I suggested earlier, the view of social reality depicted in history textbooks cannot deviate too much from that depicted in the popular press and culture without encouraging a form of cognitive dissonance among students that would itself be delegitimating. This means that while American foreign policy always ends up being validated in the textbooks, it is only after at least some 'pro' and 'con' presentation of issues in most of the textbooks. Even if oppositional viewpoints remain without the bounds of a liberal-conservative debate over state policy and offer no radical options, and even if less space typically is provided for oppositional than affirming viewpoints, they are presented in some form in most of the textbooks surveyed. Furthermore, in several textbooks this concern with editorial neutrality and the presentation of alternative viewpoints is significant enough to provide a basis for a critical assessment of some aspects of the dominant Cold War ideology.

As an example, in several textbooks Soviet mistrust of the American government is revealed to have some basis in reality. One textbook observes: 'The United States became convinced that the Soviets wanted not cooperation but world domination. For its part, Russia believed that the Americans, negotiating "with the atom bomb on their hip," were seeking the capitalist encirclement of the Soviet Union.' The textbook also recognizes Soviet domination of Eastern Europe as part of a trade-off involving spheres of influence: 'Churchill and Roosevelt appeared to agree that Eastern Europe should be within the Soviet sphere of influence.' Finally, the textbook acknowledges that the United States, as well as the Soviet Union, has not always kept its word: 'The United States no longer accepted the idea of a Soviet sphere of influence in this region.'

President Reagan is implicitly criticized in two of the textbooks for being overtly confrontational and simplistic in his depiction of the worldwide 'communist menace'. According to one textbook: 'Reagan soon made it clear that he would oppose Soviet expansion everywhere, *even at the risk of confrontation*.' It also describes the situation in El Salvador as a complex one, in which 'guerilla fighters, supported by some intellectuals and peasants, battled to dispossess the ruling class and to redistribute the land.' Finally, the textbook notes that Reagan has critics at home who are fearful that we might become 'involved in another war like that in Vietnam.' The other textbook critical of Reagan notes, for example, that 'many people thought that Reagan was not concerned about the dangers of nuclear war.'

Some indication of the diversity among the textbooks in their treatment of events in the post-war era is provided by a comparison of textbook descriptions of the Marshall Plan. In one textbook we read simply that: 'This aid was offered to the Soviet Union and the Communist countries of Eastern Europe too, but they refused it. The Western European countries accepted the American offer.' The reader is left with the impression that a very generous and altruistic offer of assistance by America was snubbed by communist countries. Yet in another textbook we learn that the Soviets 'formed their own plan to help Eastern European countries they controlled. The Soviets, however, had lost so much during the war that they could give little aid to others. Because of this, their plan did not have the impact of the Marshall Plan.' According to still another text, the Marshall Plan was designed to appeal to liberals in American politics (who 'liked the idea of helping the people of other countries defend their independence . . .') as well as conservatives (who 'liked the idea of resisting communism and thus preserving the free enterprise system . . .'). The textbook notes, however, that critics of the Plan 'argued that it was a disguised form of imperialism.' Furthermore, 'Marshall's offer to include Russia was a bluff, or at least a gamble. If the Russians had accepted it, Congress would probably not have provided the money to make the plan work.' While the first of these three interpretations of the Marshall Plan is highly simplistic, one sided and overtly legitimating, the second is almost neutral in its treatment; and the third arguably serves to delegitimate more than legitimate a major component of post-war American foreign policy.

Beyond the Cold War Curriculum

I have argued in this essay that the social studies curriculum assumes an ambiguous and potentially contradictory position in the struggle over legitimation of state policy, even though its overriding purpose from the perspective of state leadership is to affirm the wisdom of that policy: including the 'need' for a strong nuclear defense posture and an ever-expanding military share of state expenditures. I have also sought to show how this contradiction in the curriculum is reflective of a broader contradiction and crisis of legitimation in advanced capitalism, in that state policy is only successfully validated as the result of an 'open' public debate and national consensus, with the independent press assuming an essential role in this process. The social studies curriculum is not independent of these dynamics to be found in the non-school, independent press, and in fact cannot be if it is to successfully legitimate. The journalistic treatment of the world pervades the general form as well as specific ideological content of the curriculum. While this enhances the legitimating potential of textbooks in most regards, it undermines state validity claims in a number of more subtle ways that are significant.

One important implication of this line of research is a better understanding of whether, or more precisely to what extent, curriculum predetermines interpretations of sociohistorical reality presented to students, or conversely presents students with an opportunity to see beyond simplistic, ideological interpretations of social phenomena. This study indicates that while several American history textbook series are strongly ideological and provide little room for alternative interpretations, several other textbook series provide some limited room for students to deconstruct various viewpoints and construct their own. The choice of a history textbook series by school districts and by teachers will not, therefore, be an insignificant one.

Aside from the room or space textbooks allow for the demystification of state policy, we also need to know more ethnographically about how teachers and students 'use' textbooks in legitimating and delegitimating ways. Here it may be useful to draw upon the distinction Habermas (1973, p. 15) makes between non-reflexive and reflexive learning. The former type of learning, he argues, takes place in contexts in which validity claims are naively taken-for-granted and accepted or rejected without discursive consideration by the participants. This represents an extreme form of taking the textbook as the unquestioned authority. On the other hand, reflexive learning, according to Habermas, takes place in contexts in which discourse — in the full sense of that term — is the vehicle through which understanding develops. In such cases validity claims are 'rendered problematic through institutionalized doubt', so that they may be redeemed or dismissed on the basis of their true merits.

There are several implications of this distinction between reflexive and non-reflexive learning that bear on the role of teachers in helping their students make better use of texts. First, teachers need to help students penetrate the ideological sub-texts embedded in their history textbooks, and also the contradictions within these ideologies. As Apple (1982) has written: '(I)deologies are filled with contradictions . . . . They are not coherent sets of beliefs . . . . Because of this, ideologies are contested, they are continually struggled over' (p. 15). For example, with regard to the Cold War ideology there is the contradiction of ever-larger military expenditures to preserve our international position, and a growing state deficit that threatens to undermine our international position. Of course, the ultimate contradiction in Cold War logic is that nuclear war must be planned for and believed in if it is to be an effective defense strategy, yet nuclear war itself would have no winners. By helping to reveal these contradictions, teachers help students understand that ideologies may also be contested.

Second, teachers need to promote the use of several rather than a single text, each with its own perspectives, insights and particular focus — much as is done in college history courses. Only when students are exposed to varied perspectives and interpretations can they develop critical thinking skills and a more complex under-standing of historical events and developments. There is no reason financially why schools cannot replace their one, expensive textbook series with a variety of paperback histories and collections of essays. That, however, is not likely to happen so long as state schooling is designed primarily to promote non-reflexive rather than reflexive learning. But teachers do have some rights to supplement texts (at their own expense, of course), and they should take as much advantage of these rights as possible. Finally, teachers need to help students relate the concrete events of history they read about in their texts to a theory of history and society. Unless students can understand the larger forces at work in situations, they will fall prey to simplistic historical analysis and ideological manipulation. To lead students beyond the narrow ideological confines of the Cold War will thus necessitate new ways of thinking about history that are profoundly delegitimizing to the status quo.

Notes

1 See Horvat (1979, pp. 81–100). The concept of legitimation is most fully developed in classical sociology in the work of Max Weber, although his conception is not based on a model of the state as serving class-linked interests and legitimation in the Weberian sense does not take on the negative connotations that it has in the Marxist tradition. For a critique of Weber's theory of legitimation see Habermas (1973, pp. 97–101).
2 The textbooks surveyed included: Herbert Bass, George Billias and Emma Lapansky, *America and Americans, Volume II: From Reconstruction to the Present.* Morristown, N.J.: Silver Burdett, 1983; Henry Drewry, Thomas O'Connor and Frank Freidel, *America Is.* Columbus, Ohio, Charles Merrill, 1984; John Garraty, *American History.* New York: Harcourt Brace Jovanovich, 1982; Robert Green, Jr., Laura Becker and Robert Coviello, *The American Tradition: A History of the United States.* Columbus, Ohio: Charles Merrill, 1984; Anatone Mazour, John Peoples and Theodore Rabb, *People and Nations: A World History.* New York: Harcourt Brace Jovanovich, 1983; Sidney Schwartz and John O'Connor, *The New Exploring Our Nation's History.* New York: Globe Books, 1979; Boyd Schafer, Everett Augspurger and Richard McLemore; adapted by Milton Finkelstein, *A High School History of Modern America.* Irvine, Calif.: Laidlaw Brothers, 1977; Clarence Steeg and Richard Hofstadter, *A People and a Nation.* New York: Harper and Row, 1978; Lewis Todd and Merle Curti, *Rise of the American Nation.* New York: Harcourt Brace Jovanovich, 1982; Wilder, Ludlum and Brown; prepared by Susan Roberts, *This is America's Story.* Atlanta, Ga.: Houghton Mifflin, 1983.
3 For an insightful analysis of the consensus theory in American history textbooks see Apple (1979, pp. 82–104).
4 See in particular Anyon (1979), especially for her discussion of the treatment (or lack of treatment) of labour and labour history in textbooks. See also Apple (1979) and Taxel (1981).

References

ANYON, J. (1979) 'Ideology and United States history textbooks,' *Harvard Educational Review*, 43, 361–85.

APPLE, M. (1979) *Ideology and Curriculum*. London: Routledge and Kegan Paul.

APPLE, M. (1982) *Education and Power*. London: Routledge and Kegan Paul.

CLARK, G. and DEAR, M. (1984) *State Apparatus: Structures and Language of Legitimacy*. Boston: Allen and Unwin.

DAVIS, M. (1984) 'The political economy of late-imperial America,' *New Left Review*, 43, 6–38.

HABERMAS, J. (1973) *Legitimation Crisis*. Boston: Beacon Press.

HORVAT, B. (1979) 'The delegitimation of old and the legitimation of new social relations in late capitalist societies,' in B. DENITCH (Ed.), *Legitimation of Regimes: International Frameworks for Analysis*. New York: Sage.

LONDON, H. (1985) *Why Are They Lying to Our Children?* New York: Stein and Day.

TAXEL, J. (1981) 'The outsiders of the American revolution: The selective tradition in children's fiction,' *Interchange*, 12, 2–3, 206–28.

Chapter 5

Hegemony and the Selective Tradition

Raymond Williams
University of Cambridge

The Concept of Hegemony

Gramsci made a distinction between 'rule' (*dominio*) and 'hegemony'. 'Rule' is expressed in directly political forms and in times of crisis by direct or effective coercion. But the more normal situation is a complex interlocking of political, social, and cultural forces, and 'hegemony', according to different interpretations, is either this or the active social and cultural forces which are its necessary elements. Whatever the implications of the concept for Marxist political theory (which has still to recognize many kinds of direct political control, social class control, and economic control, as well as this more general formation), the effects on cultural theory are immediate. For 'hegemony' is a concept which at once includes and goes beyond two powerful earlier concepts: that of 'culture' as a 'whole social process', in which men define and shape their whole lives; and that of 'ideology', in any of its Marxist senses, in which a system of meanings and values is the expression or projection of a particular class interest.

'Hegemony' goes beyond 'culture', as previously defined, in its insistence on relating the 'whole social process' to specific distributions of power and influence. To say that 'men' define and shape their whole lives is true only in abstraction. In any actual society there are specific inequalities in means and therefore in capacity to realize this process. In a class society these are primarily inequalities between classes. Gramsci therefore introduced the necessary recognition of dominance and subordination in what has still, however, to be recognized as a whole process.

It is in just this recognition of the *wholeness* of the process that the concept of 'hegemony' goes beyond 'ideology'. What is decisive is not only the conscious system of ideas and beliefs, but the whole lived social process as practically organized by specific and dominant meanings and values. Ideology, in its normal senses, is a relatively formal and articulated system of meanings, values, and beliefs, of a kind that can be abstracted as a 'world view' or a 'class outlook'. This explains its popularity as a concept in retrospective analysis . . . , since a system of ideas can be abstracted from that once living social process and represented, usually by the selection of 'leading' or typical 'ideologists' or 'ideological features', as the decisive form in which consciousness was at once expressed and controlled (or, as in Althusser, was in effect unconscious, as an imposed structure).

The relatively mixed, confused, incomplete, or inarticulate consciousness of actual people in that period and society is thus overridden in the name of this decisive generalized system . . . . It is the fully articulate and systematic forms which are recognizable as ideology, and there is a corresponding tendency in the analysis of art to look only for similarly fully articulate and systematic expressions of this ideology in the content . . . or form . . . of actual works. In less selective procedures, less dependent on the inherent classicism of the definition of form as fully articulate and systematic, the tendency is to consider works as variants of, or as variably affected by, the decisive abstracted ideology.

More generally, this sense of 'an ideology' is applied in abstract ways to the actual consciousness of both dominant and subordinated classes. A dominant class 'has' this ideology in relatively pure and simple forms. A subordinate class has, in one version, *nothing* but this ideology as its consciousness (since the production of all ideas is, by axiomatic definition, in the hands of those who control the primary means of production) or, in another version, has this ideology imposed on its otherwise different consciousness, which it must struggle to sustain or develop against 'ruling-class ideology'.

The concept of hegemony often, in practice, resembles these definitions, but it is distinct in its refusal to equate consciousness with the articulate formal system which can be and ordinarily is abstracted as 'ideology'. It of course does not exclude the articulate and formal meanings, values and beliefs which a dominant class develops and propagates. But it does not equate these with consciousness, or rather it does not reduce consciousness to them. Instead it sees the relations of domination and subordination, in their forms as practical consciousness, as in effect a saturation of the whole process of living — not only of political and economic activity, nor only of manifest social activity, but of the whole substance of lived identities and relationships, to such a depth that the pressures and limits of what can ultimately be seen as a specific economic, political, and cultural system seem to most of us the pressures and limits of simple experience and common sense.

Hegemony is then not only the articulate upper level of 'ideology', nor are its forms of control only those ordinarily seen as 'manipulation' or 'indoctrination'. It is a whole body of practices and expectations, over the whole of living: our senses and assignments of energy, our shaping perceptions of ourselves and our world. It is a lived system of meanings and values — constitutive and constituting — which as they are experienced as practices appear as reciprocally confirming. It thus constitutes a sense of reality for most people in the society, a sense of absolute because experienced reality beyond which it is very difficult for most members of the society to move, in most areas of their lives. It is, that is to say, in the strongest sense a 'culture', but a culture which has also to be seen as the lived dominance and subordination of particular classes . . . .

A lived hegemony is always a process. It is not, except analytically, a system or a structure. It is a realized complex of experiences, relationships, and activities, with specific and changing pressures and limits. In practice, that is, hegemony can never be singular. Its internal structures are highly complex, as can readily be seen in any concrete analysis. Moreover (and this is crucial, reminding us of the necessary thrust of the concept), it does not just passively exist as a form of dominance. It has continually to be renewed, recreated, deflended and modified. It is also continually resisted, limited, altered, challenged by pressures not at all its own.

Traditions, Institutions and Formations

Hegemony is always an active process, but this does not mean that it is simply a complex of dominant features and elements. On the contrary, it is always a more or less adequate organization and interconnection of otherwise separated and even disparate meanings, values and practices, which it specifically incorporates in a significant culture and an effective order. These are themselves living resolutions — in the broadest sense political resolutions — of specific economic realities. This process of incorporation is of major cultural importance. To understand it, but also to understand the material on which it must work, we need to distinguish three aspects of any cultural process, which we can call traditions, institutions, and formations.

The concept of tradition has been radically neglected in Marxist cultural thought. It is usually seen as at best a secondary factor, which may at most modify other and more decisive historical processes. This is not only because it is ordinarily diagnosed as superstructure, but also because 'tradition' has been commonly understood as a relatively inert, historicized segment of a social structure: tradition as the surviving past. But this version of tradition is weak at the very point where the incorporating sense of tradition is strong: where it is seen, in fact, as an actively shaping force. For tradition is in practice the most evident expression of the dominant and hegemonic pressures and limits. It is always more than an inert historicized segment; indeed it is the most powerful practical means of incorporation. What we have to see is not just 'a tradition' but a *selective tradition*: an intentionally selective version of a shaping past and a pre-shaped present, which is then powerfully operative in the process of social and cultural definition and identification.

It is usually not difficult to show this empirically. Most versions of 'tradition' can be quickly shown to be radically selective. From a whole possible area of past and present, in a particular culture, certain meanings and practices are selected for emphasis and certain other meanings and practices are neglected or excluded. Yet, within a particular hegemony, and as one of its decisive processes, this selection is presented and usually successfully passed off as 'the tradition', 'the significant past'. What has then to be said about any tradition is that it is in this sense an aspect of *contemporary* social and cultural organization, in the interest of the dominance of a specific class. It is a version of the past which is intended to connect with and ratify the present. What it offers in practice is a sense of *predisposed continuity*.

There are, it is true, weaker senses of 'tradition', in explicit contrast to 'innovation' and 'the contemporary'. These are often points of retreat for groups in the society which have been left stranded by some particular hegemonic development. All that is now left to them is the retrospective affirmation of 'traditional values'. Or, from an opposite position, 'traditional habits' are isolated, by some current hegemonic development, as elements of the past which have now to be discarded. Much of the overt argument about tradition is conducted between representatives of these two positions. But at a deeper level the hegemonic sense of tradition is always the most active: a deliberatively selective and connecting process which offers a historical and cultural ratification of a contemporary order.

It is a very powerful process, since it is tied to many practical continuities — families, places, institutions, a language — which are indeed directly experienced. It is also, at any time, a vulnerable process, since it has in practice to discard whole areas of significance, or reinterpret or dilute them, or convert them into forms which support or at least do not contradict the really important elements of the current hegemony. It is significant that much of the most accessible and influential work of the counter-hegemony is historical: the recovery of discarded areas, or the redress of selective and reductive interpretations. But this in turn has little effect unless the lines to the present, in the actual process of the selective tradition, are clearly and actively traced. Otherwise any recovery can be simply residual or marginal. It is at the vital points of connection, where a version of the past is used to ratify the present and to indicate directions for the future, that a selective tradition is at once powerful and vulnerable. Powerful because it is so skilled in making active selective connections, dismissing those it does not want as 'out of date' or 'nostalgic', attacking those it cannot incorporate as 'unprecedented' or 'alien'. Vulnerable because the real record is effectively recoverable, and many of the alternative or opposing practical continuities are still available. Vulnerable also because the selective version of 'a living tradition' is always tied, though often in complex and hidden ways, to explicit contemporary pressures and limits. Its practical inclusions and exclusions are selectively encouraged or discouraged, often so effectively that the deliberate selection is made to verify itself in practice. Yet its selective privileges and interests, material in substance but often ideal in form, including complex elements of style and tone and of basic method, can still be recognized, demonstrated and broken. This struggle for and against selective traditions is understandably a major part of all contemporary cultural activity.

It is true that the effective establishment of a selective tradition can be said to depend on identifiable institutions. But it is an underestimation of the process to suppose that it depends on institutions alone. The relations between cultural, political and economic institutions are themselves very complex, and the substance of these relations is a direct indication of the character of the culture in the wider sense. But it is never only a question of formally identifiable institutions. It is also a question of *formations*; those effective movements and tendencies, in intellectual and artistic life, which have significant and sometimes decisive influence on the active development of a culture, and which have a variable and often oblique relation to formal institutions.

Formal institutions, evidently, have a profound influence on the active social process. What is abstracted in orthodox sociology as 'socialization' is in practice, in any actual society, a specific kind of incorporation. Its description as 'socialization', the universal abstract process on which all human beings can be said to depend, is a way of avoiding or hiding this specific content and intention. Any process of socialization of course includes things that all human beings have to learn, but any specific process ties this necessary learning to a selected range of meanings, values and practices which, in the very closeness of their association with necessary learning, constitute the real foundations of the hegemonic. In a family children are cared for and taught to care for themselves, but within this necessary process fundamental and selective attitudes to self, to others, to a social order and to the material world are both consciously and unconsciously taught. Education transmits necessary knowledge and skills, but always by a particular selection from the whole available range, and with intrinsic attitudes, both to learning and social relations, which are in practice virtually inextricable. Institutions such as churches are explicitly incorporative. Specific communities and specific places of work, exerting powerful and immediate pressures on the conditions of living and of making a living, teach, confirm and in most cases finally enforce selected meanings, values and activities. To describe the effect of all institutions of these kinds is to arrive at an important but still incomplete understanding of incorporation. In modern societies we have to add the major communications systems. These materialize selected news and opinion, and a wide range of selected perceptions and attitudes.

Yet it can still not be supposed that the sum of all these institutions is an organic hegemony. On the contrary, just because it is not 'socialization' but a specific and complex hegemonic process, it is in practice full of contradictions and of unresolved conflicts. This is why it must not be reduced to the activities of an 'ideological state apparatus'. Such apparatus exists, although variably, but the whole process is much wider, and is in some important respects self-generating. By selection it is possible to identify common features in family, school, community, work and communications, and these are important. But just because they are specific processes, with variable particular purposes, and with variable but always effective relations with what must in any case, in the short term, be done, the practical consequence is as often confusion and conflict between what are experienced as different purposes and different values, as it is crude incorporation of a theoretical kind. An effective incorporation is usually in practice achieved; indeed to establish and maintain a class society it must be achieved. But no mere training or pressure is truly hegemonic. The true condition of hegemony is effective *self-identification* with the hegemonic forms: a specific and internalized 'socialization' which is expected to be positive but which, if that is not possible, will rest on a (resigned) recognition of the inevitable and the necessary. An effective culture, in this sense, is always more than the sum of its institutions: not only because these can be seen, in analysis, to derive much of their character from it, but mainly because it is at the level of a whole culture that the crucial *interrelations*, including confusions and conflicts, are really negotiated.

Chapter 6

Text Analysis and Ideology Critique of Curricular Content

Rob Gilbert
James Cook University of North Queensland

In the preceding chapter (Chapter 5) Raymond Williams stipulates that ideology in its normal sense is 'a relatively formal and articulated system of meanings, values and beliefs, of a kind that can be abstacted as a "world view" or a "class outlook"' (p.56). He points out that ideological analysis has conventionally consisted of identifying significant features of these systems as the means by which consciousness is expressed and, at the same time, controlled. The contributions by Wald, Carlson, Christian-Smith and Taxel (Chapters 1–4) are important examples of this work and the variety of concepts and techniques which characterize it, but as these authors themselves indicate, there is some discontent with the conventional approach, and a number of recent developments offer fresh avenues for research.

This chapter traces developments in ideological critique through analysis of curricular texts. A brief review of traditional approaches leads to a commentary on more recent structuralist approaches which have sought a more explicit theory of the production of textual meaning. Criticisms of structuralist theory, and of the concentration on text analysis itself lead to a consideration of present problems and future directions for ideological analysis in the curriculum.

Traditional Approaches

In much traditional educational debate informed by accepted views of truth, objectivity or science, critical analysis of curriculum content addressed itself to ideas of bias or distortion, and the critic's task was to identify those elements of curriculum materials which departed from the ideal of objective description, analysis and explanation of 'the way the world is'. However, objectivity has come to be seen as a highly problematic concept, and this traditional perspective is now regarded as a narrow view of how ideology can operate in school texts. Some studies were nevertheless quite sophisticated. For instance, Dance's classic study, *History the Betrayer: A Study in Bias* (1960), identified aspects of English schoolbooks which denigrated other nations, focusing on the omission of important information through biased selection, lack of balance in curricular topics and prejudiced vocabulary in describing other nationalities. Dance is quite aware of the insidious and pervasive nature of these elements of bias, and he acknowledges that there is no such thing as objective history. Nonetheless, he sees these manifestations of ethnocentric and racist bias as isolated instances of error reflecting group prejudices, rather than systematic patterns of denigration produced by social and political movements such as imperialism and jingoism. What is lacking in all countries, according to Dance, is 'the will to see things the other way around' (Dance, 1960, p. 21).

Studies of this kind were few, for the close critical interpretation of textual meaning demonstrated by Dance was overtaken by quantitative content analysis as the most widespread research method for textual analysis in the social sciences. Aiming for an objective, systematic and statistically reliable method, researchers developed techniques for the quantitative description of text meaning content. Often these were simple frequency counts of the occurrence of prespecified words, phrases or other semantic units. For instance, in a study of values expressed in American children's readers from 1800 to 1950, de Charms and Moeller (1962) counted occurrences of imagery in narrative to compare the incidence of affiliation motivation and achievement motivation as indicators of a developing American ethos. They also measured the amount of moral teaching in the books by counting the number of 'explicit or implicit statements of judgment between right and wrong' (p. 138). The trends identified were interpreted as evidence of cultural change over the period.

There are, however, important difficulties with this approach to content analysis. First, the unit of analysis must be chosen, whether it be a word, a phrase, a sentence, a paragraph, a page, a chapter or some other unit. This decision involves identifying the limits within which a statement's meaning is fully and discretely established. Given that meanings are progressively constructed in the course of reading a text, through such processes as iteration, recursivity and anticipation, to suggest that a meaningful unit can be isolated in this way oversimplifies the way textual meaning is produced by the reader. It also ignores the way a text is sequenced and organized, which is no less important in the construction of meaning than the individual elements of a text. A related problem for quantitative content analysis is that the units of analysis are treated as discrete centres of meaning unaffected by their location in a continuous discourse, or what de Saussure (1966) has called their syntagmatic relations. In content analysis a word or phrase is taken to have an identical meaning each time it occurs in a text. More presumptuously, this assumption of constant meaning applies not only within a text, but also across texts, when comparisons of frequencies are made. In the study by de Charms and Moeller (1962), for example, these identities of meaning are also taken to be timeless, so that comparisons are made across documents spanning a century and a half, ignoring the complex ways in which meanings change in history.

The reliability of quantitative analysis can be high, given close definitions of rules of classification, training of coders and other steps designed to produce so-called low inference measures. However, the selection of textual elements to be counted is of course a high inference step, since there is no low inference way of deciding what aspects of a text are in fact the important ones to identify and analyze. The apparent 'objectivity' of content analysis is, even on its own terms, spurious, as the highly controlled frequency counts can be based only on earlier arguments of interpretation. Finally, content analysis assumes that frequency of occurrence is the central feature of the construction of meaning, ignoring the fact that importance and frequency can be entirely separate aspects of a text.

Content analysis and earlier forms of interpretation were therefore theoretic-ally reductionist and methodologically superficial. Small units were seen as the raw material for the linear and additive process of the production of meaning. Frequent presence was the focus to the neglect of absence and omission, and texts were seen to cohere through simple addition of elements rather than underlying schematic structures. Although some applications of quantitative content analysis remain useful, as in the numerous studies of sex-role stereotypes (Tibbetts, 1979), this paradigm has proven inadequate as a comprehensive theory and method. In the critique of curricular content — as in textual theory in general — it has been overtaken by attempts to analyze texts in ways that emphasize their structured and contextually grounded character.

Structuralist Analyses

A landmark in the analysis of school textbooks was Jean Anyon's paper, 'Ideology and United States Textbooks' (1979), for while Anyon does not discuss her method in detail, her approach demonstrates many of the features of what can generally be called a structuralist method. For Anyon ideology is 'an explanation or interpretation of social reality which, although presented as objective, is demonstrably partial in that it expresses the social priorities of certain political, economic, or other groups' (Anyon, 1979, p. 363). This has similarities with Dance's notion of group prejudices, but recognizes much more closely the relation-ships between textual representation and the social forces that produce them.[1] Thus Anyon's paper reviews the concentration of ownership of school text publishing and the economic interests served by particular representations of economic history. In Anyon's view, to understand how ideologies operate we must analyze the connections between the texts and the conflicting social practices and competing interests they represent. The presupposition here is that meaning cannot be adequately interpreted if ideas are abstracted from their material contexts.

Much of Anyon's text critique uses techniques found in Dance's study of 1960 discussed above. Processes of selection by omission or emphasis, the prejudicial effects of descriptive vocabulary, and overt expressions of sympathy are aspects of textual meaning pointed to in both studies. Again, Anyon sees value in some quantitative measures as well, referring to numbers of paragraphs, pages and books

Part II
Textbook Form

Chapter 7

Literacy Instruction: Technology and Technique[1]

Suzanne de Castell
Simon Fraser University
and
Allan Luke
James Cook University of North Queensland

Since World War II the tendency among both national and international develop-ment agencies such as Labour Canada (1979) and UNESCO (1976, 1980; cf. Gray, 1956) has been to assume that increasing rates of literacy further the economic interests, and the political and social participation of a given populace. The desire to modernize and expand schooling in developing countries makes the kind of cost-efficient and scientifically-based reading textbook programmes used in developed countries appear very attractive. Paradoxically the public educational systems of developed countries, and of the United States and Canada in particular, are charged now with responsibility for what is widely perceived as a 'literacy crisis'. It seems timely, therefore, to reconsider the technical form of literacy curricula currently used in postindustrial countries, and the kinds of literacy to which it gives rise.

In this chapter we examine a preferred strategy for dealing with the perceived literacy crisis: the mass production and mass implementation of 'teacher-proof' curricular programmes to teach the basic skills of reading and writing. We discuss the relation of contemporary technologies to teacher and student technique, and conclude with some exploratory observations on the goodness of fit between what technocratic literacy textbooks teach and the functions and uses of literacy in contemporary North American society.

The Crisis Reconsidered

Claims of crisis arise when contradictions within the social system have become visible, when the system in question is shown not to have met the criteria and objectives which it has publicly set for itself (Habermas, 1975). This situation can lead to a withdrawal of public confidence in the authority and legitimacy of the system itself. These perceptions of crisis, and the ensuing withdrawal of public confidence, create a demand for rational justification of and by the institution in question. Such justifications must either explain the perceived failures as remediable within the existing system, or show them to be inevitable and inescapable hardships caused by surface structure contingencies, not internal system defects (cf. Wilden, 1980). For while a system *problem* can be resolved by modifications — in Kuhn's words 'fine tuning' — of the existing system, a systems *crisis* requires further reaching structural changes.

Currently, the popular press, mass circulation periodicals, scholarly journals and, most importantly, government and industry-sponsored assessments and reports accuse the public educational system of failing to provide 'functional literacy' and basic general education.[2] For, despite ongoing increases in educational investment in the United States and Canada, levels and patterns of literacy acquisition remain *apparently* unimproved. Judged by its own criteria of success and failure, the public school system appears to have failed.

In the face of diminishing public confidence, the educational system must attempt to persuade the public that perceived failures result from a temporary and remediable problem, and not from any structural deficiency inherent in the public system itself. If this attempt at self-justification is unsuccessful, the education system faces what Habermas (1975, p. 49) has called a 'legitimation crisis': a situation in which the dominant culture cannot maintain the requisite level of mass loyalty to its secular and non-secular institutions to eliminate, diminish, or deflect attention away from perceived failures. The current self-justificatory tactic of North American public school systems consists largely in attributing these apparent problems to remediable human failures, in the form of individual, if widespread, teacher incompetence, deficiencies in teacher education, school administration and the like. Fault thereby can be assigned to the performance of human subjects who work in the educational system and not with system defects. The strategy of choice for dealing with apparently declining standards of literacy has been the continuing development and mass-scale implementation of so-called 'teacher proof' curriculum packages and standardized testing programmes.

Whether this strategy succeeds in restoring public confidence remains to be seen. From an analysis of these programmes we will suggest that, public opinion aside, such curricular reforms offer little hope of dealing with the literacy problems disclosed by recent studies.

The Legacy of Educational Science: Standardization and Skills

> If, by a miracle of modern ingenuity, a book could be arranged that only to him who had done what was directed on page one would two become visible, and so on, and much that now requires personal instruction could be managed by print. (Edward Thorndike and Arthur Gates, *Elementary Principles of Education*, 1929)

The move to standardize and teacher-proof curriculum began in the late nineteenth century, and three major developments conditioned its emergence. First, there was a slow but steady shift in the emphasis of school textbooks from a traditional focus on content — on national ideology and religious morality — to an emphasis on scientific methods of literacy training (Smith, 1965). In the United States the two earliest best-selling textbooks were Noah Webster's *American Spelling Book* (1783) and the various versions of *McGuffey's Readers* (1848–1879). These texts tried to capture and reflect what Webster called 'the American Character' (cf. Rollins, 1978) and, according to historians Soltow and Stevens (1981), largely were successful at embedding the teaching of reading and writing within an identifiable 'ideology of literacy'. In Canada colonial authorities feared the movement of American 'radical' sentiments northwards, and Lord Durham's 1839 *Report to the British Parliament* recommended that American textbooks be banned from the schools of English Canada (Robinson, 1976, p. 6; Lorimer, 1984). The *Irish National Readers*, used in other British colonies, were imported into Canadian classrooms in 1842. Well-suited to the aims of loyalist school promoters, these readers stressed allegiance to the Crown, Christian self-sacrifice and traditional British values. Like the American readers of the same era, such content was geared to the creation of a local cultural consensus, though in this case that consensus was closely aligned with the political and economic aims of the British Empire. Until the rise of progressivism in the late nineteenth and early twentieth centuries, the overt moral, religious and ideological content of readers remained a primary criterion for textbook development and adoption.

A second development which influenced the production of standardized curricula was the emergence of experimental psychology in the late nineteenth century, the later expansion of applied psychology and, by the middle of the twentieth century, the systematic application of behavioural psychology to various domains of educational practice. Early research and experimentation, premised on the view that reading was a measurable psychological and physiological process (e.g., Huey, 1909; Thorndike, 1917), provided a scientific basis from which changes were proposed in textbooks and teaching methods. Using lists of commonly occurring words (e.g., Thorndike, 1921; Gates, 1926), measures of syntactic complexity, lexical density and eye movement relative to different kinds of text and typefaces, children's readers could be designed scientifically to be more 'readable', more developmentally appropriate and thereby, it was presumed, more effective. Begun in the interwar period, packaged reading curriculum had its most significant impact in the late 1940s and early 1950s, when William S. Gray and May Hill Arbuthnot's 'Dick and Jane' series — with a host of derivative competitors — was used throughout the United States, Canada and English-speaking 'colonies' like the Philippines (Luke, 1988a). During this time public school enrolments had risen dramatically with the post-war 'baby boom' and an unprecedented shortage of qualified teachers enhanced the appeal of instructional programmes which promised to compensate for a lack of specialized training.

By the mid-1960s B.F. Skinner was proclaiming the virtues of a 'technology of teaching', which in practice ranged from Skinner's proposed 'teaching machines' to increasingly comprehensive programmed and packaged curricula. He contended that 'It would, no doubt, be better if all teachers were specialists in the things they teach . . . but there are administrative problems that can be solved only if the teacher need not know what he is teaching' (Skinner, 1968, pp. 257–8). For, he explained, 'teachers must often be assigned to fields in which they are not experts.' In fact, Skinner simply was reframing in technological terms what had become curricular practice two decades earlier: this practical approach certainly appealed to public school administrators who, from the 1950s onward, had to defend the public system against renewed criticism that the unstructured curriculum and permissive socialization of progressive educational practices had rendered the public schools inefficient, at best, if not actually left wing in ideology (Cremin, 1961). The logical solution lay with further standardization and centralized control over the teaching and learning process, and educational science promised precisely what was needed: increased teacher efficiency and heightened public accountability. Gradually, the basal reader had undergone a profound historical transformation to become, in the words of Chall (1967, p. 187), the 'total reading program'.

A third factor in the development of a technology of literacy training was the marketplace. In the early days of public schooling teachers had few textbooks from which to choose. But the educational textbook market flourished as the public school system expanded. By 1890 the 6·5 million dollar textbook market had become glutted: school districts could choose from 159 grammar texts, 134 readers and 116 spellers (Madison, 1966, p. 124). This expanded competition put smaller publishers out of business. In Canada only three major publishers survived: Copp-Clark, Ryerson and Gage (Hindley, Martin and McNulty, 1977, p. 15; see Lorimer, 1986). In the US five of the larger houses and a dozen smaller publishers joined forces to form the American Book Company, which in time came to be known as the 'Schoolbook Trust'. By 1908, however, a series of influence peddling and bribery allegations induced the State of New York to legislate new controls over textbook adoption policies in an attempt to deter financially rewarding collaborations between public education officials and textbook entrepreneurs of the Trust. The American Book Company failed to keep pace with production of the kinds of modern and scientifically-based readers sought by the emergent generation of university trained and progressive educational administrators, gradually losing their monopoly to innovative companies like Scott-Foresman and Ginn (Madison, 1966, p. 125).

These surviving publishers forged a new alliance with the public school system, this time involving university-based and corporation funded educational researchers.[3] This new collaboration, the virtual reinvention of the reading process by educational psychologists, and the rejection of traditional school texts and methods by the rising progressive movement provided publishers with innovative development and promotional strategies needed to compete for what had become a multi-million dollar domestic and international market. Publishers were quick to capitalize on the latest fashions in educational science, presenting scientific reading series as panaceas (e.g., the 'Sonsil' approach), as foolproof methods of literacy instruction. The presumption of scientific progress, moreover, accelerated the highly profitable cycles of curriculum development and obsolescence which remain with us today (see Apple, Chapter 12, this volume).

By the mid-1960s smaller independent publishing firms increasingly were unable to shoulder the costs of developing and marketing basal reading series. The publishers which diversified corporate support, however, were better able to finance the expensive research and development process (cf. Lorimer, 1986). Beginning in 1963, the purchase of textbook publishers by industrial corporations began in earnest. IBM acquired the phenomenally successful SRA company, pioneers of the totally 'individualized' reading programme. Shortly thereafter, Random House was purchased by RCA, Holt, Rinehart and Winston by CBS, and Ginn and Co. by XEROX (Lorimer, 1986; Locke and Engler, 1972). The mandate for these multinational corporations was the packaging and marketing of the latest instructional materials for sales on both domestic and foreign markets. By 1964 an estimated 92–98 per cent of US primary teachers were using such basal readers as the principal basis for literacy instruction (Jenkins and Pany, 1980, p. 557). Canada and other English-speaking countries had begun to look to American publishers for an increasing percentage of their educational materials (see Lorimer and Keeney, Chapter 13, this volume).

Commenting in the early 1970s on the role of technological approaches to education, executives of McGraw Hill predicted that

> As a corporation, we must respond to the realities of the marketplace and not simply to our visions of it. . . . The majority of the schools will demand systems of instructional materials with precisely stated behavioral objectives, diagnostic tests of pre-instructional behavior, criterion-referenced tests of achievement (in Locke and Engler, 1972, p. 409).

About the same time, in a report of the Committee on Reading of the National Institute of Education, reading researchers Carroll and Chall (1975) argued that it was indeed modern curricular technology which held the potential for producing universal literacy in America.[4] Not one of the researchers, noted Olson (1975), questioned the basic assumption that psychologically designed instructional technology was equal to that task.

What, then, of the legacy which educational science and the enterprise of modern publishing has bequeathed to the public schools? Contemporary curricular products, despite publishers' claims to the contrary, are not so very different from the first total reading programmes offered to educators in the post-war period. In its 1948–49 version David Russell's *Ginn Basic Reader* provided twelve graded texts with adjunct materials such as fill-in-the-blanks and multiple choice exercise booklets and sheets; picture, word, phrase and sentence cards; glossy display boxes; a teachers' manual; and a standardized testing programme (Smith, 1965, pp. 284–5). A recent update, XEROX's *Ginn 720*, is much the same in basic structure.[5]

The programmes are adapted for multinational markets (e.g., Canada, Australia, the Philippines) by changing place names, illustrations and historical figures (see Lorimer and Keeney, Chapter 13, this volume). Token literary selections are substituted to reflect local and culturally relevant situations: the Australian versions of multinational readers, for example, typically feature local folklore and historical narratives alongside the standardized selections included in all versions of the series. In Canada this editorial process is called 'Canadianization'.

Accordingly, such programmes treat literacy as a universal, culturally neutral information processing skill, which can be broken down into different cognitive/skill 'domains'. Though essentially designed to teach reading literacy, these programmes extend to cover the range of language arts: *DISTAR Reading*, for example, is accompanied with a *DISTAR Language* curriculum (cf. Herriman, 1986, pp. 164–5). As a result, many teachers consider the reading programme the sum total of their literacy curriculum, despite teacher educators' warnings of the limitations of strict, lock-step adherence to basal programmes (e.g., Durkin, 1983). In the *Ginn 720* series the 'domains' or 'strands' include 'decoding, comprehension, vocabulary, study skills, literature and creativity'. Each is taught, piece by piece in a thoroughly scientific manner guaranteed to succeed with all but the learning disabled child.

In the accompanying teachers' guides the use of medical and managerial models encourages teachers to see themselves as 'professionals', and to see literacy instruction as the efficiently managed elimination of pathology (cf. Mills, 1976). Students are literally diagnosed, prescribed for, treated and checked at regular instructional intervals (e.g., Ginn, 1979, p. ii). From ages 5 to 13 the *Ginn 720* programme processes students through fourteen discrete 'skill levels', each of which corresponds to a theoretical level of literate competence. The teachers' manual attempts to guide classroom discourse and interaction by specifying discussion topics, teacher questions and the parameters of correct student response (see Luke, de Castell and Luke, Chapter 19, this volume). The programme's effectiveness is premised upon students' *and* teachers' success at decoding and following oral and written instruction. For example, 'Suggested *Independent* Activities' (our emphasis) for a story in Holt Rinehart and Winston's *Language Patterns* (1969), a CBS product, include: 'have the child choose the correct homonym'; 'have the child write the correct form of the verb'; and 'have the children choose the *correct emotional response*' (emphasis added, pp. 38–9).

So enacted, the process of language acquisition is indeed the acquiring of an 'instrument of personal behaviour control', as promised to the teachers of *Language Patterns*. Success in the performance of such exercises depends on how well both students and teachers can conform to the instructional script of the programmes. These instructional sequences are based on stages of reading development (Chall, 1983) which in turn presuppose universal stages of cognitive, linguistic and moral development. For if literacy is viewed as a body of universal, cross-cultural and cross-situational 'skills' or 'habits', to borrow terms from Huey and Thorndike, its optimal pedagogical techniques likewise can be universalized. The practical result of these theoretical presuppositions is that lessons lack context specificity: they are designed to be taught to any group of children; they can be applied to virtually any narrative, and they are usable by virtually any teacher, even one who is unfamiliar with the particular text in question or with the discourses of reading psychology, psycholinguistics and so forth. Hence, such teacher-proof technology is premised on the elimination of the very need for teacher (theoretical) knowledge and (practical) technique and on the minimization of variables of student background knowledge and cultural difference.

The aforementioned activities are designed to transmit what are considered 'lower order' reading skills, the fundamentals of literacy. Yet even when 'higher order' comprehension is stressed, there is little difference in basic approach. For example, the following instructions to teachers are part of a lesson designed to teach students to 'make inferences about story characters' — a commonly taught comprehension skill.

> Remind pupils that they may make inferences about characters even though an author doesn't specifically describe them. . . . Write the following sentence on the chalk board. . . . Ask pupils to reread page 31 and find a sentence or two to support the inference expressed by the sentence. . . . Tell pupils that the following activity contains inferences that can be supported by what the author has implied in the story. Explain to them that they may copy lines directly from the book or use their own words. . . . Have pupils complete activity page 8. . . . (Ginn, 1979, p. 28)

The goal here is reasonably sophisticated, for the student must enlarge on the meaning of a narrative by identifying implications and connotations rather than literal denotations (Donaldson, 1978; Olson, 1986); this is often referred to as 'forward inferencing' (Smith, 1983). But inferring motivations and character traits must call upon the reader's background knowledge of personalities, norms and situations (Bruce, 1980, p. 370). This exercise, nonetheless, is as standardized, linear and mechanistic as those used to teach lower order literacy skills; no accommodation of the students' schematic prior knowledge is made by the instructional script. Consequently, the student is caught in a kind of paradoxical injunction: at once enjoined to 'make inferences . . . even though the author doesn't specifically describe them', while at the same time tethered to (and assessed on) the particular inferences sought on page 8 of the workbook and simulated by the teacher.

Thus the skills orientation of these programmes preoccupies both teacher and student with the minutiae of strictly delimited tasks, thereby 'diverting attention from meaning' (Smith, 1983), and preventing spontaneous, divergent or critical responses to texts. Because texts must follow rules of 'readability', lexical and syntactical complexity, and story structure, much of what the students read in elementary literacy training is too often repetitive, formulaic and insignificant. Programmes like *Language Patterns* and *DISTAR* (1972), with phonics emphases, are particularly guilty of sacrificing meaning for skills acquisiton.

We have described the effects of basal reading programmes on basic literacy instruction in elementary schools, noting at the onset that such programmes often tended to monopolize instructional time in other areas of the language arts as well. But what of basic writing instruction? First and foremost, it is worth noting that the advances in systematized approaches to the teaching of reading and in sophisticated curricular packages have not been paralleled by developments in the teaching of writing until recent years. Certainly post-war educational policy has reflected the conceptual equation of functional literacy with basic reading skills thought to be necessary for rudimentary social participation (Kirsch and Guthrie, 1977; cf. de

Castell, Luke and MacLennan, 1986). Though the 'process' approach to early writing instruction advocated by Graves (1983), Calkins (1983) and colleagues is not by any means a recent invention (Haley-James, 1981), the very point of this recent work is well taken: that basic research and curriculum development in the teaching of writing has been sorely neglected. Given the foregoing reading of the effects of modern curricular technology, this might appear a blessing. However, surveys of historical and current trends in basic writing instruction tend to indicate otherwise.

In historical terms the advent of educational progressivism certainly led in the 1940s and 1950s to a change in textbook approaches from autocratic, rote learning approaches to writing towards a more 'experience-based curriculum'. Nonetheless, in her study of trends in twentieth century writing curricula, Donsky (1984, p. 197) reports that 'those nineteenth century die hards, grammar and sentence construction, plodded unerringly along, oblivious to changing times and changing educational currents.'

Donsky's observation is confirmed in a 1978 NCTE survey of the teaching of writing in elementary schools. Petty and Finn (1981) examined the use of 'language arts' instructional time apart from the teaching of reading which remains, as noted, centred on basal programmes. They report that 86.6 per cent of primary teachers surveyed spend 'at least 30 minutes daily' on language arts, though the 'practices reported as being used more frequently' centred on 'having students do punctuation and capitalization exercises' and 'requiring completion of grammar exercises' (p. 23); 75 per cent of grade 4 teachers reported that they 'almost always' administer objective tests in writing and language study. This leads Petty and Finn to query the extent to which — despite younger teachers' tendency to stress such innovative approaches as 'writing conferences' — the 'filling in of blanks' may remain the central component of writing and language arts programmes (p. 27).

There is evidence that many teachers periodically undertake what could be construed as progressive, and 'whole language' activities (e.g., creative drama, creative writing, shared book experience, language experience). But it seems obvious that for a majority of students, basic literacy instruction consists of the basal reading programme, augmented by correlatively mechanistic approaches to the teaching of writing: weekly spelling lists following the Monday through Friday pre- and post-test format pioneered in the 1930s (cf. Luke, 1988); worksheet exercises on grammar and punctuation; objective tests on usage. Though the work of Graves *et al.* undoubtedly is having some impact on elementary literacy instruction (see Gilbert, Chapter 15, this volume), the basal approach to reading continues to be augmented by a 'skills orientation' to the teaching of writing, handwriting, spelling and other language arts. In too many elementary classrooms the teaching of writing as rhetorical, meaningful communication remains subordinated to rote learning of discrete skills.

It is not our present purpose to describe such approaches to basic literacy instruction in greater detail. Rather we wish to isolate one factor which we think is crucial for explaining perceived declines in 'higher order' literacy: the development in both teacher and student of an uncritical and mechanical relation to the reading of text, the writing of text and the acquisition of knowledge from text.

Curricular Form: Technology and Technique

> I say moreover that you make a great, a very great mistake, if you think that psychology, being the science of the mind's laws, is something from which you can deduce definite programmes and schemes and methods of instruction for immediate schoolroom use. Psychology is a science, and teaching is an art; and sciences never generate arts directly out of themselves. An intermediary inventive mind must make the application, by using its originality. (William James, 'Psychology and the Teaching Art,' 1899)

To the degree that literacy instruction approaches the technocratic ideal, to that degree it eradicates the possibility of its modification by both student and teacher alike.

What is unique in this kind of instruction is that technology, the skills orientation of the packaged curriculum, appropriates the technique of teachers and learners. For the technocratic curriculum embodies both the *means* of knowledge production and the *social relations* of the production process. In order to achieve this, intervening variables of human action and social situation must be eliminated, including both the prior knowledge of teacher and learner and the interactive situation of both in the classroom context. Sociolinguistic strategies for negotiating personal identity, material and social context — which constitute the real relations of teacher and learner in the processes of acquiring knowledge — are rendered irrelevant by the programme. They are restructured into artificial relations manifested in the prespecified linguistic exchanges of teachers' guides, mass duplicated worksheets and exercises.

The contemporary classroom has become the setting for a simulation of the 'art' of teaching and learning referred to by James. The programme provides a script whereby language, thought and action are stage managed. The players are stripped of their off-stage identities. Language acquisition and use are removed from their real pragmatic context and resituated as an empty formalism in a no-man's land where thought and action are detached from authoritative thinking and acting. The programme has the final authority, even to the extent of tacitly engendering kinds and levels of teacher and student resistance.

What occurs in many modern classrooms is a mechanistic reduction of literacy into a hierarchy of constituent skills. In order to become 'skilled', students must suspend their own particular world view, background knowledge and existing linguistic competence. As important is the fact that teachers must undergo a parallel transformation, sacrificing technique to the directives of curricular technology. Both teachers and students are thus 'deskilled' and 'reskilled' by that technology, as previously acquired knowledge and competence are replaced by externally defined, transmitted and tested skills (Apple, 1983; cf. Braverman, 1974). From an educational standpoint this scenario is profoundly unsatisfactory.

For technique is embodied. It refers to human activities, perceptions, interpretations, goals and intentions. Technique can be emulated and acquired by apprenticeship, or it can be discovered through *bricolage*. Technology, by contrast, is material. It is embodied and functions independently of its human creators. Its operation — though overseen by human subjects – is mechanical; in and of itself it is incapable of interpreting its context on its own initiative (Ellul, 1980; Ihde, 1976). Technology per se is devoid of purpose or intention. While technique can achieve goals independent of technology, technology can be used to attain goals but it is not autonomous; its use depends on the *mediation* of technique. Techno-logical literacy programmes attempt to bypass human fallibility, to embody technique — the 'teaching art' — mechanically in a prepackaged and decontextualized system of instruction.

Here we want to focus on the restructuring of authority relations which result from reliance on such programmes, for this restructuring is central to the replace-ment of technique by technology. Teacher authority, traditionally accorded in recognition of superior knowledge of what is to be mastered, loses its foundation to the extent that teachers become supervisors in a production process over which they have no control. Institutional authorization, that is to say, comes to replace epistemic authority (de Castell, 1982). With this transfer of authority from the teacher to the textual script (and indirectly to the multinational publisher), students lose organic and embodied models of the goals of classroom activities. Instructional aims and standards become non-negotiable, and as a result many of the activities and evaluative criteria appear to students and teachers to be quite random. For example, when those of us involved in teacher education ask teachers why they are teaching a particular lesson, basal unit, or language 'skill', all too often they respond that 'it's in the curriculum', that they are simply following an authorized instructional sequence laid out in the teachers' guide. With the press for increased accountability and the diminished role of the humanities and educational foundations in teacher training, this trend towards uncritical acceptance of textbooks and curricula is likely to continue. The result is that both teachers' and students' intellectual efforts and potential are sacrificed to routines of following instructions (cf. Donaldson, 1978, p. 103), whose rules are explicit but whose meaning and purpose remain a mystery. Within many of the instructional programmes criteria of success are invariant: subjective gradations of more or less, better or worse, are disregarded in favour of quantifiable, if impoverished, judg-ments of technical correctness.

We are not advocating educational laissez faire, such that literacy instruction should be entirely defined by the teacher. And we certainly recognize that many teachers if left entirely to their own devices might do a far worse job than they would if they followed the directives of programmes such as we have described. Nor are we suggesting, incidentally, that even the finest teacher should have sole authority over classroom literacy instruction. But we maintain that authority is necessarily a human attribute, not a mechanical one, that teachers must share with learners the authority jointly to negotiate meaning in the classroom, and that all participants in such negotiations must be both sensitive and responsive to specific contextual considerations in any educational process (Freire, 1970; see Baker and Freebody, Chapter 21, this volume; Cazden, Chapter 22, this volume). What is needed in reading, language arts and English instruction is a continuous modification and adaptation of both content and method, in the light of highly variable learning styles (e.g., Edelsky, Draper and Smith, 1983), environmental, cultural and linguistic differences (e.g., Au, 1980; Valadez, 1981) and specific classroom and community characteristics (e.g., Heath, 1983; Fiore and Elsasser, 1981). Accordingly, the kind of whole-scale standardization and uniformity in the teaching and learning process we have described precludes meaningful and thereby effective literacy instruction. For what is lost in such a process is profoundly simple, and profoundly damaging. It is the exchange of meanings between teachers and learners, between readers and writers, an exchange which enables both cultural transmission and cultural renewal.

It would appear, then, that the quality of literacy achieved by those who 'succeed' does not indicate a failure of the educational system, but rather ironically signals instructional and curricular effectiveness. Those students have learned precisely what technocratic curricula have taught: mechanical skills of contending with text.

Participation in a literate cultural tradition requires far more than this. It requires the ability to grasp meaning by reading and listening, and to transform meaning by writing and speaking. The first is essential for cultural transmission, the second for cultural renewal. At present the possibility of public education generating cultural renewal in industrial and postindustrial nation states is slight. We have argued here that many students rarely are encouraged to read or write anything of substance, or to enlarge upon the standard set of interpretations designated as 'correct' by programmed textbooks, skill exercises and worksheets. It should come as no surprise that the range of meanings students are exposed to in textbooks remains extremely limited (Freebody and Baker, 1985; Baker and Freebody, 1988): to meet the demands of the regional text adoption policies, local and national policy lobby groups, authors deliberately avoid text content which might be construed as 'controversial' (see Arons, Chapter 16, this volume); to meet the demands of a burgeoning multinational market, publishers design texts which are intentionally context-neutral and content-free (see Lorimer and Keeney, Chapter 13, this volume).

The sacrifice of meaningful content to efficiency of method and the subordination of technique to technology, which have shaped early literacy instruction since World War II, make even the transmission of culture problematic. For the kind of reading and writing taught stresses literal decoding and formulaic information processing, while a literate cultural tradition is precisely non-literal, stressing the abstract, the symbolic and the imaginative (Olson, 1977). A literary tradition offers children a vast range of possible meanings to be worked with, to be brought to bear upon the lived experience of the reader and to work, in turn, on the everyday world so that it can be seen as only one of an infinite range of 'possible worlds' (Olson, 1986). By standardizing and conventionalizing literacy training we relegate students to the role of passive recipients, rather than active participants in a culture — consumers of textual and curricular products who are too often not introduced to the competences, insights and inclinations to revitalize, transform or even preserve literate culture.

The crisis in literacy is a result of a curious admixture of educational failure and success: technocratic teaching has successfully opted against those linguistic and cultural minorities who have historically failed in the public system, and it has succeeded in transmitting to others an educationally limited and culturally disempowered form of literate competence. But what are the social consequences of this kind of literacy instruction? It is instructive to examine, finally, the literate demands of North American society. We shall try to show that the quality of literacy in North American schools, and students' acquired sense of the values and uses of literacy, fit *well* with most of its present-day functions and uses.

Some Remarks on the Functions and the Uses of Literacy

Contrary to predictions by educators, researchers and economists, in some cases technological progress has resulted in a widespread 'deskilling' of literate labour (Apple, 1983, 1986; Heath, 1986). The deskilling of teachers, traditionally expected to be highly literate, is a case in point. Reading and writing are still required for a good deal of white-collar work, but the types of reading and writing increasingly involve literal information processing, requiring standardized responses to routine texts (Coe, 1978; Berland and McGee, 1977; Heath, 1986; cf. Braverman, 1974, pp. 424–49). Clerical work has been affected similarly, particularly through the increasing use of word processing technology (Menzies, 1981; Glen and Feldburg, 1979, pp. 62–3). Even among the most rapidly growing group of professionals, computer programmers, a deskilling is underway: the 'artist programmer' of a decade ago is being replaced by several programmers, each performing a limited and specialized function (Kraft, 1979, p. 5).[6] Furthermore, it appears that semi-skilled and unskilled workers — though their job descriptions may require literate competence — often are talked through work tasks orally rather than instructed in print. For example, Heath (1986) documents how such limited writing tasks as the filling in of application forms typically are completed by employment officers for prospective employees.

By contrast, the role that literacy plays in everyday social and recreational activities remains central. In addition to daily communicative uses of literacy in the form of notes, bills, greeting cards, labels, recipes, street signs, cheques and the like (Heath, 1983), North Americans continue to devote a good deal of leisure time to reading. By one estimate Americans spend roughly twenty to thirty minutes of each day reading books, magazines, newspapers (Robinson, 1980, pp. 147–9). While newspaper readership appears on the decline, there is a corresponding increase in the reading of periodicals and books. Studies of American readership also indicate the persistence of a 'small core of non-readers', a disproportionate percentage of which is non-white and did not complete high school (McEvoy and Vincent, 1980, p. 137). These surveys also give us some sense of who is reading: McEvoy and Vincent note that 'heavier volume book readers . . . were more likely to be women, between the ages of 20 to 49, and white' (p. 136).

These indicators of what we might call 'elective literacy' do not, of course, tell us what is actually read, but they do serve to indicate the distribution and consumption of print materials.[7] A diversity of texts is available in increasing quantities: 'how to' books, popular fiction, self-improvement manuals and specialized 'hobby' magazines are enjoying unprecedented levels of mass circulation, in spite of widespread use of home computers, teletext and videotape (Corbett, 1981; cf. Suhor, 1984). In Canada Harlequin Enterprises Ltd, publishers of popular romances, has become one of the nation's largest publishers, and one of the few to make substantial inroads in the American and Australian markets (Bureau of Management Consulting, 1977; cf. Christian-Smith, Chapter 2, this volume). Yet this apparent diversity of print materials conceals a sameness, a redundancy. What kind of literacy is demanded of its consumers?

The Texts of Everyday Life

> She had read Paul and Virginia, and had dreamed of the bamboo cabin, of the Negro Domingo and the dog Fidele: and especially she dreamed that she, too, had a sweet little brother as a devoted friend, and that he climbed trees as tall as church steeples . . . . (Gustave Flaubert, *Madame Bovary*)

Flaubert had a keen sense of the mystifying functions of the popular text: his characters Bouvard and Pecuchet lived according to the latest 'how to' manuals. Emma Bovary lost herself altogether in the rapture of romantic fiction.

Magazines and popular fiction today remain sources of what Barthes (1972) has called cultural 'mythologies'. Barthes differentiates between 'myths', which serve to reconcile social and cultural anomalies, and the 'mythologies' of popular media, which suppress, deny and conceal genuine social problems and contradictions. So doing, the mythologies of popular culture serve to 'naturalize' and thereby render beyond criticism what are in fact historical sources of social and political conflict. The mythologies of the social text — be they of celebrities' lives, fictions of sexual intrigue, fashion trends and the like — represent the present as an ahistorical ideal.

Harold Rosenburg (1960) has suggested that we live within a 'tradition of the new', that the cultural tradition which is passed on through print and non-print media is a continual reinvention, a repackaging of the same basic themes and schemata, each under the guise of the new. This is an ironic twist on what Havelock (1976; Chapter 17, this volume), Goody and Watt (1969), Olson (1977; Chapter 18, this volume) and others have noted is the bias of literate culture towards the preservation of the civic and historical record. For the social text of our particular postindustrial culture is in some way more ephemeral than traditional oral history: yesterday's news is just that, and text's intrinsic property of permanence is cancelled by the planned obsolescence and discardability of both the ideational content and physical substance of trade paperbacks, periodicals and newspapers, junk mail and business forms and, for that matter, textbooks.

The cultural tradition conveyed by popular fiction and mass circulated magazines like *People* and *National Enquirer*, moreover, is designed for the consumption of popular belief, conventional wisdom, as well as actual textual product (cf. Lowenthal, 1961).[8] Consumption of products, whether material or textual, becomes the great equalizer, that which enables every (wo)man to vicariously participate in the lives of the famous and wealthy. All of this, according to Lowenthal, serves to mollify any anxiety one might have regarding real political and economic or ontological issues. In *Newsweek* and *Time*, for instance, sandwiched between a particular version of political events are fashions, vogues and commodities. While the text may generate anxieties over, say, the Middle East or inner-city crime, it also offers the reader a way out of these and any other apparent dilemma: products to buy, trends to follow.

Much of the text which North America readers read is effectively redundant and disempowered. Enabled is private participation in a set of collective social mythologies, requiring consumption rather than interpretation. Literacy does indeed enable access to 'culturally significant knowledge' (Olson, Chapter 18, this volume), yet the complexity and interpretive demands of the texts of contemporary culture are minimal. Eco's (1979) distinction between open and closed texts is a useful one here. The open text, says Eco, is one which challenges and expands known schematic structures and thereby requires what we called earlier 'higher order' abilities of comprehension and interpretation. Such texts require a systematic rewriting on the part of the reader; reading becomes a knowledge-constitutive activity (cf. Barthes, 1977). It was this kind of reading — reading as rewriting — that Borges addressed in his 'Pierre Menard': Borges's fictional reader rewrote, word for word, the *Quixote* in order to experience the text. Closed texts, by contrast, are those which are consumed in large quantities and require minimal participation from the reader (cf. Luke, 1988b). They represent limited 'causal chains' operating, like TV narratives, on the basis of wholly predictable narrative structures. According to Eco, these texts — popular fiction, detective novels, gothic romances, television situation comedies, superhero comic books and so on — satisfy the public's 'hunger for redundancy': 'narrative of a redundant nature would appear the only occasion of true relaxation offered to the consumer' (Eco, 1979, p. 121).

Bearing in mind Eco's distinction between closed and open texts, we can reflect on the nature of the social text typifying North American culture. It is redundant, requiring mere recognition rather than reasoning, and rarely calling for more than literal 'processing'. For its consumption the public schools provide all that is required. Claims that the kind of literacy public education provides the roughly 80–90 per cent literate fails to meet the needs of contemporary North American labour and culture seem, then, to be unfounded. This is not surprising, since private sector industry today largely defines labour force needs, controls the production of mass media, and has appropriated increasingly both the contents and the methods of public education. If we are dissatisfied, our dissatisfaction must be, then, with the character of both labour and literate culture in contemporary society.

Notes

1 The authors wish to thank Kelleen Toohey for her critical comments and suggestions and to acknowledge the support of the Social Sciences and Humanities Research Council of Canada. An earlier, more extensive version of this paper appeared in the *American Journal of Education*, 95, 3, 1987, 413–40.

2 See, for example, the National Commission on Excellence in Education (1983); Task Force of the Business-Higher Education Forum (1983); New England Board of Higher Education (1982); Twentieth Century Fund Task Force on Federal Elementary and Secondary Education Policy (1983); and the Task Force on Education for Economic Growth (1983); see Apple (1986) for critical commentary on the current debate.

3 A considerable body of research details the financial and political support of university-based psychologists from the beginning in the twentieth century (e.g., Callahan, 1962; Karier, 1976). Tyack and Hansott's (1982) study of the rise of educational administration points to the development of national networks of academic and financial interests. See also Hamilton's (1977) analysis of the industrial structure and corporate support of scientific approaches to curriculum development.

4 Carroll and Chall's *Towards a Literate Society* (1975) was part of a national literacy campaign entitled 'the Right to Read'. This 'compensatory' programme, which received $23.8 million in 1976 alone, was a Federal response to widely documented claims that illiteracy and educational failure were concentrated among lower socioeconomic and minority students. It was cited by UNESCO (1980, pp. 68–9) as a 'noteworthy experiment' in mass literacy transmission,.

5 The *Ginn 720* series is among the most widely used in North America. In British Columbia, for example, approximately 78 per cent of elementary school teachers use *Ginn*, following a province-wide adoption in the early 1980s; most of the remaining 22 per cent use Holt Rinehart and Winston's *Language Patterns* (1969), a CBS product with a phonics emphasis. The *Ginn 360* series, replaced by *720* in most US and Canadian schools, remains among the most popular American basals used in Australia.

6 The effects of computer technology on patterns of social reproduction and on structures of literate discourse have been the subject of widespread speculation and polemic. For discussion of educational implications and alternatives, see Griffin and Cole (1987).

7 Heath's (1983) ethnographic study of a range of socioeconomic groups in the Carolinas comprehensively details daily functions and uses of literacy. She notes also that many of the literate competences taught in schools rarely were used in out-of-school occupational and social settings and that, conversely, actual daily uses of literacy rarely were featured in the conventional curriculum (Heath, 1986).

8 A recent television advertisement for *People* magazine frames the mystifying element of popular texts and the diminution of critical interpretation: 'And if it's in *People*', the ad runs, 'you know it's true!' This is, in Flaubert's words, the propagation of 'accepted ideas'.

References

APPLE, M.W. (1983) *Education and Power*. London: Routledge and Kegan Paul.

APPLE, M.W. (1986) *Teachers and Texts: A Political Economy of Class and Gender Relations in Education*. London: Routledge and Kegan Paul.

AU, K. (1980) 'Participant structures in a reading lesson with Hawaiian children: Analysis of a culturally appropriate instructional event,' *Anthropology and Education Quarterly*, 11, 2, 91–115.

BAKER, C. and FREEBODY, P. (1988) 'Possible worlds and possible people: Interpretive challenges in beginning school reading books,' *Australian Journal of Reading*, 11, 2, 95–104.
BARTHES, R. (1972) *Mythologies*. London: Jonathan Cape.
BARTHES, R. (1977) *Image-music-text*. New York: Hill and Wang.
BERLAND, J. and McGEE, D. (1977) 'Literacy and the atrophy of competence, pts. I and II,' *Working Teacher*, 1, 1–2.
BRAVERMAN, H. (1974) *Labor and Monopoly and Capital: The Degradation of Work in the Twentieth Century*. New York: Monthly Review Press.
BRUCE, B.C. (1980) 'Plans and social actions,' in SPIRO, R.J., BRUCE, B.C. and BREWER, W.F., (Eds), *Theoretical Issues in Reading Comprehension*. Hillsdale, N.J.: Erlbaum.
Bureau of Management Consulting (1977) *The Publishing Industry in Canada*. Ottawa: Department of the Secretary of State.
CALKINS, L.M. (1983) *Lessons from a Child*. Exeter, N.H.: Heinemann.
CALLAHAN, R.E. (1962) *Education and the Cult of Efficiency*. Chicago, Ill.: University of Chicago Press.
CARROLL, J.B. and CHALL, J.S. (1975) *Towards a Literate Society*. New York: McGraw Hill.
CASTELL, S.C. DE (1982) 'Epistemic authority, institutional power, and curricular knowledge,' *The Journal of Educational Thought*, 16, 1, 23–8.
CASTELL, S.C. DE, LUKE, A. and MacLENNAN, D. (1986) 'On defining literacy,' in CASTELL, S.C. DE, LUKE, A. and EGAN, K. (Eds) *Literacy, Schooling and Society*. Cambridge: Cambridge University Press.
CHALL, J.S. (1967) *Learning to Read: The Great Debate*. New York: Random House.
CHALL, J.S. (1983) *Stages of Reading Development*. New York: McGraw Hill.
COE, R.M. (1978) 'Writing skills: White collar control,' *The Journal of the British Columbia English Teachers' Association*, 19, 1.
CORBETT, E.P. (1981) 'The status of writing in our society,' in WHITEMAN, M.F. (Ed.), *Writing: The Nature, Development, and Teaching of Written Communication, Vol. 1, Variation in Writing: Functional and Linguistic-Cultural Differences*. Hillsdale, N.J.: Erlbaum.
COSER, L.A., KADUSHIN, C. and POWELL, W. (1982) *Books: The Culture and Commerce of Publishing*. New York: Basic Books.
CREMIN, L. (1961) *The Transformation of the School*. New York: Random House.
DONALDSON, M. (1978) *Children's Minds*. New York: Norton.
DONSKY, B. (1984) 'Trends in elementary writing instruction 1900–1959,' *Language Arts*, 61, 8, 795–803.
DURKIN, D. (1983) *Teaching Them to Read*. 4th ed. Boston, Mass.: Allyn and Bacon.
ECO, U. (1979) *The Role of the Reader*. Bloomington, Ind.: Indiana University Press.
EDELSKY, C., DRAPER, K. and SMITH, K. (1983) 'Hookin' em in at the start of school in a "whole language" classroom,' *Anthropology and Education Quarterly*, 14, 1, 257–81.
ELLUL, J. (1980) 'The power of technique and the ethics of non-power,' in WOODWARD, K. (Ed.), *The Myths of Information: Technology and Postindustrial Culture*. Madison, Wisc.: Coda Press.
FIORE, K. and ELSASSER, N. (1981) 'Through writing we transform our world: Third world women and literacy,' *Humanities in Society*, 4, 4, 395–418.
FREEBODY, P. and BAKER, C. (1985) 'Children's First Schoolbooks: Introductions to the Culture of Literacy,' *Harvard Educational Review*, 55, 4, 381–98.
FREIRE, P. (1970) *Pedagogy of the Oppressed*. New York: Heder and Heder.
GATES, A.I. (1926) *A Reading Vocabulary for the Primary Grades*. New York: Teachers College Press.
GINN and Co. (1949) *The Ginn Basic Readers*. Boston, Mass.
GINN and Co. (1979) *Reading 720*. Boston, Mass.
GLEN, E. and FELDBURG, R.L. (1979) 'Proletarianizing clerical work: Technology and

organizational control in the office,' in ZIMBALIST, A. (Ed.), *Case Studies in the Labor Process*. New York: Monthly Review Press.

GOODY, J. and WATT, I. (1969) 'The consequences of literacy,' in GOODY, J. (Ed.), *Literacy in Traditional Societies*. Cambridge: Cambridge University Press.

GRAVES, D.H. (1983) *Writing: Teachers and Children at Work*. Exeter, N.H.: Heinemann.

GRAY, W.S. (1956) *The Teaching of Reading and Writing*. Paris: UNESCO.

GRIFFIN, P. and COLE, M. (1987) 'New technologies, basic skills, and the underside of education: What's to be done?' in LANGER, J.A. (Ed.), *Language, Literacy and Culture: Issues of Society and Schooling*. Norwood, N.J.: Ablex.

HABERMAS, J. (1975) *Legitimation Crisis*. Boston, Mass.: Beacon.

HALEY-JAMES, S.M. (1981) 'Twentieth century perspectives on writing in grades one through eight,' in HALEY-JAMES, S. (Ed.), *Perspectives on Writing in Grades 1–8*. Urbana, Ill.: National Council of Teachers of English.

HAMILTON, D. (1977) 'Making sense of curriculum evaluation: Continuities and discontinuities in an educational idea,' *Review of Educational Research*, 5, 318–50.

HAVELOCK, E. (1976) *Origins of Western Literacy*. Toronto: Ontario Institute for Studies in Education.

HEATH, S.B. (1983) *Ways with Words*. Cambridge: Cambridge University Press.

HEATH, S.B. (1986) 'The functions and uses of literacy,' in CASTELL, S. DE, LUKE, A. and EGAN, K. (Eds), *Literacy, Society and Schooling*. Cambridge: Cambridge University Press.

HERRIMAN, M.L. (1986) 'Metalinguistic Awareness and the Growth of Literacy,' in CASTELL, S. DE, LUKE, A., and EGAN, K. (Eds), *Literacy, Society and Schooling*. Cambridge: Cambridge University Press.

HINDLEY, P., MARTIN, G. and MCNULTY, J. (1977) *The Tangled Net: Basic Issues in Canadian Communications*. Vancouver: Douglas and McIntyre.

HOLT RINEHART and WINSTON. (1969) *Language Patterns*. New York.

HUEY, E.B. (1909) *The Psychology and Pedagogy of Reading*. New York: Macmillan.

IHDE, D. (1976) 'A phenomenology of man-machine relations,' in FEINBERG, W. and ROSEMONT, H. (Eds), *Work, Technology and Education*. Urbana, Ill.: University of Illinois Press.

JAMES, W. (1899) 'Psychology and the teaching art,' in *Talks to Teachers on Psychology*. New York: Holt.

JENKINS, J.R. and PANY, D. (1980) 'Teaching comprehension in the middle grades,' in SPIRO, R.J., BRUCE, B.C. and BREWER, W.F. (Eds), *Theoretical Issues in Reading Comprehension*. Hillsdale, N.J.: Erlbaum.

KARIER, C.J. (1976) 'Testing for order and control in the corporate liberal state,' in DALE, R., ESLAND, G., and MACDONALD, M. (Eds), *Schooling and Capitalism: A Sociological Reader*. London: Routledge and Kegan Paul.

KIRSCH, I. and GUTHRIE, J.T. (1977) 'The concept and measurement of functional literacy,' *Reading Research Quarterly*, 4, 484–507.

KRAFT, P. (1979) 'The industrialization of computer programming from programming to "software production",' in ZIMBALIST, A. (Ed.), *Case Studies in the Labour Process*. New York: Monthly Review Press.

Labour Canada (1979) *Education and Working Canadians*. Ottawa: Ministry of Labour.

LOCKE, R.W. and ENGLER, D. (1972) 'Run, strawman, run: A critique of run, computer, run,' in DELECCO, J. (Ed.), *The Regeneration of the School*. New York: Holt Rinehart and Winston.

LORIMER, R. (1984) *The Nation in the Schools*. Toronto: Ontario Institute for Studies in Education.

LORIMER, R. (1986) 'The business of literacy: The making of the educational textbook,' in CASTELL, S. DE, LUKE, A. and EGAN, K. (Eds), *Literacy, Schooling and Society*, Cambridge: Cambridge University Press.

LOWENTHAL, L. (1961) *Literature, Popular Culture, and Society*. New York: Prentice-Hall.

LUKE, A. (1988a) *Literacy, Textbooks and Ideology*. Lewes, Sussex/Philadelphia, Pa.: Falmer Press.

LUKE, A. (1988b) 'Open and closed texts: The semantic/ideological analysis of textbook narratives,' forthcoming in the *Journal of Pragmatics*, 12, 6.

MCEVOY, G.F. and VINCENT, C.S. (1980) 'Who reads and why?' *Journal of Communication*, 30, 1, 134–40.

MCGUFFEY, W.H. (1962) *McGuffey's Fifth Eclectic Reader (1879)*. New York: New American Library.

MADISON, C.A. (1966) *Book Publishing in America*. New York: McGraw Hill.

MENZIES, H. (1981) *Women and the Chip: Case Studies of the Effects of Informatics on Employment in Canada*. Montreal: Institute for Research on Public Policy.

MILLS, C.W. (1976) 'The professional ideology of social pathologists,' in BECK, J., JENCKS, C., KEDDIE, N. and YOUNG, M.F.D. (Eds), *Towards a New Sociology of Education*. New Brunswick, N.J.: Transaction.

National Commission on Excellence in Education (1983) *A Nation at Risk: The Imperative for Educational Reform*. Washington, D.C.: US Department of Education.

New England Board of Higher Education (1982) *A Threat to Excellence: The Preliminary Report of the Commission on Higher Education and the Economy of New England*. New England Board of Higher Education.

OLSON, D.R. (1975) 'Review of *Towards a Literate Society*,' *Proceedings of the National Academy of Education*, 2, 109–78.

OLSON, D.R. (1977) 'From utterance to text: The bias of language in speech and writing,' *Harvard Educational Review*, 47, 3, 257–81.

OLSON, D.R. (1986) 'Learning to mean what you say: Towards a psychology of literacy,' in CASTELL, S. DE, LUKE, A. and EGAN, K. (Eds), *Literacy, Society and Schooling*. Cambridge: Cambridge University Press.

PETTY, W.T. and FINN, P.J. (1981) 'Classroom teachers' reports on teaching written composition,' in HALEY-JAMES, S. (Ed.), *Perspectives on Writing in Grades 1–8*. Urbana, Ill.: National Council of Teachers of English.

ROBINSON, J.P. (1980) 'The changing reading habits of the American public,' *Journal of Communication*, 30, 1, 134–40.

ROBINSON, P. (1976) *Where Our Survival Lies: Students and Textbooks in Atlantic Canada*. Halifax: Atlantic Institute of Education.

ROLLINS, R.M. (1978) 'Words as social control: Noah Webster and the creation of the American dictionary,' in ZUNDERLAND, L. (Ed.), *Recycling the Past: Popular Uses of American history*. Philadelphia, Pa.: University of Pennsylvania Press.

ROSENBURG, H. (1960) *The Tradition of the New*. New York: Horizon Press.

SKINNER, B.F. (1968) *The Technology of Teaching*. New York: Appleton-Century Crofts.

SMITH, F. (1983) *Understanding Reading*. 2nd ed. New York: Holt Rinehart and Winston.

SMITH, N.B. (1965) *American Reading Instruction*. Newark, Del.: International Reading Association.

SOLTOW, L. and STEVENS, E. (1981) *The Rise of Literacy and the Common School in the United States*. Chicago, Ill.: University of Chicago Press.

SUHOR, C. (1984) 'The role of print as a medium in our society,' in PURVES, A.C. and NILES, O. (Eds), *Becoming Readers in a Complex Society: Eighty-Third Yearbook of the National Society for the Study of Education*. Chicago, Ill.: University of Chicago Press.

Task Force of the Business–Higher Education Forum (1983) *America's Competitive Challenge: The Need for a National Response*. Washington, D.C.: Business-Higher Education Forum.

Task Force on Education for Economic Growth (1983) *America's Competitive Challenge: The Need for a National Response*. Washington, D.C.: Business-Higher Education Forum.

THORNDIKE, E.L. (1917) 'Reading as reasoning: A study of mistakes in paragraph reading,' *Journal of Educational Psychology*, 8, 323–32.

THORNDIKE, E.L. (1921) *The Teacher's Word Book*. New York: Teachers College.

THORNDIKE, E.L. and GATES, A.I. (1929) *Elementary Principles of Education*. New York: Macmillan.

Twentieth Century Fund Task Force on Federal Elementary and Secondary Education Policy (1983) *Making the Grade*. New York: Twentieth Century Fund.

TYACK, D. and HANSOTT, E. (1982) *The Managers of Virtue: Public School Leadership in America, 1820–1980*. New York: Basic Books.

UNESCO (1976) *The Experimental World Literacy Programme: A Critical Assessment*. Paris: UNESCO.

UNESCO (1980) *Literacy 1972–1976: Progress Achieved in Literacy throughout the World*. Paris: UNESCO.

VALADEZ, C.M. (1981) 'Identity, power and writing skills: The case of the Hispanic bilingual student,' in WHITEMAN, M.F. (Ed.), *Writing: The Nature, Development, and Teaching of Written Communication. Vol. 1. Functional and Linguistic-Cultural Differences*. Hillsdale, N.J.: Erlbaum.

WEBSTER, N. (1978) *The American Spelling Book*. Boston, Mass.: Isiah Thomas.

WILDEN, A. (1980) 'Changing frames of order: Cybernetics and the machina mundi,' in WOODWARD, K. (Ed.), *The Myths of Information: Technology in Postindustrial Culture*. Madison, Wisc.: Coda Press.

Chapter 8

The Shape of the Science Text: A Function of Stories

Kieran Egan
Simon Fraser University

Whatever else may remain in dispute about Kuhn's thesis concerning the 'paradigmatic' development of scientific understanding, his exposition of the radical rewriting of the history of scientific disciplines has not been disputed. He has shown how scientists at any particular time reinterpret their predecessors' work as though the predecessors were interested in the same kinds of questions, worked by much the same methods and accepted similar kinds of conclusions as appropriate terminations of their inquiries. By studying the work of earlier scientists in a number of disciplines, and carefully locating it in the context of its time and the interests, hopes, methods and aims of those scientists, he has been able to show how the typical textbook's rendering is seriously anachronistic (Kuhn, 1970). One product of such anachronistic readings is a rather simple, linear, progressive view of science; a view that is commonly presented to children through the textbooks used to teach science in schools. This contributes to a kind of unitarian view of science — a suggestion that science as we now practise it has always been the same everywhere and in all times. The only significant difference acknowledged is that of accumulating knowledge. So the history of science is commonly seen as discontinuous with whatever preceded it; things like myth, alchemy, astrology and so on. They receive attention only to indicate the kinds of fundamental errors which prevented them from being science. The story of science begins typically with the earliest methodological statements that look like modern scientific method, such as Bacon's, and the earliest successes in making scientific sense out of phenomena that had previously been the subject of mythic or religious speculation, such as Galileo's work.

The progressive, positivist view of science that Kuhn challenged has had, no doubt obviously, a profound influence on the textbooks used to teach science to children. The unitarian view of an unchanging, except accumulating, science leaves the educator only one dimension to deal with. The educational problem becomes how to initiate children into the scientific view of things and accumulate as much as possible of the knowledge and the methods that constitute science. If one believes, with Kuhn, that there have been many different conceptions and practices of science, and that the presently dominant conception is changing constantly, then a further dimension is added to the task of education in science. If one believes, furthermore, and relatedly, that science did not emerge complete in early modern Europe, but that it is connected with a long history and even pre-history of human inquiry, then one begins to conceive of the educational task rather differently than is presently common.

In this chapter I want to explore how taking some variant of a Kuhnian view of science might affect how one can go about differently initiating young children into scientific understanding. I shall deal very briefly with just the earliest years and discuss the potential effects of a 'paradigmatic' view on both the curriculum and methods of teaching. I shall contrast these effects with the recommendations common in the typical introductory science textbook provided for children on the one hand, and the textbooks provided for pre- or in-service teachers on the other.

Curriculum

If we begin to see scientific understanding as having various 'dimensions', that is, as being something other than a monolithic, unchanging, unitary and immensely authoritative thing, then we begin also to see the educational task somewhat differently. Or, at least, we raise some questions about currently dominant assumptions, and those questions lead us to explore some alternative possibilities for the curriculum. The standard textbook today treats science as its present practice is conceptualized — imprecisely understood of necessity, as it is imprecisely under-stood also by philosophers of science who dispute its nature — as the given form into which children must be initiated. Consequently the task facing the designer of the science curriculum and of the textbook that will help define that curriculum is how to bring the young child to understand what the scientific enterprise is about and how to communicate as much as possible of the achievements of science. At the beginning of the curriculum, then, the textbook accommodates to the child's ignorance and perhaps to some more or less precise notion of the child's 'stage of development'. What science is, however, is not considered problematic.

By insisting that what science is should also impinge on the construction of the curriculum and on the structure of the textbook we add further dimensions both to the task of the curriculum designer and, potentially, to the child's understanding of what science is. If we adopt a Kuhnian position about the changing nature of science and, for the sake of this exploratory article, accept a somewhat contro-versial recapitulationist view, we can see our way to a significantly different kind of elementary science programme.

The notion of recapitulation I would like to adopt provisionally here (argued for in Egan, 1988) is that the historical layers in the development of scientific understanding reflect a combination of logical and psychological constraints of the growth of knowledge. That is, certain developments in scientific understanding required particular knowledge to be in place before they could occur; scientific development shows layers of logical prerequisites in logical sequences. But that is not the whole story. Any adequate account of the development of scientific understanding must also include reference to psychological factors. The process of scientific development followed particular directions rather than others because of human hopes, fears, interests, expectations and so on, and their expressions through history. That is, psychological factors play a necessary part in the story. The recapitulationary thesis concerns the connection of this historical process to that of the individual child. The claim is that the same logical and psychological constraints on the growth of scientific understanding also constrain the sequence in which children can learn science. The same logical and psychological constraints operate on children's developing understanding. It is difficult to characterize either the necessary logical sequences in the accumulation of scientific knowledge or the psychological constraints on that process. They do operate, however. Neither the logic of the subject nor human psychology lets up. While attempts to deal with both these areas separately — studies of the structure of knowledge on the one hand, and of stages of psychological development on the other — leave us with considerable opaqueness, uncertainty and highly contentious theories, we do have another resource. This is the resource of the history of science. In that history we can see the effects of logic and psychology working together — which is, of course, how they work in the child trying to master science. From the study of those effects we can get some guidance that might help us construct a curriculum and design textbooks that might be more in tune with the child's developing ways of making sense of the world and with the nature of science itself.

Now I need to acknowledge that I am asking the reader to take a considerable leap. An adequate defence of such a claim would occupy vastly more space than is available here (see also Egan, 1987). But it is not entirely implausible, and has the virtue of showing how a view of science such as has been elaborated by Kuhn and others can have interesting implications for the curriculum. Also, when I refer to 'the' history of science, I do not mean to suggest that there is some uncontentious account we can refer to. Rather I want only to suggest that there is a *dimension* to the growth of scientific understanding that is significantly different from the story of accumulating knowledge. I want also to see this dimension as reflecting psychological concerns that affect how we can make sense of scientific knowledge at different stages of our individual development. (I want also to adopt in what follows a Vygotskian view in which higher psychological functions, such as are involved in developing scientific understanding, entail internalization of previous social/historical functions. I mention this only to suggest that while I shall be largely focusing on psychological matters I am not thereby ignoring the social conditions that have influenced the changing nature of scientific inquiry.)

A further step in this direction away from the currently dominant textbooks is the perception of science growing, or changing, while preserving features of earlier practices as constituents of newer views. That is, changes in science are not so radical that there is no continuity with what preceded any particular paradigm. Indeed, I suspect that recognizing how certain features of previous paradigmatic practice remain constituents of later practice helps to account for the progressive appearance of science. (This is, of course, something of an anti-Kuhnian view). What we might begin to focus on for our elementary science curriculum, then, are those constituents of scientific understanding that were historically foundational to the development of science. We do this because they are the logical and psychological foundations of science, and it is our reasonable hypothesis that as such they will provide the best introduction to science for children. What are these foundations? Where shall we find them?

might be considered its present logical foundations, but rather to its historical foundations. Its foundations do not occur with the first articulations of what we currently recognize as scientific method. Those grew out of, and on top of, a long history of inquiry. That inquiry may look peculiar in some of its forms — myth, alchemy, astrology, etc. — but we falsify the origins of science if we ignore these and ignore the constituents of modern science that we find in distinctive ways within these. That is, alchemy, for example, is not simply an irrelevant precursor to be forgotten once scientific methods have been discovered. Within alchemy vital features of science were first developed and elaborated. They have not gone away, but remain foundational to all scientific inquiry. By studying their forms in alchemy, astrology and myth, we can get a better grasp of how children might be introduced to these foundational constituents of scientific understanding.

This is not to suggest that we teach alchemy, astrology and myth in our elementary science course, but rather that we excavate what it was about those activities of the human intellect that were so engaging, and why science should have grown out of them. In brief, foundational to alchemy, astrology and myth are careful observation of complex phenomena, classification of those according to criteria of usefulness or personal or social relevance, and the expression of the results of inquiry in some memorable form. We can say these things at least, and no doubt much else. Let us hold these items in abeyance for a while, and explore some potential implications of this different approach to science for teaching. Then we can consider an example that will try to draw a number of these observations together.

Teaching

In discussing teaching the foundations of science we shall want to bear in mind the above issues. One of the elements that will become of particular interest is myth. Myth stories are to be found at the beginnings of human inquiry and seem a universal form developed in oral cultures for the encoding and expression of lore of various kinds, whether about social customs, economic practices and also what we would consider — in a quite different form — observations about natural science. If we are to learn something from the mythic foundations of inquiry and the organization and dissemination of its results we need to take a closer look at these peculiar kinds of stories and their uses.

The invention of the story was a crucial stage in the discovery of the mind. What was invented was a narrative form that worked at increasing the memorability of its contents. In oral cultures what one knew was what one remembered. Those techniques that could make knowledge more easily memorable were thus of enormous social importance (Ong, 1982). Such techniques include rhyme, rhythm and meter. More generally and more importantly they included the story, that great holder of meaning in memorable form. In recognizing its power and refining it through millenia, people discovered something remarkable about how the human mind works. We are a storying animal; we make sense of things prominently in story forms; ours is a largely story-shaped world. Rational and empirical science inquiries, of course, are not generally story-shaped, seeking as they do to reflect the logic of their subject-matter, but they provide in their results further material out of which we make stories. It seems we have to in order to make their results more generally meaningful. But even this is to concede too much; it is increasingly being realized that physics does not expose purely the logic of reality, rather it exposes reality in terms already informed by our ways of making sense.

These are rather opaque observations. A crucial role of the story in oral cultures was to ensure that the main cultural messages were retained in living memories and that the rememberers were emotionally committed to those messages (Havelock, 1963; Chapter 17, this volume; Ong, 1982). But while we may be ready to acknowledge the persisting power of stories at even the most sophisticated levels of our literate culture, it seems obvious that they have not survived to play for us the same roles as in oral cultures. Indeed, we might feel somewhat uncomfortable with a technique devised to enchant and commit the unreflective mind to the conventions and dogmas of a particular society. It is a technique designed to suppress precisely the reflective rationality that we prize so highly in education. Clearly we do not need stories to perform the pragmatic task of sustaining our social institutions, but equally clearly they remain of great psychological importance for us. Mind you, what made stories of social importance in the first place was the psychological functions they performed, so perhaps techniques such as the story that were of fundamental importance in the early history of our culture may have a continuing importance at the foundational level of our education.

In this chapter, I shall explore a few features of the kind of stories children seem to find most readily engaging and consider some implications of that engaging power for education. Heath (see Chapter 9, this volume) has focused on the undermining of the communicative role of fictional stories in 'composition' textbooks, and there is a considerable literature on the importance of folk tales and the classic fairy stories for children's moral, social and intellectual well-being. I want to point out that retaining some of the characteristics of the oral communicative forms Heath discusses, and particularly the shaping of knowledge into story forms, can be a powerful technique for making it meaningful for young children. I shall focus here on how introductory science texts can also benefit from shaping their contents into story forms.

The story form clearly provides a comfortable and hospitable environment for children's imaginative lives. I shall consider why it provides so hospitable an environment and why children find stories so readily accessible, engaging and meaningful. 'Environment', we may note from the beginning is perhaps an appropriate word here. We know that things generally become meaningful within contexts, within boundaries and limits. Very generally we may say that young children's experience of the world is such that they have very little sense of the limits, the boundaries, the contexts in which much of their experience is meaningful. And they have an urge to make sense of their experience, asking endless questions, eager to learn. The story is the linguistic unit that, as it were, brings its boundaries with it. Within the story, as within the game, the world is limited, the context is created and given and so the events of a story can be grasped and their meaning understood more readily than can the events in the less hospitable, imprecisely bounded world. Equally applicable to stories is Huizinga's observation about play and games; each 'creates order, *is* order' (Huizinga, 1949, p. 29).

What Is a Story?

I shall begin with a partial definition, one that will need some unpacking: 'a story is the linguistic unit that can ultimately fix the affective meaning of the events that compose it.' A number of elements here have implications for children's learning and need elaboration. First, the story blends the disparate events that compose it into a unit of some kind; then stories fix meaning in some way; and the kind of meaning they fix, which is in turn to some degree definitional of stories, is 'affective'.

Let us take an event from story: 'She walked into the rose garden.' By itself this event may set off more or less random associations, but its meaning is unclear. It has too many possible meanings, one might say. We know what the words mean but we don't know, most crucially for an event in a story, how to feel about it. Should we feel glad or sorry, ecstatic or horrified that she walked into the rose garden? If we add, 'and she found the money', we begin to limit the possible meanings of the event, though not by much. As events are added to the story one by one, the possible meanings are reduced until, in the end, only one meaning is possible. If we add events that tell us she had been desperately searching for money to give to her sad Irish grandfather, we might begin to feel, tentatively, glad that she entered the rose garden. Further events might reveal that the Irish grandfather is sad because his plan to hook all the local kids on heroin has not been going as well as he had hoped, and that he wanted the money to buy up a recent shipment of the drug. With this elaborated context we may now begin to feel sad or horrified that she entered the rose garden and found the money. When we know finally what to feel about the event, we know that we have reached the end of the story. In other words we know we have reached the end of the story not when we are told that all lived happily ever after but when we know how to feel about all the incidents that make up the story.

A crucial aspect of stories is that they are narratives that orient our affective responses to events. As we read a well-crafted story, the senses of expectation or puzzlement or fear that are set up in the beginning are played and shaped by the movement of the story. The story is like a musical score and our emotions are the instrument it plays. As long as we remain unsure how to feel about the events, we know we have not reached the completion of the larger unit. We know we have reached completion when we know finally how to feel about 'She entered the rose garden', and the rest of the events of the story. If we are to separate out the kind of meaning proper to the story, then, it is something that involves our emotions. Obviously such meaning requires lexical meaning — knowing the proper referents of terms like 'she' and 'entered' and 'rose garden' — and also semantic meaning — making sense of the sentences as one reads or listens. Both are necessary to make sense of a story, but both are equally necessary to make sense of an essay. The kind of meaning that is unique to stories, and that stories are uniquely responsible for organizing, is what I am calling 'affective meaning' (Egan, 1978).

A connected crucial aspect of stories is that they are narratives that end. They do not just peter out or stop at some arbitrary point. What makes them stories is that their ending completes and satisfies whatever was raised in their beginnings and elaborated in their middles (Kermode, 1966). In doing this they fix the meaning of their contents; they show us how to feel about the events we have been following. In this, stories are radically unlike history. A problem with meaning in history is that we cannot fix our affective responses to events. They have too many sides, too many contexts, to allow the reduction of possible meanings to one precise meaning. As new things happen we constantly reassess the meaning of all past events. The only people who can fix for themselves *the* meaning of historical events, and who are therefore confident of how to feel about them, are ideologues who assert an ending which they claim is inevitable for the historical process. In an unsophisticated Marxist view, for example, the laws of history are known, and so the future progress towards the classless society is allowed to give meaning to the present stage of history. They then 'know' the meaning of history by transforming it into a story. Knowing the end, they can know the meaning of all the events that are a part of the process. As Kafka pointedly observed, 'The meaning of life is that it stops.' The ancient Greeks make a similar observation: 'Call no man happy until he is dead.'

One attraction of stories is that they grant us the satisfaction, which history and our experience withhold from us, of being sure how to feel about events and characters. The world of the story, like the world of the game, reduces reality — of which humankind cannot bear very much — to a scale that mimics it on the one hand, and allows us a certain comfort in dealing with it on the other. This attraction and its satisfaction seem to be felt keenly by children. The circumscribed worlds of story and game within which meanings are clear and determinate provide a haven from the conceptually less apprehensible world of everyday experience. While children's stories and games seem to be simpler than adults', articulated more starkly on binary poles of good and bad, love and hate, fear and security and so on, they share with adults' the purpose, which is the focus of attention here, of fixing how to feel about the events that make them up. (I am concerned here only with the basic story form. I realize that this analysis works less well or, rather, needs to be supplemented if we consider all the ambivalences built into sophisticated narratives, and if we consider the mixing of elements of history and present realities into fictional narratives. My point, however, needs only the simpler story form.)

If we consider the kind of meaning children seem to find in their stories and fantasy worlds, and if we accept even some part of Piaget's image of the primitive nature of young children's logico-mathematical operations, we may see that the most prominent tools children have for making sense of things are strongly affective and moral. Children grasp the world, that is to say, by means of such concepts as good and bad and all the variants of these, with joy, sorrow and anger, with love and hate, with fear and security and so on. One is tempted to suggest that children's grasp on the world is affective and moral rather than logical and rational, but this would be to accept the restricted and misleading contrast inherited from the Greeks. Rather, in young children what we call the rational and logical are intricately tied up with what we rather vaguely call the affective. In early childhood, thinking and feeling have not yet been schooled down divergent paths. Or rather, we might say, the oral techniques of thinking most accessible to young children and most useful for making sense of their lifeworld do not find any advantage in systematically separating out thinking from feeling. One may say that we think with our feelings no less effectively and sensibly than with the particular cognitive tools usually focused on when rational thinking is referred to.

Common acceptance of the age-old distinction between the rational and the affective has not only tended to remove children's imagination and fantasy from educational discourse and research, but it has also inhibited educational programmes and curricula focusing on the development of Dionysus's contributions to thinking — generating and elaborating the second, poetic, world apart from nature and encouraging greater precision of our emotions. Refinement and sophistication of our affective orientation to the world and knowledge are, I am arguing, a crucial and neglected part of education in rational thinking. The affective and the imaginative are not to be considered distinct elements from rational thinking; they are necessary *parts of* proper rational thinking. It is to the early development of these affective aspects of thinking that the story-form in general can contribute so richly.

One implication of this discussion is that the story-form, which is responsible for organizing and fixing affective meaning, has more important contributions to make to children's learning than are made by its casual use in fictional narratives during language arts classes. Even people who accept the importance of stories, in other words, often fail to see that underlying them is a tool of immense power and importance for education. It is a tool that is underused if it is wheeled out only during story-times that are separated from 'real learning' and academic 'work'. If our concern is with the communication of meaning, and children seem able readily to grasp the world affectively, and the tool we have for affectively organizing meaning is the story-form, then it would seem that use of the story-form in the planning of lessons and units might yield some important benefits.

Stories in Education

The story is a technique for organizing events, facts, ideas, characters and so on, whether 'real' or imagined, into meaningful units that shape our affective responses. It is a basic conceptual tool for providing coherence, continuity, connectedness and meaning to its contents, and building from their coalescence a further level or kind of meaning. Stories, after whatever transformations, reflect a mental predisposition. One implication of these conclusions for education is that we would be sensible and courteous to organize what we want to teach children in this form that can make its contents engaging and meaningful. This is one of the implications that might do with teasing out a little.

The trick here is to abstract elements of the story form from the typical content of, say, the classic fairy tales or myth stories and see how those elements might be used to shape the content of lessons or units of study across the curriculum. Important elements of such stories that we have already considered include a beginning that sets up an expectation; this expectation has an affectively engaging quality, and such a quality is most commonly achieved by setting binary opposites into conflict with one another. (For the role of binary opposites in myth see Levi-Strauss, 1966). The central part of the story involves the elaboration of this binary conflict, and the end comes with its satisfaction or resolution. If we concentrate on these principles and consider how we might convert them into a technique for use in planning teaching, an initial general implication concerns our very approach to our subject-matter. We must start seeing knowledge of the world and of human experience as good stories to be told rather than, or as well as, sets of objectives to be attained.

The beginning, then, involves searching the content for what is most affectively engaging about it. We may phrase this as asking what is most important about it or why does it matter. We must locate what is of deep human significance about our subject. Saying simply that children ought to know it in order to become educated is insufficient. We must, these principles imply, find what is most important about the topic and frame that importance in the form which children are predisposed to find engaging and meaningful.

Such an approach may seem possible in history or social studies, but more remote from science and mathematics. The main reason mathematics and science seem to present such difficulties to so many children is because their place in human understanding is still taken in largely unreflective educational practice in a nineteenth century positivist sense, unmediated by anything like the Kuhnian view mentioned above. Mathematics and science need to be re-embedded in contexts of human meaning, with their hopes, fears, intentions; the human emotions among which they came to birth, continue to progress and that give them life and meaning. Of course, we can impress mathematical and scientific facts and operations into children's superficial memories without any of this, but, as has been pointed out by educationalists for centuries, this achievement is educationally useless. The problem is to engage children's understanding. That engagement of understanding, I am arguing, is accessible to young children by presenting material in a manner that draws on elements of the story form.

The Curriculum and Teaching

If in science we are required to teach a unit on heat, to bring together the earlier discussion of the curriculum with the observations about stories, it is not enough — either in terms of courtesy or pedagogical sensitivity — to organize the knowledge we want acquired into a neat logical sequence; setting up perhaps a set of interesting experiments whose results build gradually the basic knowledge about heat that constitutes the objectives of the unit. The implication of the earlier discussions is that we must first embed the topic in a foundational context of human meaning accessible to, and vividly engaging for, the child. We must begin by finding something that is affectively important about heat, and finding a way, perhaps by means of binary opposites, of embodying that affective importance in clear and engaging terms. The question about identifying the affective importance of the topic is not to be interpreted in some 'childish' sense. Rather, the teacher can ask simply what he or she finds most affectively important; at what point does the topic engage an emotional response in him or her. In addition we shall consider the historical foundations of our understanding for clues about how to make this engaging and meaningful.

Let me quickly sketch an outline for a unit on heat appropriate for young children that uses the principles identified above. One way of answering the beginning question is to see heat as destroyer or heat as helper. How can we show destroyer/helper opposites in conflict in a way that will enable us to show vividly the content of our unit in an engaging and meaningful way? We might begin by setting up our context, preparing the bedding, for the facts, experiments and so on. And we might borrow the way the Greeks did this themselves in their mytho-logical representations. (These were the bases from which their and subsequent rational and scientific inquiries grew.) So we might begin with the myth stories that explain affectively the vital importance of heat to human life, and its dangers. We can thus tell the stories of Prometheus and Zeus, and of Sol and Phaeton, and see Haephestus limping around his constructive workshop. The daring of Prometheus, giving fire to humans, and the terrible punishment of Zeus show the importance controlled heat has played in human civilization. It is a power that has made us more like the gods. Phaeton's escapades show what destruction can follow when this terrible servant gets out of control.

The middle of our unit needs to elaborate the theme of heat as destroyer/heat as helper, and needs to be seen as like the middle of a story. It is not to be developed by simply putting in relevant content in some logical sequence. Rather, the teacher must think more as a story-teller developing a theme. So the content selected will be influenced by the theme. We shall choose as experiments, for example, not so much those that get at key facts, but those that expose key facts in light of our theme. It is what they expose about the constructive/destructive forces of heat that matter now. (Obviously we could have chosen different binary pairs and consequently developed different themes.) Experiments with heating water and generating steam can tie in with the stories of Hero of Alexandria's steam engine and then that of James Watt. These stories need to catch the human purposes, hopes, fears, struggles, of the individuals, and embed their discoveries and inventions in them as they relate to our theme. It is by embedding the facts that events in a story-form context that we can establish their meaning. Experiments using silver or matt black reflectors over glasses of water and measuring the temperatures of the water after they have stood in the sun for some time can be engaged with the theme through wondering how space ships and astronauts can best be protected from Sol's burning rays in space. The difference in this approach is more a matter of context, and its affective quality, than in the typical content of such a unit.

A conclusion to such a unit might come in considering the constructive and destructive potentials of heat in nuclear power. This urgent present issue is still grasped in the terms given vivid form in the ancient Greek myth of Prometheus and Zeus. Nuclear energy promises a Promethean gift to human beings, but Zeus may wreak vengeance for our attempts to harness his godly power. The myth catches a way in which we still affectively orient ourselves to the constructive and destructive potentials of heat. This sketch of a unit is not intended to be any more than an indication of how it is possible to take some of the principles discussed above and turn them to pedagogical use.

Conclusion

The story, I have argued, is the archetypal form in which narrative bits are pulled together into coherent wholes to create a larger meaning. This is a fundamental featfure of our sense-making. We see it in embryonic form in very young children's chattering narratives and in another form in sophisticated theories in the physical sciences. Our minds, that is, do not simply mirror the world, they construct an image of it out of mind-stuff — concepts, or whatever we want to call it. That constructing is our ever-active sense-making, which involves crucially the constant and shifting coordination of contexts and contents, the making of our images of the world in the context of our patterns of understanding and our emotions and so on, and the matching of these with the further knowledge we derive from the world (Gombrich, 1960). The ability to follow a story entails the most fundamental form of this process. We assume its existence in young children when we tell them the story of Cinderella or Robin Hood, confident that the story will generate a kind of pleasurable, satisfying meaning. This basic capacity is not something we learn, it is something we *are*. We do not, then, need to teach it.

What we can usefully do is stimulate it, elaborate it, develop it and, of course, use it.

Stories can draw into the bright circle of their recognition a huge range of knowledge about the world — the distinctive character of particular places, flora, fauna and geographical details, people past and present, and a set of norms, values and expectations attached to roles and relationships within one's culture. One might enrich this by adding Ted Hughes's observation that stories are 'in continual private meditation, as it were, on their own implications. They are little factories of understanding. New revelations of meaning open out of their images and patterns continually, stirred into reach by our growth and changing circumstances' (Hughes, 1987, pp. 34–5). Stories can expand knowledge and experience, and can do so in an exploring, enriching way (Rosenblatt, 1976). They can enhance the meaning of the particular places in which they are set, and can enrich one's perception of the human possibilities of similar kinds of places. A common difficulty for early settlers in North America was the sense of alienness of the natural environment. The landscapes of Europe were infused with human meaning by their being the settings of so many stories. The incorporation of Indian legends and the writing of their own stories, songs and poems about their new environments and experiences shaped by them humanized and made comprehensible what had previously been alien.

The primary stuff of stories is human emotion. As the landscape becomes humanized by being placed in contexts of human hopes, fears, loves, hates and so on, so even more vividly do we understand other characters through the behaviours caused by these common emotions. Stories have the power to enable us to feel with others. We can see the world through others' eyes, through their emotional responses to events. Such a way of dealing with the typical content of the early science curriculum is rather alien to the normal textbook. But it is a way that seems possibly to make science less alien by introducing it to children the way it developed in human culture generally.

This has been an exploration of how the typical science textbook might be reformed if we were to adopt a Kuhnian view of changing science, and then add to that an assumption that it makes sense to introduce science to children using some of the means whereby it developed in the first place. This kind of recapitulation does not lead us to recapitulate the *content* of science in some historical sequence, but leads us rather to focus on the forms of sense-making that were historically foundational to scientific inquiry and remain foundational constituents of science as a human activity.

References

EGAN, K. (1978) 'What is a plot?' *New Literary History*, 9, 3, 455–73.
EGAN, K. (1987) 'Literacy and the oral foundations of education,' *Harvard Educational Review*, 57, 4, 445–72.
EGAN, K. (1988) *Primary Understanding*. London and New York: Routledge and Kegan Paul.

GOMBRICH, E. (1960) *Art and Illusion*. Princeton, N.J.: Princeton University Press.

HAVELOCK, E.A. (1963) *Preface to Plato*. Cambridge, Mass.: Harvard University Press.

HUGHES, T. (1988) 'Myth and education,' in EGAN, K. and NADANER, D. (Eds), *Imagination and Education*. New York: Teachers College Press.

HUIZINGA, J. (1949) *Homo Ludens: A Study of the Play Element in Culture*. London: Routledge and Kegan Paul.

KERMODE, F. (1966) *The Sense of an Ending*. Oxford: Oxford University Press.

KUHN, T. (1970) *The Structure of Scientific Revolutions*. Chicago, Ill.: University of Chicago Press.

LEVI-STRAUSS, C. (1966) *The Savage Mind*. Chicago, Ill.: University of Chicago Press.

ONG, W.J. (1982) *Orality and Literacy*. London: Methuen.

ROSENBLATT, L.M. (1976) *Literature as Exploration*. New York: Noble and Noble.

Chapter 9

Talking the Text in Teaching Composition

Shirley Brice Heath
Stanford University

During the eighteenth and nineteenth centuries of Anglo-American societies, literature — broadly defined to include not only fictional works, but also political treatises, biographies and history — served as the prompt for most classroom discussion and student writing in English courses. The stories of literature were reconceived by students asked to talk and write about their responses to their reading. Interpreting and reinterpreting the motifs, themes and situations of literary writings became the primary means in English classrooms by which students demonstrated their speaking, reading, writing and thinking abilities. In the past three decades, however, curricular reforms, the rise of the textbook industry and expanded uses of standardized tests of comprehension have combined with shifts in literary criticism to close the innate openness of literary texts. Textbooks — or books of texts — no longer invite students to compare their own or others' life experiences or to offer multiple reflections on how and what literary writing can mean. The current textbooks of English courses have followed the course of basal readers to become collections of writings from which teachers test students on their knowledge of formal terms, specifics about the content of the writing and facts about authors and the period of the writing.[1] Within the broad sweep of secondary and college-level English classes over the past century, this chapter examines the diminishing role that schools allow the prior knowledge and talk of students to play in their interpretation of written texts and in their preparation for writing.

From Parlour to Classroom

For any worker the means of making a livelihood strongly influences the uses of leisure time. Together work and play determine what, how and why individuals read, and what they do with what they read. Do they talk about their reading, store, transform, apply, or forget ideas gained from reading, and do they write about what they have read? For most of the history of public schooling in Anglo-American society, many families across occupations and classes chose to use their leisure time to read and then to talk about or apply ideas gained from their reading.[2] Farmlife, long distances between households, strong community sanctions on work on the Sabbath, and ample opportunity in community affairs to use what one could learn from print drew families to reading at home, even when the jobs of adult members were such that no immediate benefits came from reading. The structuring of leisure time came at the local level, where families and communities worked together to create ways of entertaining family members of all ages. Without highly specialized activities, commercial entertainment and numerous public gathering places, families became their own recreation resources. Books, cardgames and pencil-and-paper games were inexpensive, flexible and multi-purpose. Institutions, such as churches, workplaces and unions, pulled together as community resources to clear fields and city lots for ballgames, to plan county fairs and bazaars and to stage parades or support community plays. All of these activities depended in large part on the interpretive powers individuals had gained in the hours spent in their homes talking about what printed materials meant and how ideas gained from reading could be turned into actions. The recreational resources of books and other printed materials thus extended beyond their actual first reading to their *re-creations* in theme floats in city parades, church pageants and community plays or operas.

Abundant documentary and artifactual evidence tells us that families gathered in the parlour, around the kitchen table, or on the front porch to read and talk.[3] Beyond the home, men and women collected in sex-segregated groups to read and talk as they participated in church affairs, planned ethnic celebrations, or organized unions. Across Canada and the United States local library and historical society records make it clear that both book publishers and newspaper editors expected readers to talk about what they read and to reinterpret, expand and debate print materials. Thus for most of the history of public schooling, from the 1860s into the 1950s, children from those families who included reading in their home and community leisure time went to school having taken up the habit of talking about written texts and recasting them into new forms. One-room schools for the elementary grades continued this practice while older students helped younger ones. In secondary schools English courses focused on literature as the basis of class discussion and written assignments, and thus built on habits that many students had developed at home. Contrary to the myths that have come down to us, more people read outside the workplace than within job settings. A great portion of those who read did not see reading as an activity to be taken up primarily as the means to obtain a job. Instead, individuals found reading and the social activities it engendered — especially talking — to be a primary incentive for becoming an active participant in family reading circles, literary clubs, church guilds and the many other family and community-based occasions for reading that American life offered.

Public writings about schooling, as well as textbooks used in English class-rooms, support the view that reading was a prime facilitator of debate, conver-sational skills and argumentative powers.[4] Literature, generally regarded as written to stimulate identification on the part of readers with the morals, characters and situations of the text, became the primary prompt for discussion and essay writing. It is no accident that the essay, the literary form in which writers *try out* their ideas, became the favourite genre of the English classroom. Ideally, this form captured the openness of letters and conversations, while also allowing room for including narratives or stories, and promoting a particular direction of argument (Heath, 1987).

Eighteenth and nineteenth century textbooks that addressed the teaching of composition (as well as articles on language in American periodicals) illustrate how closely linked those who expressed their view in these sources considered spoken and written language to be. Talking ideas through came as a natural preface to well-organized ideas expressed in writing. These writers regarded form and content as interdependent: form could not be taught apart from content. If one had nothing to say, no amount of dressing up the grammar in written formalities could hide that fact. A slow and gradual shift away from these hard-nosed views during the final decade of the nineteenth century speeded up considerably in the twentieth century. A focus on language competence as personal expression, cultivated through oral performance, and fundamental to the intellectual and social benefit of society, came to be replaced by a strong emphasis on the specialized pedagogical practice of teaching writing or 'composition'. The move was from recognizing an essential relationship between the experience of learning and the linguistic expression of knowledge to asserting the need to lay out criteria and procedures for teaching how to form or 'compose' written language. The stories or the multiple interpretations that students could re-create from literature to reinforce their arguments and enliven their essays disappeared in favour of rules that schooled students in the technical skills of writing compositions and drilled them on the content matter of literature as facts to be stored along with those of social studies and geography.[5]

The Place of Talk

Reviews of the history of language education in the United States have focused primarily on rhetoric and the teaching of grammar and literature (Lyman, 1922; Murphy, 1982). Perceptions of curricular debates that took place before the twentieth century have been formed to a great extent by current divisions of labour in departments involved in language education; speech departments hold responsibility for oral language performance, departments of rhetoric and English for written language development. Thus historical overviews have examined either the course of public oratory or the teaching of grammar and literature. To be sure, within Anglo-American societies in the nineteenth century there came the general recognition that the meaning of the term 'rhetoric' which had earlier meant oral delivery, had shifted to mean written composition. However, few historians have asked the question of what happened to expectations of spoken language when this shift occurred.

The answer lies partly in a practice that Americans have not considered part of the school curriculum — conversation. Yet when we look closely at eighteenth and nineteenth century writings on language, it is clear that the public and educators alike expected the art of conversing — sharing experiences and ideas in dyadic or multi-party oral exchanges — to lay the groundwork for the craft of writing.

It was in conversation that common people and élites alike could test their own reasoning against that of others. In conversation individuals could test directly the powers of their own thinking processes and give proof of an immediate grasp of both knowledge and logical organization. Central to the early national dependence on such talk was the view that 'Men [and women] should learn to doubt before they learn[ed] to believe' (*The Instructor*, I:8:29, 24 April 1755). In conversation an individual could pass from premises to conclusions and apply the 'faculty of reasoning'; such talk allowed the communication of ideas and the possibility of doubt to be addressed openly by all parties (*Monthly Miscellany and Vermount Magazine*, I:1–6.13, 1794). This 1790 poem takes up the rewards of conversation:

> Hail, conversation, heav'nly fair,
> Thou bliss of life, and balm of care,
> Call forth the long-forgotten knowledge
> Of school, of travel, and of college
> . . .
> Let Education's moral mint
> The noblest images imprint;
> . . .
> But 'tis thy commerce, Conversation,
> Must give it use by circulation;
> That noblest commerce of mankind,
> Whose precious merchandize is MIND.
> (*Universal Asylum and Columbia Magazine*, IV.251–2, March–June 1790)

This anonymous poet reminds readers that it is in conversation that the knowledge of school, travel and college becomes the stories or core narratives of conversation. Written materials alone cannot engage the mind in active give and take, and books cannot unite kindred sympathies to seal social relations. Through conversation, speakers could exhibit a special merchandising, a 'trade' that kindled lively pleasures, sought allusions, used quick memory, traced images to their source and allowed the exhibition of wit.

In conversation one could not mask ignorance for long. Society judged conversationalists more by the logical connections of ideas and less in terms of the correctness of their forms of speaking. The successful conversationalist was not expected to speak formally or to carry into conversation the strict application of grammar rules learned in school for public oratory or writing exercises. Speaking with 'careless cheerfulness', simplicity of manner and with the 'grace, ease, and vivacity natural to youth' was desirable in conversation (*Weekly Magazine*, I.121–11, February–April 1798). Short sentences, colloquial language — 'not that of books' — should mark conversation; to be avoided were extravagances in language — clichés, satire, sarcasm, artifice and fillers, such as 'you know', and 'you say' (*How to Be a Lady: A Book for Girls*, 1850).

With the mid-nineteenth century spread of formal schooling and newspapers from urban centres to rural communities came repeated debates about the relative merits of conversing and writing. During the first decades of the nineteenth century, periodicals had often tried to claim a conversational character, and to invite readers to feel they were part of a two-way exchange (Heath, 1981 b). Columns of these periodicals offered hints on how to be a good conversationalist, and etiquette manuals advised readers on ways to handle conversation in a wide variety of situations (Heath, 1978). Those who 'spoke out' in written form argued that writing could become a solitary, arrogant exercise that allowed the rule-governed display rather than the test of ideas.

Early in the nineteenth century, some of those who wrote grammar textbooks for schools similarly argued against artificial rule-making and for 'common communication' among men and women, those of trade and interest in practical matters as well as professionals (Ash, 1785). One grammarian, writing in 1803, prefaced his grammar with the admonition that schoolmasters should not spend time on rules and examples of the principles of language and of English grammar; instead they should emphasize language uses that would expand ideas and exercise their [students'] understandings (Adams, 1803). Grammarians of the 1830s increasingly pointed out the lack of emphasis in school instruction — especially in the teaching of grammar — on practical communicative skills. The simple principles of speech stood in contrast with the 'artificial, perplexing, contradictory, and impracticable systems taught in schools and colleges' (Cardell, 1825, p. vii).

Textbooks on the teaching of composition did not come along until the second half of the nineteenth century and then not without considerable acknowledgement that they could only artificially induce what might more naturally flow from genuine conversations around written texts with which students could argue and debate. Students could not only sharpen their wits in conversation, but also their understanding of the principles of language. Talk provided instant challenge and highly motivated opportunity for expressing one's own ideas and experiences; speech offered 'an exhaustless source of practical facts and principles, which go far beyond all abstract reasoning, in teaching to man the great lesson "know thou thyself"' (Cardell, 1825, p. 26). To move most easily and 'genuinely' from conversation to written forms, students should write letters, for they allowed writers to retain a conversational mode and a rapport with a clearly imagined audience. Numerous letter-writing manuals gave advice on ways to achieve a conversational tone that evoked a reciprocity of emotional, intellectual and moral response from the correspondent.[6]

Early Composition Textbooks

With more and more schools came more grammar books, spellers and dictionaries that were soon joined by books devoted primarily to the teaching of 'English composition'. The commitment of earlier eras to the benefits of conversation began to weaken. The most widely used composition texts just after the mid-nineteenth century (that offered a philosophy of composition) acknowledged that writing letters was a primary initial step and form of practice to enable learners to retain many of the desirable qualities of conversation — spontaneity, fluency and a sense of the reader's role. These earliest American books devoted entirely to the teaching of composition reflect in their apologetic tone something of an ambivalence about the offering of aids or instruction for composing. They recommended letter-writing to students or offered practice exercises along with numerous other types of compositions. Models of famous letters helped fill the back portions of these composition books; for example, *First Lessons in Composition*, by G.P. Quackenbos, as well as his later *Advanced Course of Composition and Rhetoric*, included letters as the first of the models placed at the end of the book.

These early textbooks noted what numerous late twentieth century critics of the teaching of writing in schools have come to announce as new revelations: 'Compositions' — and their variants of 'themes' and 'essays' — are genres contrived by and for formal schooling. To make connections between these and the practical writing tasks outside school is to strain the reader's credulity, and thus these early textbook authors apologetically passed off composition as merely one way of offering another form of *practice* in using language. Quackenbos pointed out that he wrote his first book because school personnel told him there was a need for such a resource. As early as 1844, a superintendent of schools had 'regret[ted] the almost entire neglect of the art of original composition in our common schools, and the want of a proper textbook upon this essential branch of education.' The super-intendent continued his plea with the commentary that 'Hundreds graduate from our common schools with no well-defined ideas of the construction of our language' (Quackenbos, 1866, preface, n.p.). Quackenbos and other authors felt that books of texts of various genres, from letters to essays, would help overcome this problem. By the 1860s, when he wrote his advanced book-of-texts or textbook for composition students, Quackenbos had some competitors who had gone farther than he in establishing rules and formal approaches to composition. Though no doubt in the interest of promoting the sales of this second venture, Quackenbos noted the extraordinary success of his first book and then offered some cautions about the rapid move of schools to formalize and overly instruct composition. He suggested that many teachers still preferred no aid or instruction of any kind, and he himself reminded readers that humans were creatures in possession of reason, intellect and imagination, and they were not to be regarded fundamentally as 'rule-followers'. To those who would use his book, Quackenbos opened by noting that students had to have something in their heads — thoughts, ideas, information — to compose. Substance had to precede form; he warned that composition was first 'the process of Invention, which furnishes the thoughts to be clothed in a dress of words, and which constitutes the most difficult if not the chief branch of the art . . .' (Quackenbos, 1862, p. 6).

Similarly, Richard Parker, whose *Aids to English Composition Prepared for Students of All Grades* rivalled the books of Quackenbos in popularity in mid-century, reminded his readers: 'Genius cannot be fettered, and an original and thinking mind, replete with its own exhuberance, will often burst out in spontaneous gushings, and open to itself new channels, through which the treasures of thought will flow in rich and rapid currents' (Parker, 1853, preface, n.p.). He denied the usefulness of a curriculum that set out composition along a pattern of progressing systematically from one stage to another. He repeatedly reiterated the importance of 'a disciplined and cultivated mind, in the exercise of vigorous thought, on reading and observation, and an attentive study of the meaning and the force of language' (Parker, 1853, introduction, n.p.). In short, if there was indeed any first step in composition, it was 'to obtain ideas'.

The sources of ideas, imagination and thought that these early pedagogues of composition pointed out were, to be sure, the writings of others, but a close examination of the texts selected as models for these early composition books and of the other routes to obtaining ideas reveals some fundamental values of democracy and individual resourcefulness. Models included letters, descriptions and arguments of the élite and famous, but also those of children and individuals in different stations of life. Moreover, the resources of the individual learner, called up simply in observing carefully one's own daily life and surrounding environment, could provide the fundamentals of vigorous thought, an analytical perspective and a capacity for synthesis. Students were urged to learn to attend to what was going on about them — objects, events, dialogues — and to bring the richness of their own sources of knowledge and ways of perceiving into their writing first and foremost. Students thus guided would learn the powers of description possible in language not through memorizing lists of adjectives, but through describing the 'qualities, uses, operations, and effects, together with their relation to other things' of objects and events in their own personal experience. The goal was to 'teach the learner to describe, in easy sentences, any circumstances which happen to himself and others. He should be directed to write the incident just as he would relate it to his parents or a young friend . . .' (Parker, 1853, p. 4).

All composition textbooks published between 1845 and 1865 reflected in one way or another the concern that formal schooling acknowledge students' experiences in both life and language as the basis of learning to write compositions. To be sure, some voiced their concerns more directly and strongly than others did. For example, Parker noted the role of dialogues and conversations as the familiar exemplars of children's expertise:

> Young persons are seldom at a loss for topics of conversation, when left unrestrained to themselves. But as soon as they are required to write what is called a *composition*, they feel at a loss what to say [sic]. This arises from no inability to form ideas, nor from want of words to express them, but rather from a vague apprehension that something is required of them, which they have never done before; and to which they know not how to address themselves. (Parker, 1853, p. 7)

His list of subjects that teachers might ask students to write about included many that would be based solely on their powers of direct observation, recall of events, and analysis of the styles and meanings of what had been said in dialogues they had either heard or participated in themselves.

How-to-write books in series that offered 'home improvement' in a variety of activities echoed the convictions of early composition textbooks that the resources of the direct experiences and everyday language of students must be the fundamental building blocks of composition. One such book combined both Quackenbos' admonition that substance had to precede form in composition and Parker's wish to rely to a great extent on students' primary source knowledge — or that gained directly through personal experience, careful observation and delayed analysis. The anonymous author of this pocket manual wrote:

> We will presume that every young man or woman who shall look into this little book for instruction in the art of composition, has thoughts and feelings to express, facts to state, arguments to advance, reasons to urge — in a word, *something to say*. To those who have not, our teachings will be of no use. If you have nothing to say, say nothing. We cannot furnish ideas. We aspire simply to aid the young writer in molding into available shape, and clothing in fitting language, those he may already possess. (Anonymous, 1857, p. 16)

The blunt tone directed to those who would presumably have taken up this manual outside a formal school setting contrasts sharply with the softened reminders and cautions of textbook writers of this same era. However, the authors of both seemed aware that reification of writing as school composition took away much that had been fundamental in the language uses of American society: ideas and arguments based on individual experience and conviction, as well as the spontaneity and immediate testing of ideas that conversation offered. The wedge that seemed to be driving spoken and written language further and further from each other also separated substance from form and individuals from the sources of their own experience as authority (compare Taxel, Chapter 3, this volume, on the 'privileging' of texts).

Relinquishing Composition to a 'Course of Study'

By 1880, words of caution about what the individual and his or her habits of spoken language use might contribute to the writing of school compositions had all but disappeared in educational materials (see de Castell and Luke and van Peer, Chapters 7 and 10, this volume, on the decline of 'higher order' literacy skills across the history of Anglo-American schooling). 'School compositions' — that genre written by individuals in isolation and solely in connection with classwork, generally in courses of Rhetoric or Literature — had become the focus of 'courses of study'. Many viewed this move as a 'rational remodelling' (Swinton, 1876, preface, n.p.) and a move toward making teaching 'scientific'. Proponents argued that if language were to receive its due attention, composition must join grammar and spelling in being subject to rules and principles. Textbooks of this era began splitting definitional hairs, sometimes separating 'composition' as distinct from either a 'theme' or an 'essay'. Similarly, the parts of a composition or theme came in for prescription, and progress from introduction to the delineation of definitions, origins, and progressions, and finally to effects and conclusions, were set out as the rational and logical way for an individual to think about any subject or topic. Many authors acknowledged their debt in their rule formation to Rhetoric, which they admitted had referred originally 'not to writing, but to speaking', and urged that holding this notion in mind might enable students to forget all the mechanical approaches that now accompanied writing and 'to think simply of the sending of thought from one mind to another' (Anderson, 1894, preface, n.p.).

Several scholars have outlined the sociological and pedagogical history of the shift in the last two decades of the nineteenth century to objectives of science and standardization (e.g., Tyack, 1974). Changes in the economy and population distribution created demands for factory workers in urban industrial zones; unschooled adult immigrants and Blacks became part of a workforce that was highly visible to educators who faced their children in classrooms. Schools responded to the strange languages and unfamiliar experiential backgrounds of these students with carefully prescribed school subjects and demands that students demonstrate knowledge of these subjects in regimented and routinized ways. Terms that had carried positive force in the mid-nineteenth century — spontaneity, genius, original, practical, vigorous, and collaborative — came to characterize negative behaviours that called for stern discipline imposed from outside the individual. Vocational, ordered, moral, and above all, predictable, were terms now used to describe courses of study; gone was the former era's talk of learners talking and debating together in their preparation for writing (see Gilbert, Chapter 15, this volume, for a description of the renewal of emphasis on the 'individual' learner in writing reform movements of the mid-1980s). Systematic instruction with careful attention to rules became the means for redeeming the inferior status of knowledge about language of each subsequent school generation. 'Good language' was the mark of character, diligence, discipline and appropriate allegiance as an individual citizen (Heath, 1981 a).

By the beginning of the twentieth century, the science of teaching writing could tolerate no longer any reminders that spoken language uses and the observation and analysis of one's own experiences could lie at the core of learning. The term *composition* came to substitute for *rhetoric*, and the few whispers that might have reminded English teachers of the curious habit of teaching in school a genre that bore no relation to either writing demands outside of school or even literary models went unnoticed. The Scottish logician, Alexander Bain, set education out as a science (1897), and his books reminded school teachers that it was 'knowledge imparted', not knowledge experienced, that was the work of the school. He completely stripped considerations of subject-matter from teachers, arguing that definition, logic and placement of the parts of the composition and its units (sentence, paragraph, etc.) supplied the essential points. 'Ordering', 'managing' and 'proportioning' became the terms of teaching as well as merchandising and industrializing.

The Legacy

After 1880, more and more textbook writers focused on the teaching of composition, and the history of the introduction of this activity into American colleges and universities as well as into consideration by the Modern Language Association has been told by several scholars (for example, Murphy, 1982, Part 2; see Stewart, 1985, for a review article and bibliography of such studies). Certain individuals early in the twentieth century, such as Sterling Andrus Leonard, took note of both the recurrent pattern of tightening rules and focusing on form, especially when the public seemed to believe language was deteriorating, and the tendency increased for schooling to move away from students' direct experiences with life and language (for a review of Leonard's reform efforts, see Myers, 1986).

In the 1980s, the social history of their own profession has become a topic of English teachers at their professional conferences. Books and articles have documented reform efforts in English teaching (on topics ranging from attitudes toward standardization to the competition between literature and writing in the curriculum) and their relative patterns of success (e.g., Finegan, 1980; Baron, 1982; Stewart, 1986). Several of these historical treatments remind us that almost all 'new' proposals (such as those for collaborative writing, conferencing, etc.) emerged earlier in the twentieth century as reform efforts and could not be sustained in the face of 'teacher-proof' textbooks, standardized testing and the intense focus on the evaluation of the individual performance — of both teacher and student. However, while some of these historical examinations minimally acknowledge the strong influence of the general economic environment and the social climate on earlier pedagogical entrenchments (see Applebee, 1974; Piche, 1967, for example), few current proposals for reform take any account of the contemporary labour market into which high school graduates will move. What types of language skills and problem-solving abilities will the workplaces of the next century need, and can schools help students learn these? There is abundant evidence that the domesticity and passive rule-following rewarded by the factory workplace became the norm for classrooms during the early twentieth century. Is it possible therefore that the late twentieth century shift in workplace needs might similarly influence the school in the future?

The current combined efforts of some literacy experts, educators and labour economists suggest a growing awareness that if schools continue to educate for 'basic skills', passivity and individual effort, they will condemn the bulk of students to either the bottom levels of the labour market or no access at all (National Academy of Sciences, 1984; Carnegie Forum on Education and the Economy, 1986). Studies of the communicative and decision-making demands of cutting-edge industries in the 1980s help substantiate predictions about the nature of the workplace (National Academy of Sciences, 1984). Needed in the wide variety of jobs that will be available from computer systems analysts to building custodians will be workers who know how to learn and are 'well grounded in fundamental knowledge and who have mastered concepts and skills that create an intellectual framework to which new knowledge can be added' (National Academy of

Sciences, 1984, p. 17). Individuals must be able to draw inferences from a variety of types of information, to understand and transmit instructions, to develop alternatives and reach conclusions and to 'express their ideas intelligibly and effectively.' These skills are required for entry-level; advancement depends on the ability to *compose* both tables and reports, consult source materials, handle mathematical concepts, control complex equipment and address groups. Fundamental to these descriptions of future workers is the recognition that workplaces must depend on collaboration and the joint construction of interpretations and alternative identifications of problems and their solutions.

Arguments made in the late 1970s that technology would deskill a majority of sectors in the modern workplace failed to take into account the centrality of communication and computation in the rapidly growing human service institutions. From building contractors to nursing aides, workers need specialized knowledge about how information and experience relate to decision-making, and they must work cooperatively. Workers must be able to act on information by taking it down, repackaging it and sending it on to others, or combining different kinds of information to make decisions. The fact that a machine records and even transmits the information does not relieve workers from checking for accuracy and facing the challenge of combining different kinds of information to make interpretations. Workers must be able to apply analogical and inferential thinking to new problems that arise; to work together collaboratively to identify problems and arrive at solutions; to plan ahead and predict consequences of actions before they actually commit themselves to a course of action. The switch from heavy to service and information industries ironically now requires *in the workplace* many of the skills gained and practised in earlier centuries *in leisure activities* of the family and the community.

Thus, the tasks and settings of these modern workplaces send us back to the criteria of conversation and composition in the eighteenth and early nineteenth centuries — clearness, unity, observation, fluency, and substantive ideas subject to argument, debate, coherence and analogous reasoning. Results of the 1980s National Assessment of Educational Progress studies of writing report that these are the qualities students have not mastered. A study conducted by the National Council of Teachers of English (1987) on basal readers came to a similar conclusion. Basal readers deprive both teachers and students of opportunities to test, exchange, create and debate ideas. Dependent on the central premise that a 'sequential all-inclusive set of instructional materials can teach all children to read *regardless of teacher competence and regardless of learner difference*', basals have their roots in the same industrial management technology that put composition textbooks in place.

History, Voltaire once quipped, is the way the living have of playing tricks on the dead. He might well have added: and on the living as well. In the late 1980s, a considerable amount of mythology prevails about the need to 'return to the basics' while depending increasingly on technology and 'scientific' standardized approaches to helping individual students improve their communicative skills. Proponents of 'teacher-proof' textbooks and workbooks would have us believe on the other hand they must find out these rules for themselves. In this sense they confront an 'invisible' textbook, and the learning process is a continuous quest for a cultural practice hidden from them. Thus social knowledge is at once assumed and suppressed. One obvious solution to this problem would be the introduction of textbooks dealing with essays. The existence of composition textbooks would seem to be such a solution. It remains to be seen, however, to what degree such textbooks concern themselves with familiarizing pupils with the text type they are trained to write. On the basis of Heath's analysis (see Chapter 9, this volume), one would expect different emphases in different epochs. It should be pointed out, moreover, that composition textbooks are mainly an American invention; in Europe such books are virtually absent. Presumably this may be related to a different status of the essay in these different cultures.

The initial description of canonical writing forms now needs a further specification. The educational reforms which most (European) countries have seen over the past decades have also affected the position of the essay. In a number of cases this has led to severe criticisms, or even to efforts to break away from the essay altogether. Such instances provide interesting cases to study, because the very fact that the structures of interaction are in such moments prone to change allows us to perceive more clearly their anchorage within the institution and within society as a whole. In The Netherlands two major innovations have been introduced alongside the traditional essay. One was geared toward more literary types of texts, so-called *creative* writing. The other was aimed at non-literary and everyday types of text, and could be labelled *pragmatic* writing: pupils were expected to gather and process information on a particular (usually realistic) topic, and subsequently to structure ensuing the information into a text not altogether unlike a kind of report.

What interests us here is the precise way in which this new type of writing instruction attempts to set up its own distinctive profile. Three central ingredients of pragmatic writing appear as constants in the relevant literature: its *informative* content, its *goal-directed* nature and its *audience*-orientation. The traditional essay, by implication, would thus seem to be *not* informative in content, *not* goal-directed and *not* audience-oriented. But this would seem to be counter-intuitive. Surely there is a particular goal and a particular audience involved in essay-writing. And there can be little doubt that the traditional essay attempts to convey some kind of information. Thus it would seem to be the case that the communicative intent of new alternatives to the traditional essay, rather than being new in themselves, are but a reformulation of a number of ingredients which were (and have always been) present in the traditional forms of essay writing. The crucial point here is that the fundamental goal, audience orientation and informative intention of the essay, are no longer *perceived* as such by participants; that is, they are no longer part and parcel of youngsters' discursive backgrounds. Nor do they belong to teachers' general and professional equipment, either. Thus the dissatisfaction of teachers with the essay demonstrates the historical breakdown of the communicative presuppositions upon which it has traditionally been based.

One is left then, with a paradox: on the one hand the essay is a canonical form of writing instruction; on the other hand the necessary conditions for its operating successfully are no longer fulfilled. This requires further analysis, for the paradox needs a solution in practical terms: writing instruction must go on. We shall return to this solution of the paradox, but first we must outline the situation in social terms in more detail.

The new forms of instruction for learning to write have not been limited to instances of pragmatic writing. Another strand has stressed the importance of creative writing (see also Gilbert, Chapter 15, this volume). In this case heavy emphasis is placed on the development of fantasy, emotional involvement, originality of composition and formulation, exploration of the self in relation to others, spontaneity and expressive quality, and the integration of various perspectives into an 'organic' whole of the text. One could ask again whether these qualities are not also inherent in the conventional practice of essay writing. More important still is the fact that this alternative stresses the individual's expressive potential *at the expense* of the more informative qualities proposed by pragmatic writing. Apparently, dissatisfaction with the traditional essay goes in two directions simultaneously: one move (creative writing) goes *against* objectivity (or its presumed intent to this effect), while the other (pragmatic writing) is *in favour* of heightened objectivity, and thus (by implication) against a presumed subjectivity of the traditional essay. From a logical point of view the two moves must be considered contradictory. The conclusion may therefore be warranted that both approaches take issue with only *a part of* the traditional practice against which they react. That is, the two movements described can only have come into being if the original practice of essay writing contained *both* a subjective and an objective moment. One group of educational reformers is dissatisfied with the degree of subjectivity it possesses (and consequently demands a more informative kind of writing), the other takes issue with its objective ingredients (and therefore strives toward a higher degree of subjectivity in pupils' writings).

In as far as these arguments in favour of new forms of writing are based on an incomplete and often also incorrect understanding of essay writing, they must be said to be invalid. The interesting point here is that creative writing has hardly succeeded in acquiring a firm footing in educational practice generally. One reason for this may be that it is itself too ambivalent to replace the (perceived) vagueness and the half-forgotten postulates of essay writing. Hence few maxims as to its practice may be operationally formulated. With pragmatic writing these diffi-culties may be more easily overcome. Apart from the differences in their didactic applicability, however, there may be other reasons of a more sociological kind that have influenced the course of events. It may be noticed that present-day society hardly needs, for its everyday functioning, a high degree of creative writing skills. Alternatively, where one may observe writing activities to function socially, the demand will be for more 'objective' forms of writing, coming close to the kind of reports involved in pragmatic writing. Thus the affinity between essay writing and social situation displays the fluctuations in value attributed to this practice. It is therefore necessary to study this relationship in more detail.

The essay, in the form that we know it now, finds its origin in the rise of the new class at the beginning of modern times. In fact the creation of the new literary

Table 1. Some Factors Affecting Textbook Use

School/Classroom Context Factors
  Hands-on in-service with the text/familiarity
  Textbook availability
  Curriculum objectives and guides
  Social studies assignments, activities
  AV availability
  Holidays
  Tests
  School finances
  Interruptions during class
  School policies

Teacher/Student Factors
  Perceptions of the text
  Attitudes/expectations for the teacher/student
  Belief system, philosophy about content, teaching, learning
  Prior knowledge of content, language, form
  Reading strategies
  Teaching strategies
  Future goals
  Curiosity
  Absenteeism
  Academic ability
  Personality traits/mental states
  Ethnic background
  Boredom/interest

Textbook/Materials Factors
  Text characteristics (teachable, readable, questions, etc.)
  Concept appropriateness
  Workbooks/worksheets
  Textbook subject-matter
  Publisher assumptions

the social studies textbook selection committee. Analysis of this form helped bring to light the assumptions of the curriculum committee concerning textbooks and their use: (1) the student textbook and teacher's manual are essential for the curriculum; (2) the textbook should be used instructionally to present concepts and principles, build skills, serve societal need or policy (equality for all groups), apply traditional thinking strategies, and give a 'hands-on' approach to geography. In other words, the emphasis should be on cognitive learning.

This districts' textbook needs analysis form brings up, by omission, issues concerning the affective domain, the interpersonal and textual functions of language and disciplinary structures, since these areas were not represented on the form. The administrators' and learning coordinator's comments raise issues about inductive vs deductive textbooks, multiple textbooks vs a single standardized textbook, teacher in-service vs detailed teacher's manuals and the use of textbooks/workbooks to control what teachers do in the classroom.

Criteria Perceptions

One of the questions addressed in the case study of social studies textbooks in sixth grade classrooms was whether students, parents, teachers and administrators have similar criteria for an ideal social studies textbook. The same questionnaire item about criteria was given to students, parents, teachers and administrators: Name five things that make an ideal, suitable social studies textbook for (you or your child/students/teacher). When a content analysis was performed on the criteria listed by each group (see Table 2 for the most frequently mentioned), patterns emerged that formed the basis for tentative conclusions: (1) students and parents seemed more in agreement about criteria than students and teachers; (2) teachers and administrators seemed to agree closely.

Both students and parents listed criteria showing that for them affective aspects of a textbook are as important as cognitive aspects, and that psychological, social and rhetorical factors should be balanced with factual content and skills factors. They believed that interest (whether the textbook could excite or stimulate) was as important as content and clarity and that attractiveness and attention to values and feelings were very important qualities. Students and parents seemed to view the ideal textbook as a literary work of art — a text that is humanistic and that informs in a lively and friendly/interpersonal manner.

Teachers and administrators, however, in general seemed to see the textbook primarily as a non-literary piece of informative prose. They tended to perceive the ideal textbook to be well-organized/systematic, informational, appropriate in content to school objectives and readable on or below grade-level. They appeared far less concerned about interestingness and style or feelings and attitudes. Rather, they seemed to have a more objective, scientific and analytical approach to an ideal textbook. There were, of course, commonalities across all groups of respondents. For example, all wanted a readable textbook with accurate, up-to-date facts and colourful maps and pictures.

The criteria of each group were no doubt based on its experiences with the textbook in a particular context (parents and children experience the textbook at home differently from children and teachers in classroom settings, and teachers and administrators no doubt experience the textbook differently in a selection committee meeting than at their private desk), its social and cultural expectations, and its knowledge of language, form and content. The findings from this study indicated that there are discrepancies between student/parent perceptions and between teacher/administrator perceptions concerning the criteria for an ideal social studies textbook.

137

be memorized by the reader, like the multiplication tables. The role of the textbook authors, then, is to report the facts, not to explain them or their significance for the reader and certainly not to explain their plan for reporting the facts or to persuade the reader of their point of view. The corresponding role of student readers is to receive the facts passively from the truth-giving authority who wrote the text, and to memorize them, not to understand the facts or the author's attitude towards them and not to use the facts to build a larger picture or to think critically about what the author said or did in the textbook.

Another implicit assumption prevalent in much social studies pedagogy is that the realistic view of knowledge and certainty is what counts, rather than inquiry, exploration, creativity, hypothesis formation and tentativeness. Booth (1974) has pointed out the tendency of Western culture to value objectivism and to dismiss as mere belief, and therefore value, everything that is not verifiable fact. A rhetorical community which polarizes fact and value, ignoring probability — the ground between objectivity and faith or feelings — and which extols certainty and a rhetoric of conclusions, rewards the mastery of verifiable information. In such a rhetorical community, textbook authors would find no encouragement to write textbooks that promote critical inquiry, probable judgments and stance.

Both of these assumptions would no doubt have an effect on the use of metadiscourse in textbooks. Authors may not use metadiscourse at all or may use only certain types. For instance, students may not see hedges such as 'probably', 'may', 'seem' or 'apparently' used in their textbooks. In that case teachers (if they read the teacher's manual) are the 'insiders', concerning main ideas and purpose, and so on, not the student readers, who then become dependent on teachers for this information (see Baker and Freebody, Chapter 21, this volume). Or writers and publishers might assume that student readers should be semi-independent readers and that titles, text-embedded questions and end-of-chapter or unit remarks are a kind of implicit metadiscourse to be used along with teacher metadiscourse. On the other hand, authors and educators may be more likely to use explicit metadiscourse in textbooks if they believe that students should be independent readers, or that teachers probably do not use metadiscourse, or that students will not understand the implicit metadiscourse in textbooks.

Another reason textbook authors and publishers may decide not to use metadiscourse is the constraints of readability formulas. Readability formulas, based on word length, word familiarity and sentence length and complexity, are commonly used as indices of text difficulty in the US because educators assume that naturally written textbooks are too difficult for students. Although the formulas were originally intended to be applied to already written texts, they are now being used inappropriately by textbook writers as they write. The sentence length constraint often means deleting or avoiding metadiscourse since it usually increases sentence length. For marketing reasons, textbook authors and publishers decide to spend the number of words permitted them on the primary discourse, covering as many topics as possible.

When textbooks are analyzed, their form frequently reflects a wide variety of pedagogical assumptions and values (provided authors/publishers manage to

Table 4. *Reasons for the Lack of Metadiscourse in Textbooks: Publishers'*
Pedagogical Assumptions and Values.

Pedagogic theories are not sub-branches of rhetoric — the study of effective communication.

The goal of textbooks is to inform rather than inquire; subject-matter should be reported, not interpreted and should be value-free and presented as a body of conclusions.

The presentation of textbook information does not influence the way students think, read and write.

Students need an authoritative text with absolutes, flat assertions and lists of 'bare' facts, written by a flattened out, anonymous author or a committee of educationists.

Students should only be taught to read primary-level discourse; the interpersonal, social aspects of written language are unimportant; emotions, feelings and attitudes are inappropriate in textbooks.

Textbooks should not be concerned with teaching students about the domains of scholarship — where ideas come from, sources, citations, attributions and references; the textbook should be the authority and source of all statements.

Controversial topics and opportunities for critical reading should be avoided.

Textbooks do not need macrostructure; a controlling idea or thesis is inappropriate for a chapter or section; therefore, the text structure should be non-hierarchical.

Goal statements and objectives are appropriately included in a teacher's manual, but not in the student text.

Mentioning the discourse topic is important, but pointing out the discourse plan and the strategies used to produce the discourse is not.

Students' general and discipline-specific anxieties about reading and learning can be ignored.

Textbook chapters can consist of a body only, with little or no introduction or conclusion.

---

produce the books they consciously or unconsciously intended to produce). Table 4 illustrates some of these pedagogical assumptions and values suggested by textbook analyses (Crismore, 1984, 1985).

3 Text and Disciplinary Levels: Ideational, Textual and Disciplinary Considerations

Researchers have recently suggested different sets of criteria for improving the quality of textbooks based on their attempts to identify characteristics of content area textbooks that influence how well the content is learned and remembered.

Their criteria focus on the ideational and textual functions of language and on text and disciplinary structures.

The design criteria forwarded by Armbruster and Anderson (1981, 1984) are a rare example of meaningful translation of theory and research into practice. Their major premise was that ideas in informative texts must be coherent if students are to learn and remember the information and that the structure of the text is of great importance in achieving textual coherence. Therefore, they believe that authors should structure their textbooks in accordance with paradigmatic patterns of thinking found in the discipline (e.g., cause and effect or goal, action, outcome, generic frames for history) as well as with the conventions of coherent, cohesive written discourse in general. In other words, their goal was both global and local coherence. Another premise was that the more consistent and apparent the organization of ideas in a text, the more likely it is that the ideas will be learned; thus an ideal textbook would have explicit, consistent, repeated patterns and structures, both global and local. Their design criteria are incorporated into Table 5 along with those of Westbury.

Westbury (1985) attempted to sketch the beginning of a set of criteria for a 'text-rhetoric' that originates in the ideational functioning of language and in a sense of subject-matter and disciplinary structures. Westbury's concern was how to turn history into school texts, into teachable texts that provide a teacher with a resource base for classwork: exposition by the teacher, discussion, seatwork, homework and the like. He was also concerned with historical thinking, the kind of thinking which involves the when, where, who, how and why (the detail that is the characteristic medium of the historian's reasoning) and which involves the problems in historical explanations. Westbury believes that transparent teachable textbooks should appeal to the imagination of teachers and students through puzzle-posing, puzzle-solving and meaningful work in the classroom. Classrooms, then, become workplaces for teacher and student historians who use textbooks as resources for learning the necessary knowledge, skills, attitudes and conventions for the discipline.

Conclusion: What Teachers Can Do

Although, as this chapter and others in this volume have repeatedly pointed out, school texts are problematic for a host of reasons concerning content and form, we can improve their quality. By utilizing the criteria given in this chapter those of us involved in designing, selecting and using school texts can begin to re-examine our assumptions about language and knowledge, about learning and teaching, about reading and writing.

Teachers can begin to make a difference by analyzing and evaluating their current textbooks formally or informally, using the criteria suggested here. Teachers can use formal descriptive textbook analyses, for example, to investigate the extent of metadiscourse use in social studies textbooks (Crismore, 1984; Jarunud, 1986), or the considerations of content area textbooks (Armbruster and

Table 5. Criteria Synthesis and Checklist for Quality Textbooks.

Criteria categories/variables	Grade 6: Ideal Textbook	Crismore Rhetorical Textbook	Arm/And: Coherent Textbook	Westbury: Teachable Textbook	Current/ Proposed Textbook
1. *Metadiscourse level (interpersonal announcements)*					
Topic and topic shift	x	x			
Superordinate idea/thesis	x	x			
Superordinate structure	x	x			
Discourse aim/purpose	x	x			
Relevancy for readers		x			
Discourse strategies		x			
Discourse organization		x			
Discourse justifications		x			
Attributions for idea sources	x	x			
Definitions	x	x			
Readers' existence		x			
Truth condition evaluations		x			
Content evaluations		x			
Author-reader relationships		x			
Reviews of main ideas, aims, etc.	x	x			
Previews of main ideas, structure	x	x	x		
Values, emotions, attitudes	x	x			
2. *Text level (ideational/ textual aspects)*					
Accurate, recent information	x				
Information pertinent to superordinate idea/structure			x		
Systematic organization apparent to readers	x		x		
Understandable concepts	x		x	x	
Appropriate amount of major concepts	x				
Appropriate amount of detail	x		x	x	
Adequate amounts/types of examples	x				
Introductions: background information, connections between prior and present learning, content/structure relationships, text structure patterns		x	x		
Titles/headings that signal text structure (frames)			x		

Table 5 (Continued)

	Source of criteria				
Criteria categories/variables	Grade 6: Ideal Textbook	Crismore Rhetorical Textbook	Arm/And: Coherent Textbook	Westbury: Teachable Textbook	Current/ Proposed Textbook
Connectives for idea/text relationships		x	x		
Informative titles/headings for discourse which follows	x		x		
Content — appropriate, consistent, repetitive frames/patterns/structures			x		
Pronouns clearly referenced/close to word referenced			x		
Understandable substitutions for words, phrases, clauses			x		
Signalled figurative language			x		
Figurative language appropriate for readers' knowledge/experience			x		
Word choice appropriate for readers	x		x		
Clearly written prose	x		x		
Well-designed, understandable visual displays	x		x		
Visual displays that reinforce the text frame			x		
Unity — most words pertain to main idea/frame			x		
3. Discipline level (ideational aspects)					
Authors/translators with interdisciplinary perspective				x	
Inquiring approach: conveys nature, pedagogy of discipline				x	
Presents discipline as process, engages readers in the process				x	
Integrates work of discipline and the classroom				x	
Resource for engaging discipline-valid activities, puzzles	x			x	
Primary materials				x	
Concrete objects: maps, globe, charts, pictures				x	

Table 5 (Continued)

	Source of criteria				
Criteria categories/variables	Grade 6: Ideal Textbook	Crismore Rhetorical Textbook	Arm/And: Coherent Textbook	Westbury: Teachable Textbook	Current/ Proposed Textbook
Discipline-valid exercises that promote higher level thinking, reading, writing skills: analyzing, predicting, hypothesis generating/ testing/confirming, synthesis, evaluation	x			x	
Background knowledge/ issues fundamental to discipline arguments				x	
A framework that incorporates formal analysis of discipline argument structure and explication of arguments by details (discipline/expository processes)				x	
Adequate space to core generalization(s) and events	x			x	
Adequate explanations for each core generalization/event				x	
Generic frames, embedded frames specific to discipline			x		
4. Other variables					
Aesthetically pleasing: colourful, balanced prose, visuals ratio	x				
Interesting, stimulating	x			x	
Challenging scope and sequence					
Questions, answers to questions	x		x		
Conflict, controversial topics	x	x			
Framework for the course	x			x	
Materials adapted to individual differences of students	x		x		
Information about other cultures	x				
Values, emotions, attitudes	x	x			
Supplementary materials for teacher (detailed manual), students	x				

Anderson, 1981) as models for their own textbook analyses. Informally, teachers can develop textbook journals in which they and their students analyze and evaluate textbooks based on the criteria discussed here. In this approach, for each reading assignment in a textbook, both teachers and students, as they read, make notes in the margins of the textbook or on paper using the criteria as guidelines. Using these margin notes as data, students and teachers collaborate in the production of a textbook journal (Crismore, 1987).

After analyzing and evaluating their textbooks, teachers are in a far better position to decide how to use their current textbooks more effectively. If, for instance, their current textbooks have little or no metadiscourse, teachers can supply the missing metadiscourse elements themselves in their lesson plans and presentations. The teacher becomes the metadiscourser, rather than the text. To provide a more permanent form of metadiscourse and to promote independent learning, teachers and/or students can rewrite portions of the textbook inserting metadiscourse where it is needed (Crismore and Collins, 1987).

Teachers can supplement or supplant their current textbooks by providing alternative textbooks that provide what is missing in the regular textbook. By providing multiple textbooks, teachers expose students to a variety of textbook styles, formats and approaches. If they are to develop an elaborate schema for what a textbook can be, students should see a range of school textbooks written for different purposes: informative, argumentative/persuasive, expressive and literary) (Crismore and Hill, 1987; Crismore, 1985, forthcoming).

Another way teachers can make a difference is by direct involvement in the selection process itself. If teachers who have analyzed and evaluated their own textbooks are prepared to report their findings to other teachers and to adminis-trators at all levels, they help to educate them about useful selection criteria, ways to do teacher textbook research and the necessity for classroom teachers to assume ownership of textbooks. Teachers should pressure administrators for participation on textbook selection committees, insist on helping to redesign their school's textbook needs analysis forms, insist on being on state and/or national textbook adoption committees, and insist on being given the time and other resources needed theoretically to identify and practically to apply selection criteria which have proven educationally relevant and useful.

Finally, teachers can become change agents in the design of textbooks. In addition to sending letters of advice to authors and publishers, teachers informed by their textbook journals can write to publishers indicating they would be willing to help with field testing new textbooks. They might field test textbooks in progress by applying the criteria proposed here, perhaps doing an ethnographic study of the textbook in use in their own classroom or their colleagues' classrooms.

In summary, those interested in textbook design, selection and use must think clearly and carefully about their theories of language, texts and disciplines and then integrate these into a coherent model for the design, selection and use of good edu-cational textbooks. In this chapter we have tried to assist in this difficult process by providing a criteria checklist which can help teachers to systematize their subjective judgment about text quality. We have discussed the range of variables to which educators need to be sensitive, from the interpersonal, textual and ideational dimensions of language to the rhetorical form of texts and, finally, we have suggested practical activities and concrete procedures by means of which teachers can exert some influence on the selection process.

References

ANDERSON, R.C. (1977) 'The notion of schemata and the educational enterprise,' in ANDERSON, R.C., SPIRO, R.J. and MONTAGUE, W.E. (Eds), *Schooling and the acquisition of knowledge*. Hillsdale, N.J.: Erlbaum.

ANDERSON, R.C. (1984) 'Some reflections on the acquisition of knowledge,' *Educational Researcher*, 13, 9, 5–10.

ARMBRUSTER, B.B. and ANDERSON, T.H. (1981) *Content Area Textbooks* (Reading Education Rep. No. 23). Urbana, Ill.: University of Illinois, Center for the Study of Reading. ERIC Document Reproduction Service No. ED 203 298, p. 68.

ARMBRUSTER, B.B. and ANDERSON, T.H. (1984) *Producing 'Considerate' Expository Text: or Easy Reading Is Damned Hard Writing* (Reading Education Rep. No. 46). Urbana, Ill.: University of Illinois, Center for the Study of Reading. ERIC Document Reproduction Service No. ED 240 510, p. 66.

BOOTH, W.C. (1974) *Modern Dogma and the Rhetoric of Assent*. Chicago, Ill.: University of Chicago Press.

BRUCE, B. (1981) 'A social interaction model of reading,' *Discourse Processes*, 4, 4, 278–311.

CRISMORE, A. (1981) *Students' and Teachers' Perceptions of and Use of Sixth Grade Social Studies Textbooks in Champaign Middle Schools: A Case Study*. ERIC Document Reproduction Service No. ED 232 952, p. 154.

CRISMORE, A. (1984) 'The rhetoric of textbooks: Metadiscourse,' *Journal of Curriculum Studies*, 16, 3, 279–96.

CRISMORE, A. (1985) *Metadiscourse as Rhetorical Act in Social Studies Texts: Its Effect on Student Performance and Attitude*. Unpublished doctoral dissertation, University of Illinois at Urbana-Champaign.

CRISMORE, A. (1987) *Critical Thinking about Texts, Basic Writers and Textbook Journals*. Paper presented at the Penn State Conference on Rhetoric and Composition, College Park, Pa., July.

CRISMORE, A. (forthcoming) 'Improving and using instructional materials,' in HARSTE, J.C. and CRISMORE, A. (Eds), *How We Might Begin: Insights from Reading Comprehension Research*. Portsmouth, N.H.: Heinemann.

CRISMORE, A. and COLLINS, C. (1987) *Effects of Directed Instruction of Metadiscourse upon Student Comprehension and Affective Response to Reading and Writing*. Paper presented at the National Reading Conference, St Petersburg, Fla., December.

CRISMORE, A. and HILL, K. (1987) *The Interaction of Metadiscourse and Anxiety in Determining Children's Learning of Social Studies Textbooks Materials*. Unpublished paper, Indiana University-Purdue University at Fort Wayne.

CRONKITE, G.L. (1979) 'Rhetoric, pragmatics, and perlocutionary acts,' in BROWN, R.L. Jr. and STEINMAN, M. Jr. (Eds), *Rhetoric 78*. Minneapolis, Minn.: University of Minnesota, Center for the Advanced Studies in Language, Style and Literary Theory.

DILLON, G. (1981) *Constructing Texts*. Bloomington, Ind.: Indiana University Press.

FISKE, E.B. (1984) 'Quality of textbooks is the focus of a debate,' *The New York Times*, 29 July.

FITZGERALD, F. (1979) *America Revised: History Textbooks in the Twentieth Century*. Boston, Mass.: Little Brown.

GOFFMAN, E. (1981) *Forms of Talk*. Philadelphia, Pa.: University of Pennsylvania Press.
HALLIDAY, M.A.K. (1978) *Language as Social Semiotic*. London: University Park Press.
HALLIDAY, M.A.K. (1985) *An Introduction to Functional Grammar*. London: Edward Arnold.
HALLIDAY, M.A.K. and HASAN, R. (1976) *Cohesion in English*. London: Longman.
JARUNUD, S. (1986) *An Analysis of Metadiscourse in Thai Social Studies Textbooks in Secondary Schools*. Unpublished doctoral dissertation, University of Iowa.
MCCONKIE, G.W. (1983) Personal communication.
PURVES, A.C. (1984) 'The teacher as a reader: An anatomy,' *College English*, 46, 3, 259–65.
PURVES, A.C. (1986) 'The nature and formation of interpretive and rhetorical communities,' in POSTLEWAITE, T.N. (Ed.), *Essays in Homage of Torsten Husen*. Oxford: Pergamon Press.
TIERNEY, R.J. and RAPHAEL, T. (1981) *Factors Controlling the Inferences of Fifth Graders: An Extended Examination of the Author-Reader Relationship during Discourse Processing*. Paper presented at the annual meeting of the American Educational Research Association, Los Angeles, Calif.
VAN DE KOPPLE, W.J. (1985) 'Some exploratory discourse on metadiscourse,' *College Composition and Communication*, 36, 1, 82–93.
WESTBURY, I. (1985) *Text-Rhetoric: Some 'Disciplinary' Considerations*. Paper presented at the annual meeting of the American Educational Research Association, Chicago, Ill.
WILLIAMS, J. (1985) *Style: Ten Lessons in Clarity and Grace*. 2nd ed. Glenview, Ill.: Scott Foresman.
WOODWARD, A. and WESTBURY, I. (1983) *The Response of Textbooks to the Development of the Mass High School and Its Curriculum*. Paper presented at the annual meeting of the American Educational Research Association, Montreal.

Part III
Textbook Production

Chapter 12

The Political Economy of Text Publishing

Michael W. Apple
University of Wisconsin/Madison

We can talk about culture in two ways, as a lived process, as what Raymond Williams (see Chapter 5, this volume) has called a whole way of life, or as a commodity (cf. Apple and Weis, 1983). In the first we focus on culture of a constitutive social process through which we live our daily lives. In the second we emphasize the products of culture, the very thingness of the commodities we produce and consume. This distinction can, of course, be maintained only on an analytic level since most of what seem to us to be things — like lightbulbs, cars, records and, in the case of this essay, books — are really part of a larger social process. As Marx, for example, spent years trying to demonstrate, every product is an expressor of embodied human labour. Goods and services are relations among people, relation of exploitation often, but human relations nevertheless. Turning on a light when you walk into a room is not only using an object, it is also to be involved in an anonymous social relationship with the miner who worked to dig the coal burned to produce the electricity.

This dual nature of culture poses a dilemma for those individuals who are interested in understanding the dynamics of popular and élite culture in our society. It makes studying the dominant cultural products — from films to books, to television, to music — decidedly slippery, for there are sets of relations behind each of these 'things'. These in turn are situated within the larger web of the social and market relations of capitalism.

How do the dynamics of class, gender and race 'determine' cultural production? How is the organization and distribution of culture 'mediated' by economic and social structures? What is the relationship between a cultural product — say, a film or a book — and the social relations of its production, accessibility and consumption? These are not easy questions to deal with. First, the very terms of the language and concepts we use to ask them are notoriously difficult to unpack. That is, expressions such as 'determine', 'mediate', 'social relations of production' and so on — and the conceptual apparatus that lies behind them — are not at all settled. Thus, it is hard to grapple with the issue of the determination of culture without at the same time being very self-conscious of the tools one is employing.

So far I have employed some of the research on book publishing to help us understand an issue that is of great import to educators — how and by whose agency the texts that dominate the curriculum come to be the way they are. As I mentioned at the very outset of this essay, however, we need to see such analyses as constituting a serious contribution to a larger theoretical debate about cultural processes and products as well. In this concluding section, let me try to make clear this part of my argument about the political economy of culture.

External economic and political pressures are not somewhere 'out there' in some vague abstraction called the economy. As recent commentators have persuasively argued, in our society hegemonic forms are not often imposed from outside by a small group of corporate owners who sit around each day plotting how to do in workers, women and people of colour. Some of this plotting may go on, but just as significant are the routine grounds of our daily decisions in our homes, stores, offices and factories. To speak somewhat technically, dominant relations are ongoingly reconstituted by the actions we take and the decisions we make in our own local and small areas of life. Rather than an economy being out there, it is right here. We rebuild it routinely in our social interaction. Rather than ideological domination and the relations of cultural capital being something we have imposed on us from above, we reintegrate them within our everyday discourse merely by following our commonsense needs and desires as we go about making a living, finding entertainment and sustenance and so on (Apple, 1986).

These arguments are abstract, but they are important to the points I want to make. For while a serious theoretical structure is either absent from or is often hidden within the data presented by the research I have drawn upon, a good deal of this research does document some of the claims I made in the above paragraph. As the authors of *Books* put it in their discussion of why particular decisions are made, 'For the most part, what directly affects an editor's daily routine is not corporate ownership or being one division of a large multi-divisional publishing house. Instead, on a day-to-day basis, editorial behaviour is most strongly influenced by the editorial policies of the house and the relationship among departments and personnel *within* the publishing house or division' (Coser *et al.*, 1982, p. 185).

This position may not seem overly consequential, yet its theoretic import is great. Encapsulated within a changing set of market relations which set limits on what is considered rational behaviour on the part of its participants, editors and other employees have 'relative autonomy'. They are partly free to pursue the internal needs of their craft and to follow the logic of the internal demands within the publishing house itself. The past histories of gender, class and ethnic relations and the actual 'local' political economy of publishing set the boundaries within which these decisions are made and which in large part determine who will make the decisions. To return to my earlier point about text editors usually having their prior roots in sales, we can see that the internal labour market in text publishing, the ladder upon which career mobility depends, means that sales will be in the forefront ideologically and economically in these firms. 'Finance capital' dominates, not only because the economy out there mandates it, but also because of the historical connections among mobility patterns within firms, rational decision-making based on external competition, political dynamics and internal information, and, because of these things, the kinds of discourse which tend to dominate the meetings and conversations among all the people involved within the organizational structure of the text publisher (cf. Wexler, 1982). This kind of analysis is, of course, more complicated. But surely it is more elegant and more grounded in reality than some of the more mechanistic theories about the economic control of culture that have been too readily accepted. It manages to preserve the efficacy of the economy while granting some autonomy to the internal bureaucratic and biographical structure of individual publishers and, at the same time, to recognize the political economy of gendered labour that exists as well.

Many areas remain that I have not focused upon here. Among the most important of these is the alteration in the very technology of publishing. Just as the development and use of print 'made possible the growth of literary learning and journals' and thereby helped create the conditions for individual writers and artists to emerge out of the more collective conditions of production that dominated guilds and workshops (Wolff, 1981, p. 36), so too, as one would expect, the changes in the technology of text production and the altered social and authorial relations that are evolving from them will have a serious impact on books. At the very least, given the sexual division of labour in publishing, new technologies can have a large bearing on the deskilling and reskilling of those 'female enclaves' mentioned earlier (Apple, 1983; Gordon, Edwards and Reich, 1982).

Further, since I have directed my attention primarily to the 'culture and commerce' surrounding the production of one particular cultural commodity — the standardized text used for tertiary-level courses — it still remains an open question how, exactly, the economic and ideological elements I have outlined actually work through some of the largest of all text markets, those found in the elementary and secondary schools in the United States and elsewhere. Given the role played by aspects of the state apparatus (through selection committees and so on) in defining what counts as legitimate knowledge in elementary and secondary schools (see Arons, Chapter 16, this volume), however, in order to go significantly further we clearly need a more adequate theory of the relationship between the political and economic (to say nothing of the cultural) spheres in education. Thus, the state's position as a site for class, race and gender conflicts; the way these struggles are 'resolved' within the state apparatus; the way publishers respond to these conflicts and resolutions; and, ultimately, the impact these resolutions or accords have on the questions surrounding officially sponsored texts and knowledge — all of these need considerably more deliberation (see Apple, 1982 a, 1982 c; Dale *et al.*, 1981; Carnoy, 1982; Dale, 1982; Liston, 1984).

This points to a significant empirical agenda as well. What is required now is a long-term *and* theoretically and politically grounded ethnographic investigation that follows a curriculum artifact such as a textbook from its writing to its selling (and then to its use). Not only would this be a major contribution to our understanding of the relationship among culture, politics and economy, but it is also absolutely essential if we are to act in ways that alter the kinds of knowledge con-a world of idealized types and settings which mass market producers might use as norms for market planning and development. It is a generic world. Streets, parks, neighbourhoods, families, etc., all occur in generalized form. They are complemented by characters visually particular or individual but textually general. For example, mayors and contest judges, police and teachers constitute the world outside the family rather than, in contrast, named provincial premiers or even RCMP officers. Individual people are depicted in terms which do not correspond to real people but reflect a typology of psychological traits manifest in social hierarchies. Such position descriptions on the social hierarchy mean that instead of an elaborated portrayal of individuals and interaction amongst individuals, dominant and submissive behaviour pervade every story. Dramatic force is developed on the basis of anticipated movement in the hierarchy of characters. Society and institutions are both powerful and arbitrary foils for the various characters to test their mettle in order to rise to the heroic or sink to the depths of passive, ordinary citizenry. Other elements of this generic world are also noticeable. The world is one boundless, homogeneous community without distinctive subcultures or nations. The social order is the fallout of each individual competing with every other. Cooperative groupings appear as rearguard actions to cope with an arbitrary order imposed from 'outside' or 'on high'.

In general, this world was found to be almost universal in readers for grades one to three. Moreover, the majority, but not all, of the grades four to six readers displayed the same set of characteristics — slightly more subtle, slightly more diverse, but nonetheless still very much there (see Lorimer, 1984).

Evaluated in terms of the structure of the industry, these studies concluded that the pattern of content and themes observed reflect the interests of a particular set of publishers, i.e., those oriented to the mass market. While these materials respond to demands made by educators at one level, they take advantage of silence at another. Since the 1950s language arts educators have insisted, amongst other things, on expanding vocabularies and precisely laid out skill developments. Until very recently they have been quite silent on content. Or to phrase it another way, process is valued over content, thus allowing the content to follow the production and marketing criteria of the publishing industry (see de Castell and Luke, Chapter 7, this volume).

The above analysis summarizes the major thematic elements which constitute the content of the multinational textbook. Lorimer, Harkley, Long and Tourell (1978) have identified production techniques which complement that same set of interests. In one particular reading series, published by Ginn and imported into Canada from the US called *Reading 720* (Clymer, 1978), there appeared an unusual amount of non-fiction for an elementary reader. Further examination indicated that the books were made up essentially of three types of content. The first was composed of universal or generic fiction, the kind touted to be the best the English-speaking world has to offer. The second section was universal non-fiction, reportage of human interest events which could be said to have broad appeal, e.g., man conquers space, dog rescues child, etc. The third section was composed of a mixture of fiction and non-fiction with emphasis on the latter, complete with national references. Here were displayed such scenes as the Prime Minister visiting a whale in Vancouver along with other interesting journalistic items with concrete Canadian references.

This pattern of organization may be interpreted as another mass market device, one which minimizes the cost of market transferability. Thus, for example, were these books to be used in Australia, the one-third mixed 'Canadiana' fiction and non-fiction could be replaced with the equivalent 'Australiana'. In other words there appeared to be a basic generic product planned for adaptation to US specifications, Canadian specifications, Australian specifications, or any other set of specifications which might be required for a specific market.

The Multinational Social World: The Case of Social Studies

McGraw-Hill's *Social and Environmental Studies* (SES) (Vass, 1976) programme is the most stunning example of a basic generic product reflective of international market planning. Based on the 'expanding horizons' model, this programme is meant progressively to introduce the child to the individual, the family, the neighbourhood and community, the region and nation and communities and nations of the world. While such categories of content might be expected to call for an extensive amount of specific local information, the only content particular to Canada was at the grade three level. This means that were this series to be used in countries other than Canada, only one grade of the six in the programme would need to be replaced. The other subject-matter could be republished more or less as is. (Two out of twenty-seven units in the grades four to six material contained Canadian content, nothing more than would be appropriate for any English-speaking class in any country.)

McGraw-Hill's SES programme is fairly distinctive as a social studies programme. It is rare for such a low level of historically or culturally specific content to be present at any level of social studies. It seems probable that the criteria which guided the development of the SES series had more to do with marketing efficiency than education.

Other interesting patterns in content and structure emerge at the secondary level in social studies. In 1968 Hodgetts noted that a consensus version of Canadian history was being presented across the nation (Hodgetts, 1968). What we found in 1983 was consensus but with greater elaboration (cf. Carlson, Chapter 4, this volume). In ten junior high social studies textbooks examined[1] we found the perspective of recent history limited to reference to Prime Ministers, national actions and major confrontations (all successfully resolved in the name of nation-building). In short Canada is portrayed as a nation on a 'path to destiny', boiled down to its basics and with little interest in diversity, dissenting voices or alternative paths. A recognition of our growing ethnic plurality with its new internal richness and tensions, as well as the varied international liaisons which that plurality is bringing about, is quite absent. Major events of a cultural and social significance essential to have no right to call anything knowledge except where our activity has actually produced certain physical things, which agree with and confirm the conception entertained' (Dewey, 1916, p. 123). These processes do not find the individual anchored in a distinct time or culture, but rather adrift on a sea of process.

A pedagogy which unequivocally stresses the primacy of process prepares a fertile ground for the marketing strategies of the multinational publisher. Through product development, editorial policy and marketing techniques, publishers have helped legitimize an ahistorical, transnational, pan-cultural world view of education consonant with their global organizational and technological capabilities. The economies of scale dictate against the publisher addressing any cultural particularity, and if the publisher is taken to task for presenting a watered-down, common denominator view of life, undifferentiated by historical, cultural or political identities, he has a ready ally in a pedagogy which puts the method-ological categories of 'discovery' and 'experience' prior to a concern for the substantive issues of what should be 'discovered' or 'experienced'.

In Canada's case provincial and national content has been relegated to one subject area, social studies, which shows its own reflection of the dominant values inherent in other materials. The irony, of course, is that here is the very situation that provided the impetus for Dewey's theory of education: the initiation of children into a set of cultural norms which are more or less hostile to those which gave life to one's society. Abstracted from an objective social milieu, divorced from any specific notion of community or culture, the student's experience can be understood and made sense of only in terms of an ongoing technique which renders all particularities and social forms irrelevant.

Strategies for the Maintenance of Dominance

Awareness of the shortcomings of multinational-produced materials is not going to undermine their predominant position. The set of assumptions under which the multinationals operate blends nicely with the remnants of Dewey's pragmatism and they are the basic assumptions of curriculum developers, teachers and education professors, not to mention society at large. The multinationals have a powerful sales force in those who adhere to a philosophy of education in which content is placed a distant second to the primacy of technique and methods. If we are aiming in our educational institutions for the inculcation of generally applicable infor-mation processing skills divorced from any specific time or place, then what objection can there be to the products produced by the multinationals? If 'experience' and 'discovery' are the essential pedagogical categories, then surely any objection to the pan-cultural world view espoused by the multinationals is mere quibbling or short-sighted nationalism. As long as we cling to a pedagogy which puts the primacy of process (guided and abetted by the discovery of certain immutable, ineluctable psychological truths) at the centre of the educational agenda, then there is little need for writing cultural particularities into textbooks.

Additionally, the entire milieu within which curricula are developed places the multinational publisher in a very advantageous position. In addition to being able to take advantage of economies of scale, the multinationals have trained educators to expect a level of operation as well as a style of product which is only within their capability. Included here are: the presence of a publisher's representative in the province over one to two years prior to an adoption; ongoing field-testing of one or other programmes at various stages of development; the ability to respond with finished products for evaluation six weeks to six months after a call for materials (which may have taken two years to formulate); the ability to provide opportunities for teachers and education professors as editors, evaluators, etc.; to be able to choose wisely from rising 'stars' within the profession; and the ability to hire or consult with persons familiar with evaluation techniques and criteria as have been developed by, for example, Educational Products Information Exchange (EPIE). All these non-product-oriented activities are intrinsic to the maintenance of a predominant position both in the educational marketplace and in the consequent determination of basic elements of the curriculum.

Conclusion: Educators as Consumers

It has been argued that multinational publishers are a significant force in Canadian education. In creating products for the curriculum they place boundaries on its implementation by constraining the choice which educators are able to make. Moreover, the characteristics of their product, either implicitly or explicitly, actively influence the thinking of curriculum planners.

Two major factors have contributed to the success of the acceptance of market conveniences as educational desiderata. Because the interests of the multinationals are consonant with one another, competition is carried on within a narrow set of rules, and characteristics basic to mass market materials become basic pedagogical necessities for all 'good quality' products. The second major factor is the ascendancy of a pedagogy which arose in response to an industrial model of education. This pedagogy was an attempt to humanize education in the industrial society by situating the child within his or her own community. Ironically, by stressing universal and generic skills it has provided the multinationals with a rationale for producing learning materials which fail to address any aspects of particular communities and cultures.

The set of assumptions which guides the multinationals becomes most problematic where the centralist bias of the mass market ceases to speak to the specific realities of particular communities: Canada in North America, and rural and ethnic enclaves in both Canadian and American societies. Here the mass market ideology of the multinational becomes most visible, and operates most powerfully to translate curriculum into commodity, and education into consumption.

Notes

1 The texts referred to are: Collins, P. and Sheffe, N. (1979) *Exploration Canada*. Toronto: Oxford University Press; Garrod, S. (1980) *Growth of a Nation*. Toronto: Fitzhenry and Whiteside; Howard, R. *et al.* (1976) *Canada since Confederation*. Toronto: Copp/Clark Pitman; Hundley, I. (1980) *Canada: Builders of the Nation*. Toronto: Gage; Hundley, I. (1979) *Canada: Immigrants and Settlers*. Toronto: Gage; Hux, A.P. and Jarman, F. (1981) *Canada: A Growing Concern*. Toronto: Globe/Modern; Kirbyson, R. and Paterson, E. (1977) *In Search of Canada*. Toronto: Prentice-Hall; Marsh, J.H. and Francis, B. (1981) *New Beginnings: A Social History of Canada*. Toronto: McClelland and Stewart; Smith, D. *et al.* (1977) *Canada: Discovering Our Heritage*. Toronto: Ginn; Stewart, R. and McLean, N. (1977–78) *Forming a Nation: The Story of Canada and Canadians*. Toronto: Gage.
2 For an extended discussion of how American history texts neglect social movements and visions which do not fit a consensual version of history see Fitzgerald (1979). See also discussions in this volume by Carlson, Gilbert and Arons (Chapters 4, 6 and 16).
3 We are not, of course, suggesting that narrative and stories have no part to play in arriving at historical understanding. Indeed, Egan (1979; see also, Chapter 8, this volume) has argued forcefully that the story-form provides the pedagogical tool par excellence for enhancing a child's understanding of history. Our point is simply that in the multinational text those stories which digress from the dominant view of events are likely to be down-played or neglected altogether.

References

ALBERTA (1981) *Alberta Heritage Learning Resources Project*. Edmonton: Department of Education.

BARNHOLD, D.L. *et al.* (Eds) (1973) *Starting Points in Mathematics*. Toronto: Ginn Canada.

BERGER, T. (1978) *Northern Frontier: Northern Homeland*. Ottawa: Ministry of Supply and Services.

CALLAHAN, R.E. (1962) *Education and the Cult of Efficiency*. Chicago, Ill.: University of Chicago Press.

CARSCALLEN, A. (1984) Unpublished Master's thesis draft, Simon Fraser University, Burnaby, B.C.

CLYMER, T. (Ed.) (1978) *Reading 720*. Toronto: Ginn.

DEWEY, J. (1900) *The School and Society*. Chicago, Ill.: University of Chicago Press.

DEWEY, J. (1916) *Democracy and Education*. Chicago, Ill.: University of Chicago Press.

DEWEY, J. (1938) *Experience and Education*. Chicago, Ill.: University of Chicago Press.

EGAN, K. (1979) *Educational Development*. New York: Oxford University Press.

EUSTACE, C.J. (1972) 'Developments in Canadian book production and design', in *Royal Commission on Book Publishing: Background Papers*. Toronto: Queen's Printer, pp. 38–61.

FITZGERALD, F. (1979) *America Revised*. Boston: Little-Brown.

GEORGE, M. and BAGGS, T. (1984) *Textbooks in Canada: An Analysis of the Authorized Lists for the English-Speaking Provinces*. Toronto: The Association of Canadian Publishers.

GORDON, A. (1979) *The Geology of Saskatchewan*. Regina: Province of Saskatchewan, Ministry of Education.

HODGETTS, A.B. (1968) *What Culture, What Heritage?* Toronto: OISE Press.

HOWARD, J. (1974) *Strange Empire: Louis Riel and the Metis People*. Toronto: James Lorimer.

KIDD, P. (1983) Personal communication with regard to New Brunswick history.

LORIMER, R. (1984) *The Nation in the Schools: Wanted a Canadian Education*. Toronto: OISE Press.

LORIMER, R., HILL, M., LONG, M. and MACLELLAN, B. (1977–78) 'Consider content: An analysis of two "Canadian" language arts reading series', *Interchange*, 8, 4, 64–7.

LORIMER, R., HARKLEY, J., LONG, M. and TOURELL, D. (1978) 'Your Canadian reader', *Lighthouse*, 6–15.

LORIMER, L. and LONG, M. (1979) 'Sex-role stereotyping in elementary readers', *Interchange*, 10, 2, 35–45.

MOORE, B. (Ed.) (1973) *Starting Points in Reading*. Toronto: Ginn.

MOORE, B. *et al.* (Eds) (1973) *Starting Points in Language*. Toronto: Ginn.

SCOTT, G.J. (1980) *English El-Hi Publishing in Canada: 1980–1986*. Toronto: Pepperwood.

THURBER, W.A. and KILBURN, R.E. (1971) *Exploring Science*. Toronto: Macmillan of Canada.

VASS, B. (Ed.) (1976) *Social and Environmental Studies*. Toronto: McGraw-Hill Ryerson.

WOODCOCK, G. (1975) *Gabriel Dumont*. Edmonton: Hurtig.

Chapter 14

Community Publishing

Keith Kimberley
University of London, Institute of Education

Community publishing has a long and instructive history for those concerned with popular education. James (1976), for example, describes the importance of small-scale publishing ventures in early nineteenth century England and their importance in the 'battle for the mind' of the new reading public in the following terms:

> It was possible to start a periodical for as little as ten pounds, with a sympathetic printer, if one organised the sales. With determination one could get together a second-hand press and some type, and print a periodical oneself . . . . Against work on this scale the Home Office and police officials were impotent. Operating from unobtrusive premises, selling outside the normal bookselling channels through a separate sales network, Radicals with few resources could take on the might of the Establishment. It provided an 'alternative press' that operated largely outside the knowledge of the 'respectable' public . . . .(p. 36)

There is much in this account that has a contemporary ring. Indeed, the accounts of the Worker Writer and the Community Publisher's movement of the 1970s (Morley and Worpole, 1982; Gregory, 1984, 1986) place a similar emphasis on the availability of an easily used technology which could produce reasonably large quantities of cheap books or pamphlets. Indeed Worpole (1973) writes of the off-set litho in words which might, style aside, have been written of the hand-press 150 years earlier, claiming that 'the new media technology is potentially much more democratic and more amenable to local and individual control than older methods of communication.'

There is also much similarity in the purposes, broadly educational, social and political, which these ventures, separated by time, espouse. In each case publishing is perceived by its chroniclers as a radicalizing agency, operating outside the normal channels, opening up new networks of readers and offering, in relation to mainstream publishing, alternative views of reality. In both historical instances, the technological potential appears to have been combined with the presence in local communities of groups of people eager to use the means available to focus attention on the need for general social changes and thus with a particular interest in changing the relationship between those who read and those who write.

James (1976) also comments that the period 1819–1851 is noteworthy for the struggle that surrounded the cheap, printed text. He describes this as being 'between Church and State on one side, . . . Radical reformers on the other, while a third factor, commercial enterprise, was quietly making the biggest inroad of all' (p. 28). He suggests that the work done by radical reformers in opening up a market for their publications was soon matched by reactionary and commercial initiatives capitalizing on the interest in getting hold of information which the former had generated, and making available material which confirmed rather than challenged the social order. The ideological underpinning of the challenges to Church and State made by more radical publishing concerns drew much of its force from the ideas of Paine, Cobbett and the Chartists. James's reference to the Home Office, the police, and 'unobtrusive premises' is a reminder of attempts by the Establishment in the angry wake of the massacre at Peterloo to suppress critical attacks by means of a punitive fourpenny tax on all publications containing news and comment, which cost less than sixpence and appeared more frequently than every twenty-eight days.[1]

Morley and Worpole (1982) write from within the radical movements of the 1970s giving a committed, comprehensive review of output, preoccupations and purposes of community groups, writers' workshops and literacy classes from which much contemporary community publishing has originated. Worpole (1983) explicitly claims for the movement a clear line of descent from the Radicals of the nineteenth century and, writing about the 1970s, proposes that

> working-class writing, in all its forms, provides an invaluable range of understanding of the dominant forms of oppression and division, and is therefore an integral and central part of an active and participatory working-class politics. In fact it is becoming more and more clear that contemporary movements in adult literacy, people's history, and in the resurgence of working-class writing through workshops and local publishing projects, have created a very active and new kind of oppositional cultural and educational politics involving increasingly large numbers of people. (p. 23)

Gregory (1984) likewise emphasizes the *alternative* perspectives which inform community publishing, describing developments since 1970 as being characterized by 'a fresh, democratic sense of print and books as available, stripped of authority and false dignity, written by flesh-and-blood people with particular points of view and, therefore, susceptible of reply and rebuttal as well as respect and reverence' (p. 228). He notes the contemporary writers' (specifically working-class, Black and feminist) 'refusal to stay marginalised' and 'impatience at being represented, mis-represented, patronised and abused by outsiders'.

Though radical activity in the 1970s and 1980s has been subject to some surveillance by the State and community bookshops have come under attack from racist and other right-wing groups, the range of activities which Morley, Worpole and Gregory describe do not by and large have to operate in 'unobtrusive premises'. Worpole (1983) proposes that there needs to be greater recognition of the importance of the existing, legitimate sites in the community where working-class people can express their views and experience and in so doing take an increasingly active part in shaping the society in which they live. Interestingly, he contrasts the working-class, adult educational movements of the first part of the twentieth century, which were organized around what it was assumed people did not know, on their 'ignorance', with current forms of cultural struggle in and around community publishing where the emphasis is 'much more productively and radically on what people do know, and on the value and political significance of their experience and knowledge' (p. 23).

Underlying the modern community publishing movement is the central belief that opportunities to discuss, to write and to have published give ordinary people, who may hitherto have seen themselves simply as the recipients of the writing of others, a sense of their own potential for criticism, participation and decision-making.

It should be added that the 'worker writer' and community publishing movement, whose ideology Morley, Worpole and Gregory have attempted to describe, is not easily susceptible to categorization. In fact it is remarkable for the range of activities and perspectives it encompasses and, in any attempt to isolate some common features, the danger of summarizing the general achievements of a movement which takes its strength from specific settings and experiences must be acknowledged. Conversely, however, much of the strength of writing and other media (for example, photography and video) produced in the context of local communities lies in the relationship it establishes between particular instances and wider social perspectives. In a discussion of the importance of autobiographical writing and writing which has been produced by means of tape-recording the spoken word, Morley and Worpole (1982) draw attention to the way in which common experiences are given dignity and significance.

> Through such books many people are able to find large parts of them-
> selves because they shared the same or similar environment and
> experiences. The detailed autobiography can also function as a 'general
> autobiography' — one that reflects, details, analyses and critically
> validates much of what has been lived in common with others (p. 94).

In particular they note that, although most if not all of the writers published through community presses share a common class position, it is

> particularly groups affected by determinants beyond those simply of class,
> who are most evident among those consciously 'making culture' in the
> form of writing. Here we mean, for example, people for whom the
> momentum of their material lives has been severely dislocated by
> structural economic changes . . . . old people in traditional industrial
> communities threatened by change . . . . migrants who have to re-define
> themselves in a new life . . . . women trying to re-define themselves
> through new forms of consciousness (p. 102).

They conclude that 'these forms cannot be understood simply in relation to class structures — they have to be understood in their relations to patriarchy, imperialism and racism' (p. 102).

When books are produced within the perspectives outlined above, there are features of their making which differ considerably from mainstream publishing. A key feature of the community publishing movement of the 1970s and 1980s has been workshop collaboration, supporting writers through the processes of getting started, discussing and revising. Other distinctive features include knowledge of, and influence over, the production of the book by the author; launching and distribution predominantly within the community for whom it was written; and lack of financial reward! It should, however, be acknowledged that Worpole's optimism in 1973 that the off-set litho, because it would enable any writer to have full control over the means of production, provided in schools and the community 'a means of abolishing completely the distinction between writers and readers (producers and consumers)' has, he acknowledges, been tempered by experience a decade later. It is now common for community groups to make full use of available technical assistance, though maintaining as much contact as possible between writers, typists, layout people and printers (Morley and Worpole, 1982, pp. 39–52).

In concluding this brief discussion of historical and contemporary strands of community publishing it may be helpful to record that the overview by Morley and Worpole (1982) is very detailed in its coverage and includes examples of the writing referred to. This, together with Gregory's accounts (1984, 1986) and the lists of community published writing in the review pages of the *English Magazine*,[2] describe a rich and varied range of activity across the United Kingdom. It may be useful to summarize the key beliefs, insofar as there are common features, which seem to inform the movement:

1 the importance of the viewpoints of working-class people and of experience as a critical tool in understanding society;
2 the power of working-class people to write effectively about their historical, economic, social and political situation;
3 the right of access by working-class people to a full knowledge of the world and in particular to accurate reporting, commentary and speculation on all issues which closely concern them;
4 the value of humour and satire in developing alternative perspectives;
5 the importance of recognizing the distinctive experience and claims of particular groups (for example, young people, women, minorities).

Students' Writing

It will already be clear that there are factors in the past and present history of community publishing which are of particular interest to those interested in the development of a critical pedagogy in schools and an obvious overlap between the processes by which some students' writing reaches publication in school and those which predominate in community publishing. In part this overlap is the result of practical cooperation between schools and local bookshops and of the joint use of local presses, but at a more general level it is consequent on the ways in which school publication of students' work and community group distribution of local writing interact. These products form a regularly increasing range of reading material available in schools and bookshops to be read and extended by new writers from within schools and the community.

The publication of students' works in UK schools gained a considerable impetus in the early 1970s. We have already noted both the availability in schools, teachers' and community centres of technical means through which teachers and students could exert full control over the writing, illustration, layout and printing of booklets. We should note also the sympathy of a substantial number of inner-city teachers to some of the general aims of the community publishing movement. In particular these teachers shared the view that literacy is as much about writing as reading and asserted the central importance of encouraging young writers to write for a variety of audiences and purposes.

It is worth noting that some of the texts by school students which have been published and distributed widely were not produced in the mainstream of the curriculum or, in some cases, even inside schools at all and that much student writing has extremely critical things to say about schooling. Morley and Worpole (1982) note that Vivian Usherwood, a young Black writer whose book of poems[3] sold over 10,000 copies in the 1970s, was in a 'remedial' class; that Billy House and Lesley Mildiner, joint authors of *The Gates*,[4] wrote their book in a school for the 'maladjusted' where they ended up after years of truancy; and that many young Black writers have depended on agencies outside schools to give them support.[5] However, the overlap between school and community writing, publishing and distribution is such that books written and produced in schools can be found in local bookshops and community centres and inner-city schools often order books for the classroom from community publishing concerns, though it is important to remember that student writing produced in school is not identical in the conditions of its composition and presentation as that which originates in writers' workshops well away from the institutional constraints of schooling. It is arguable that the duplicated school version of Vivian Usherwood's poems is different in some of the conditions of its production and use from the glossier version later printed and circulated through the Centreprise Bookshop.

The publication of *Stepney Words*[6] in 1971 marks what must now be seen as a new era in the publication of school students' writing. Not only did its publication create a stir in the national press when the teacher involved was suspended from his teaching post, ostensibly for having published work done in the school without the governors' permission, but it contrasted in a number of ways with much previous school publishing. Typically, in the period prior to 1971, though there were exceptions, this took the form of duplicating small runs of anthologies produced in a single classroom on poor equipment or the school magazine, which often was an accumulation of sanitized reports on sporting events, school visits, together with a few pieces of self-conscious, creative writing. By contrast, *Stepney Words*, a printed collection of poems, written in school but published on a local press and distributed within the local community, broke clear of the view that school students' writing only had something to say to their parents and friends. The critical view taken by the young writers of what was happening in their locality and in the world at large was clearly one cause of the governors' anger at the possible effect of this publication on the schools' image and their decision to suspend its editor, Chris Searle, from his teaching post. If one looks through its pages today, it is difficult to see what in the students' mixture of sensitivity, gloom, humour and realistic appraisal of their situation could have raised such hackles.

The idea that children might have something to say to adults, and school students to teachers, appears to have gained considerable ground in the succeeding fifteen years (cf. Gilbert, Chapter 6, this volume). An indicator of the extent to which the publication of school students' writing has become part of the thinking and practice of teachers can be gained from the output of the Inner London Education Authority's English Centre. The writing by school students published by this teachers's centre is the outward face of far wider, classroom-based activity in which students' writing is shared across classes and schools. Autobiography, story and argument written by school students for others like themselves have all proved immensely popular. Printed as books and illustrated with phogographs, the English Centre publications, *Our Lives, Bonnie, Freda and Ann, City Lines, Say What You Think* and *Bud's Luck* and *Other Stories*[7] have achieved print runs which give pause to commercial publishers who, themselves, have little access to student writing and who are a little bemused by their popularity.

In the English Centre's publications of student writing there is an emphasis on the power students can have over texts — as readers or writers — an ideology which is overtly stated in the introduction to the books and in the Centre's information booklet.[8] Of *Our Lives* the latter says,

> Young people are often written and talked about, they rarely get a good press. In this collection they have the space to write about themselves on their own terms. The authors are from England, Ireland, Morocco, Hong Kong, Jamaica, India and Uganda, and they write about family and separation, changing home and country, accident and death, school and work. Included are *The Melting Pot, Small Accidents, My Life* and *Jamaica Child* which the English Centre used to publish as separate booklets. *Our Lives* has been used successfully to encourage students to write their own extended autobiographies (p. 9).

Similarly *City Lives*, an anthology of poems, and *Say What You Think* (some of the best entries from the English Centre's 'Say What You Think' competition) are seen respectively as means of encouraging other students to write poetry and to handle argument and discussion in writing.

Say What You Think, which is particularly interesting, has three sections. The first, 'In my experience', consists of pieces of discursive writing in which experience, through the connections it enables to be made, functions to sharpen important place and the stance towards reading and writing activities that their use can involve.

Picture, for example, classrooms where informational and literary school textbooks are available but where you may also find publications such as the following: a text written by local people about the threatened closure of a factory; a collection of autobiographical writing by school students about the experience of migration and settlement; an account of a decade drawn from the recollections of old people; or a collection of articles based on interviews with women about their experiences at work. The list could be continued but these examples will suggest the possibilities.[9] And it would be well if we assume that the classroom is also one in which students are encouraged to read all texts, fact and fiction, with critical attention.

Typically, in such classrooms students are encouraged to see themselves as able to act upon the world through their writing. In this characterization emphasis lies with the school student, both as writer and reader, having 'textual power' (Scholes, 1985). This is the power as reader to defamiliarize and interrogate and as writer to inform, excite, entertain, challenge and persuade. It is the power to understand the contexts in which published writing is produced and the audiences for whom you as school student may wish to write. In such classrooms the analysis of books written specifically for children goes hand in hand with the students writing stories for younger children; the reading of oral histories is accompanied by the school students going out and making their own taped interviews; reading published opinion is an adjunct to writing their own letters; and reading autobiography or reading fiction is often a starting point for students' own personal accounts, stories and plays.

Each of the elements of these characterizations of practice has implications for the ways in which published writing from students and community presses is produced and can be put to use. For example, with respect to the use of such texts in the classroom, it should be noted that the school students who have access to texts from the community stand in a different relationship to the texts being studied than to many other texts used in school. The students are able to supplement what is in the text from their own experience and knowledge of the community and the people in it. A booklet about an area in which you live, or written by people who may even be known to you or your friends and relatives, can be 'owned' by the reader in ways that are not possible with most other school texts, with their 'authorized', institutional formats and impersonal style. Even contemporary novels given to school students by the teacher may, initially at least, seem very distant in content and treatment from the students' concerns and experience whereas texts in which the voice of local working people can be heard are open to question and can, for instance, be challenged on grounds of historical accuracy by students who visit grandparents and other older residents. Students reading texts which rouse their anger or fuel their imagination about their own area may also develop a sense of the part they themselves might play in bringing about change. Texts whose authority lies in the experience and ideas of people in a local community often take a very different stance in terms of the politics of class, sex and race of their writers from those found in conservatively framed school texts. Some carry the resistance of the oppressed in forms which would seem awkwardly direct in the balancing acts common in educational publishing.

Similarly the writing which school students may undertake in the contexts described places the student in a position of authority and expertise. In particular, extended autobiographical writing appears to give school students an opportunity to make sense of their lives in relation to the dominant cultural and political surroundings in which they find themselves. It does this in part by enabling them to build up a body of writing which demonstrates consistent independence of thought and asserts the validity of their feelings and experience (which may, of course, include knowledge in languages and dialects other than standard English). The writing of autobiographical texts, which, in some instances, may be destined for publication, denies to teacher and school textbook the status of sole sources of authority. Such writing, at its best, offers alternative views of reality and challenges dogmatic, transmission teaching.

Rosen, in criticizing the language of school textbooks as long ago as 1967, suggests that if students are to take on 'the language of thought and impersonal observation and description, generalisation and abstraction, theories, laws, the analysis of events remote in time and space, argument and speculation' (p. 121) in other ways than by taking over whole chunks of text 'as a kind of jargon', they have to make it 'interact' with their own experience and learning. Otherwise, he argues, 'instead of the new formulation representing hard-won victories of intellectual struggle or even partial victories, they are not even half-hearted skirmishes. Instead there is empty verbalism, sanctional utterance and approved dogma' (p. 123).

This argument would appear to have relevance to the kind of interaction that can be generated in the classroom between published student and community writing and mainstream textbooks. Where there is regular use of alternative, and sometimes therefore awkward or oppositional, texts alongside those which dominate the mainstream curriculum, some of the conditions are established for real learning. Discussion of school textbooks, with good reason, tends to be formulated around the kinds of text which dominate educational discourse and around the institutionalized practices by which teachers constitute both their own authority and that of the school texts they mediate to students. It has been proposed (see Luke, de Castell and Luke and Olson, Chapters 19 and 20, this volume) that exclusive attention either to the texts or to the teacher's role in attributing authority to texts neglects an alternative view of school texts and classrooms which a consideration of the importance of student writing and community publishing brings into sharp focus. In this perspective students' capabilities as writers, readers and thinkers are placed in the foreground.

Notes

1 *Seditious Publications Act*, December 1819.
2 *The English Magazine* is produced at the Inner London Education Authority's English

Burgess's (1973) wish to conflate the concept 'writer' with the concept 'individual' emphasizes an image of the student writer popularized in the 'creative writing' movement (Langdon, 1961), the personal growth models of Subject English (Dixon, 1967) and the language and learning tracts of the early 1970s (Barnes, Britton and Rosen, 1971). All held as the centre of their positions a concept of the individual, and the individual as a writer. Kelly's personal construct theory (1963), as well as Polanyi's *Personal Knowledge* (1958), Vygotsky's *Thought and Language* (1962) and Langer's *Philosophy in a New Key* (1957) had provided a multi-disciplinary base for such a concept.

Attempts in the 1980s to blend this concept with the concept of the author (Moffett, 1981; Graves, 1983; Graves and Hansen, 1983), and to make authorship and authoring significant aspects of the writing classroom (e.g., Emig, 1983; Protherough, 1983; Hansen, 1983), extend and change the concept of the school writer in several significant ways.

Authorship and Individuality

The adoption of the concept of authorship in the classroom can be seen to strengthen a dominant pedagogical assumption that writing is the expression of individuality and personal experience (Britton, 1970; Emig, 1983). For instance Moffett (1981) argues that educators should conceive of writing as 'full-fledged authoring', as the 'authentic expression of an individual's own ideas' (1981, p. 89). His claim is that:

> True authoring occurs naturally to the extent that the writer is composing with raw material, that is, source content not previously abstracted and formulated by others . . . . Insisting on maximum authorship should stave off the construing or treating of writing as only some sort of transcription or paraphrasing or verbal tailoring from ready-made cloth. (Moffett, 1981, p. 89)

Moffett's statement is a clear example of the intertwining of the concepts of author and of authoring, with the concepts of school writer and school writing. School writing is to be regarded as 'full-fledged authoring' — with 'authentic expression', with 'original' ideas, with the 'raw material' of personal feelings and individual synthesis of experience. Authoring is a 'natural' process by which the individual gives expression to content which has not previously been 'abstracted and formulated by others'.

Moffett's rejection of a concept of writing as 'transcription', 'paraphrasing', 'verbal tailoring from ready-made cloth' emphasizes the creative power he gives to writing, now labelled 'authoring'. Authoring is about adding something unique to the world by giving original expression to personal experience. Authoring creates new material. Writing which lacks this creativity, originality and uniqueness belongs to the realm of the second-hand — 'transcription', 'paraphrasing'.

Moffett's 'tailoring' metaphor reinforces this. The material for Moffett's 'author' is 'raw' — 'source content not previously abstracted and formulated by others'. However, the material for the non-author — the 'tailor' — is 'ready-made cloth'; language that has been used before.

Used in this way, the concept of authoring reinforces many of Dixon's (1967) personal growth assumptions, by stressing the value of authenticity, originality and individuality in writing. The concept of authoring makes this emphasis possible because of the obvious connection between authoring and literature.

Authorship and Literature

When Moffett asks educators to conceive of writing as 'full-fledged authoring', he implicitly attaches to the concept of the school writer some of the traditional concepts of the literary author, and it is not surprising, given their history, that the two discourses fit well together.

An orthodox view of literature is that the literary work stems from the creative unconsciousness of the individual author. It is the author who provides the imagination, inspiration and personal vision for the work, who creates and expresses the work. It is also the author who provides the individuality and originality of a piece of literature, its claim to be treated differently from other discourse, other works. While literary study is concerned with techniques that authors use, its predominant concern is with a creative vision that guides the use of these techniques, or of a creative vision which is independent of these techniques. As a result, convention and technique — as artificial, contrived, mechanical — are opposed to authorial expression, which is regarded as individual and spontaneous. The act of creation bypasses mechanics (Macherey, 1978).

Linked with this is the modern assumption of the unique qualities of the author's vision, of the author's originality and individuality, of the author's veracity. In the name of 'truth' the author is expected to be independent of convention and free of cliché; to break rules of syntax and forge new meanings; to clear the language of the debris of 'habit'; to speak directly to the reader (Williamson, n.d.; Belsey, 1980). Language will thus be seen to be used in new and original ways, for new and original meanings, but always 'truthfully'.

The concept of the literary text as a natural, creative and honest expression from a gifted individual obscures the process of production of the text, presenting only a holistic, completed and apparently personal, spontaneous interpretation of human experience. The emphasis is not on the nature of the constructed artifact, but on its human 'truth'; not on the ideological construction of the text, but on its apparent innocence and personal vision. Feminist criticism (Millett, 1977; Fetterly, 1978) has made one of the strongest challenges to this ideological valorization of 'truth' and innocence in literature. Authority of this sort is demonstrated to be a patriarchal practice — 'truth' is seen to be male; creativity is seen to be 'male' (Gilbert and Gubar, 1979). The assumption that authors portray 'truths' which are censorship in the original decision as to what will be taught and tested for and whose image of reality will be presented in public schools and school books. In fact, by stepping back from the passion and intensity of these conflicts it can be seen that American schooling is itself a system of censorship. In the name of education it seeks to impose upon some the beliefs of others.[4]

There is, of course, a small number of basic values (perhaps those contained in a constitution) upon which virtually the entire society agrees. But in the vast majority of school value conflicts, however enlightened the ideology underlying curriculum and text may be from one point of view, it will almost always be — in either a pluralistic or a class-based society — an ideological imposition from another point of view. Just as there are no value-neutral texts or curricula, there is virtually no cultural tradition or belief structure which will command the assent of all families. Unless educational choice is secured to all equally, every school system will be an example of at least a partial imposition of values to the advantage of some and the disadvantage of others.

No particular group or movement is responsible for this systemic invasion of individual rights of conscience and belief by an agency of government. Instead, the nearly perpetual conflicts over socialization in the schools are necessitated by the very majoritarian structure of public schooling which requires that decisions made by and for the majority be imposed on the minority as well. 'Necessitated' is the right word. Forty-five years ago the US Supreme Court explained why:

> Free public education, if faithful to the idea of secular instruction and political neutrality, will not be partisan or enemy of any class, creed, party, or faction. If it is to impose any ideological discipline, however, each party or denomination must seek to control, or failing that, to weaken the influence of the educational system.[5]

As the Court suggests, if there is to be any hope of reinvigorating public education or of restoring fundamental freedoms of the mind, one must see conflicts over curriculum and books as symptoms of a deeper disorder — the compulsion to use government schooling as a tool to create or reinforce community cohesion.

Any healthy society will use some method to maintain and reinforce cohesion among its members. When this process is healthy it provides a means for every family to participate in the ongoing process of shaping and defining the culture without being coerced into abandoning their own consciences. To neglect the constant creation and transmission of culture would be to make the society sterile. It would condemn all persons to a corrosive isolation and alienating individualism. The processes by which community cohesion is maintained include forums such as schools in which families must be allowed to participate equally, voluntarily and without fear of having to trade individual conscience for a free education.

In the US, as in other societies which recognize the importance of a system of freedom of expression and conscience, the participation of the public in community building is safeguarded by denying the government any power to establish orthodoxy or sanction the content of belief and communication. In these same societies schools — as agencies of government — are a primary public forum for building community cohesion. The problem in these societies, therefore, is to maintain the vitality of schools as centres of the invigorating and constructive conflict over the nature of the community and as communicators of consensus values, while respecting the rights of conscience of the individual.

It is the premise of this chapter that a fundamental condition for easing conflicts between liberty and education is to establish an equal distribution of rights of choice in schooling across the entire community. In order for such an equality of liberty to be practical, however, it is necessary to take account of the different levels of government at which value decisions are made, and to deal first with those levels at which the erosion of rights of conscience is clearest and most damaging.

When it comes to conflicts over school textbook selection and removal, the most suspect area of dispute is not the individual case of censorship-by-removal, but the activities of textbook committees in those states which employ state-wide, political mechanisms for selecting and limiting the use of textbooks in every school district. The least suspect areas will be textbook decisions arising from the professional relationship between teacher and family or from the relationships among teachers and between teachers and families in the individual school building. In schools the struggle for a constructive, participatory and non-coercive process of building community without destroying individual conscience should begin at the most centralized point of the schooling bureaucracy, the state.

In order to address directly the conflict of individual liberty and community cohesion, which lies at the base of conflicts over school texts, the role of law in these conflicts must be considered. In fact, because the formation and expression of beliefs and world views lie at the base of most textbook conflicts, the principles of freedom of expression and belief derived from the First Amendment to the US Constitution are strongly implicated. And because the First Amendment rights of families, students and teachers are involved, it is natural to expect that the law in general and constitutional law in particular will provide guidance to the disputants and a workable resolution of their conflicts. Nothing could be farther from reality. The US Supreme Court and the other Federal courts are impaled on the same contradiction between freedom of expression and majoritarian schooling which drives the disputants to fight with each other. Each court decision deepens the contradiction; and none addresses the fundamental issue of structure which pits one family against another and leads one group of believers to view those who are different as enemies in a holy crusade. Perhaps most importantly, the entire line of cases dealing with various forms of censorship suggests no practical path to accommodating individual conscience and constructive community building.

What follows is a report on and criticism of the narrow analysis of school text and library conflicts which has characterized law to date. The aim is to recast the debate over language and authority in textbooks and to focus on the central contradiction of American schooling. The ways in which statutory and constitutional law have been brought to bear on textbook content are examined; and it is argued that law will not be constructive in this area until a radical revision of both the legal and cultural understandings of schooling is made in light of First Amendment principles.

struggle for community cohesion. But such a choice-centred restructuring of public schooling would have required the Court and the public to acknowledge that the political majority may *not* use its power over schooling to inculcate its values in the minds of dissenting children, the very power the Court went out of its way to affirm in its 'respect for traditional values' statement.[18]

When the Federal courts have gone beyond the removal of library books and directly confronted issues of textbook selection, the results have been as ambiguous and the analysis as halting as they are in *Pico*. Two cases provide the necessary background for understanding the difficult issues now before the courts. In the first case, *Loewen v. Turnispeed*, the State of Mississippi's Textbook Purchasing Board was sued for refusing to adopt a history textbook which it regarded as 'too racially oriented'.[19] In 1974 the state board had rejected a ninth grade history of Mississippi, *Mississippi: Conflict and Change* in favour of *Your Mississippi*. The effect of the decision was to require the state's public schools to continue using a text which all but ignored the existence of slavery and other forms of racism in Mississippi. The plaintiffs (editors, authors, students, parents and school administrators) charged that the selected textbook

> minimizes, ignores and degrades the roles of blacks and other minorities in Mississippi history, and presents historical events in a manner sympathetic to principles of social segregation and discrimination, black inferiority, and 'white supremacy.'[20]

In a complex decision handed down six years after the state refused to adopt the alternative, *Mississippi: Conflict and Change*, Federal District Court Judge Orma Smith required the state to adopt the text it had earlier refused. Judge Smith ruled that the failure to adopt the text had been racially motivated in violation of the Equal Protection Clause of the Fourteenth Amendment,[21] and that the plaintiff's First Amendment and due process rights had been violated in that the textbook selection process provided no 'method by which those affected by such decisions may oppose them.'[22]

The decision in *Loewen* rests in large part upon the presence of an identifiable and offensive motive — racism — driving the state's selection of texts, and upon the absence of any reliable mechanism by which all parties affected by textbook selections may have their viewpoints heard and fairly considered. Satisfying as the immediate results of this decision may be, its underlying principles provide little guidance for most challenges to textbook selection. Even when motives are constitutionally acceptable, the effect of a state-wide textbook selection process such as Mississippi's may be to require students to learn one version of history rather than another or to confess a belief in the validity of some values (e.g., free market economics), rather than others (e.g., socialism). Equally important, even if value inculcation in public schools grows out of a process which allows all parties to be heard on the question of which world views should be incorporated in required texts, there will still be dissenters. These dissenters may have their beliefs as severely contradicted by a fairly made majority selection as plaintiffs had by a skewed and racist selection in *Loewen*.

The 1984 decision of a Federal court in *Johnson v. Stuart* provides another example of the shortcomings of conventional legal wisdom for dealing with the distortions in individual education which result from textbook selection governed by political processes. Oregon state law created the state's Textbook Commission and regulated its activities by requiring, among other things, that 'No textbook shall be used in the schools which speaks slightingly of the founders of the Republic or of those who preserved the Union or which belittles or undervalues their work.'[23] Federal District Court Judge James Burus ruled that the statute unjustifiably violated the First Amendment rights of plaintiff students; and he enjoined the Textbook Commission and the State Board of Education from enforcing the challenged statute.

Judge Burus stated that the statute in question 'acts to contract the available field of knowledge and casts a pall of orthodoxy over the curriculum.'[24] But the judge did not rule that *any* state content requirement for textbook selection would cast a similar pall of orthodoxy or equally infringe First Amendment rights of the captive student audience and their families. Of course, the state's process for political specification of knowledge through text selection was not at issue in the case. Still, the Judge's comments may suggest more than he intended: '. . . it is not appropriate that the state take one side of a debate among historians concerning the founders of the Republic and preservers of the Union.'[25] One wonders whether the state would be justified in taking one side of a debate among political economists or moral philosophers, or between spiritualists and materialists, or advocates of individual competition and of collectivism. Plainly there is much work to be done before we can distinguish clearly between those kinds of value inculcation which cast a pall of orthodoxy by prescribing the basic value content of communication and conscience in school and those which do not.

Challenging the Results of the Textbook Selection System

The *Loewen* and *Johnson* cases represent narrow challenges in which particular substantive barriers to the adoption of texts are attacked. There is no attack on the validity of a state-wide political process for text selection; and what little questioning there is of those processes accepts the majoritarian premise of text selection. But with the more recent cases of *Mozert v. Hawkins*[26] and *Smith v. Mobile*[27] the conflicts take a quantum leap; and claims are made that an entire array of fairly selected public school texts systematically discriminates against the beliefs of some families while embracing the beliefs of others. These two cases do not directly challenge the power of the state to limit the texts teachers must use, but they come closer than any before them because the remedies granted in each case would require a restructuring of the text selection and use system.

The facts in the two cases are virtually the same, and in both the Christian Fundamentalist plaintiffs were victorious. The remedies chosen by the two judges, however, could not be more opposed. If *Mozert* is upheld on appeal, it presages substantially increased freedoms for all families unsatisfied with public school texts and the values they seek to impart. If *Mobile* is upheld, it will result in a major escalation of the war over value orthodoxy in American schools.

In *Mozert*, families of grade school children objected to state-selected[28] reading texts for use K-8 on the grounds that these books promoted beliefs at odds with Christian Fundamentalism[29] and violated the free exercise of religious rights guaranteed by the First Amendment. When the plaintiff's children refused to use the text in their reading classes, the Hawkins County School Board suspended the children and took legal action against their parents. The Federal district court found that the texts at issue were offensive to the plaintiff's religious beliefs:

> Plaintiff's religious beliefs compel them to refrain from exposure to the Holt series. The Board has effectively required that the student-plaintiffs either read the offensive texts or give up their free public education. . . . Accordingly, the Court finds that the plaintiff's free exercise rights have been burdened by the school board policy.[30]

Having found that requiring plaintiffs' children to learn to read from these texts amounted to a coercive and unjustified burden on the right of free exercise of religion, the court ordered that the dissenting children be readmitted to school but be excused from class when the reading texts were in use. The court further ordered the school board to permit the children to learn reading at home from books satisfactory to their parents. The defendants' claim that this kind of flexibility and choice for families would cause chaos in the schools was not accepted by the court.

The most significant obstacle overcome by the court's careful crafting of the remedy in the case was the argument that any accommodation of the plaintiff's religious beliefs in public school texts would amount to an unconstitutional establishment of their religion. By allowing the plaintiff children to learn reading at home rather than requiring all Hawkins County children to learn reading from fundamentalist textbooks, Judge Hill avoided the Establishment Clause problem and effectively disarmed the defendants.[31]

Mozert is currently on appeal and may eventually reach the US Supreme Court. If it does, it will likely be joined there by *Smith v. Mobile School Committee*, which is on appeal from the Federal District Court of Alabama. In the *Smith* case, another group of Christian Fundamentalists challenged forty-four elementary and secondary school texts selected by the state's textbook authority for use in history, social studies and home economics classes. The plaintiffs contended that the beliefs represented and taught by the texts were not only offensive to Christian Fundamentalism, but established the religion of 'Secular Humanism' in the public schools in violation of the First Amendment's Establishment Clause.[32]

Federal District Court Judge Brevard Hand agreed with the plaintiffs that the conglomeration of values found in the challenged texts constituted a religion in itself — the religion of Secular Humanism. On its face such a conclusion seems absurd. To regard all non-religious teachings as part of a single, organized, 'secular religion' inculcated in the minds of all students and therefore established by government schools is to stretch conspiratorial thinking beyond any relationship to reality. But the opinion does have the merit of recognizing that there are many non-religious values and beliefs taught in public schools and offensive to large numbers of families who attend those schools. Although couched entirely in the language of religious freedoms,[33] the judge's opinion suggests that ideological establishment may be as offensive as religious establishment where broad First Amendment freedom of belief is concerned.

It is in the fashioning of a remedy, however, that Judge Hand made his most egregious error from the standpoint of attaining a clear understanding of the conflict between majoritarian schooling and freedom of intellect and spirit. He ordered that all forty-four books be removed from Mobile, Alabama schools and prohibited their use in the state because of their religion-of-secular-humanism content.[34] Two results can be anticipated from this legal remedy. First, almost any text could be challenged as part of Secular Humanism and removed from the schools, leaving no texts at all which could be regarded as free of the establishment taint. The only way to preserve religious neutrality would then be to remove all value content from school books. Second, since the ruling does not permit dissenters to pursue their own values in schools and texts of their choice, these dissenters must struggle to have the state textbook commission foist their minority values upon the majority. If they succeed, a new group of dissenters will be created, and the conflict over textbook content would continue *ad infinitum*.

Mozert, then, expands individual freedoms of belief without creating either ideological or theological establishment, while *Smith* deals with the same kind of dispute by fuelling the conflict among all secular and religious faiths over control of the textbook selection process. Followed to its logical conclusion, the *Mozert* opinion would require so much flexibility and choice in public schools that they would need to be restructured. Followed to its logical conclusion, the *Smith* line of reasoning would result in the paralysis and eventual destruction of public schooling. The cases present an opportunity for the US Supreme Court and the public to recognize the contradiction between majoritarian control of value inculcation in government schools and individual freedom of belief and intellect. It is unlikely that anything so clear-headed and useful will emerge from the appeals of these cases as long as the majoritarian assumption is so deeply embedded in school law and culture.

After the writing of this chapter, the courts of appeals in *Mozart* and *Smith* rendered their decisions. Each case was reversed. In the *Smith* case, the appellate decision seems sound, for it rejects the replacement of an allegedly secular establishment by a clearly religious one. The decision is unsatisfying in its refusal to recognize that a secular value imposition may be every bit as offensive constitutionally as a religiously tied imposition. Secular Humanism may be a religion, the court found, but the offending texts do not establish that religion merely because there is some overlap of textbook values and religious tenets. The books are secular, and that, in the court's views, ends the inquiry: '... use of the challenged textbooks has the primary effect of conveying information that is essentially neutral in its religious content to the school children who utilize the books; none of these books convey a message of governmental approval of secular humanism or governmental disapproval of theism.'[35]

The *Mozert* decision, by overruling the district court's requirement that plaintiff families' conscience be accommodated without imposing their values on the majority in school, deepens the contradiction between conscience and majoritarianism in schooling. It is an unfortunate decision in that it misunderstands the nature of the socialization process in schooling. The court could not find in the trial record evidence of what it regarded as a requisite in making out a free-exercise claim — government coercion of students' beliefs. Merely being exposed to values which contradicted plaintiff's sincerely held religious views was insufficient. Plaintiffs would have had to have been made to confess a belief in those values for the district court's ruling to have been upheld. The court does not discuss or recognize the various ways in which textbooks, role models and hidden curriculum coerce students' beliefs without requiring that they actually make a public confession of belief. The two concurring opinions present a more realistic and sophisticated understanding of value conflict and the effect of textbooks on children and schooling alike; but they find other grounds to reverse the district court's decision. The case will have to await a possible Supreme Court review to find out whether US constitutional law will take this opportunity to try to dissolve the artificial contradiction between individual conscience and community cohesion.

Challenging the Power of the State to Select Texts

Perhaps nowhere does the assumption that what is desirable for some must be forced on all appear more broadly destructive of intellectual freedom and teacher professionalism than in the twenty-two states which have legislatively mandated, state-wide political processes for textbook selection.[36] These statutes, and the ways in which they affect the textbook publishing industry,[37] have never been directly challenged as violative of the freedom of intellect and spirit guaranteed by the First Amendment; but a strong argument can be made that state power over text selection undermines the most fundamental principles of constitutional democracy. In fact, state-wide textbook selection processes are the most vulnerable to attack of the forms of 'censorship', because it is here that political pressures are most insensitive to individual family values and most likely to create a pall of orthodoxy.

There are not great differences among the various state textbook statutes. All arose at least partly in response to problems of variable and unreliable quality in text materials (paper, covers, bindings, useful life) as well as economic irregularities such as conflicts of interest among text ordering officials, favouritism and even an occasional bribe. In addition to regulating the incidental, non-content aspects of text selection and use, each state statute creates a political mechanism for control of content. All the statutes create a textbook selection committee whose members are appointed by a public official and which sometimes includes teachers and other professional educators as well as community members. This committee either selects the texts in each subject-matter area itself, or recommends adoptions to the state board of education or superintendent of education. Most statutes call for the selection of more than one text in each subject, leaving the choice among approved texts to local education authorities.

Texts and materials not approved by the state-wide textbook committee or its parent authority may not be used in any state public school and are not available to private schools in those states which provide free texts for non-public schools. In some states (e.g., Texas) the existence of state text funds creates the leverage which effectively requires use of approved texts. In other states there are penalties for teachers or principals who use or permit the use of unapproved texts.[38]

There are only a few content requirements in the state textbook statutes themselves; but enormous discretion is left to the textbook committee in determining which texts to select and what criteria to apply in making those selections. Among the specific legislative mandates on content are the invalidated Oregon requirement that no text cast aspersions on the founders of the Republic,[39] Tennessee's prohibition against the adoption or use of any text which 'contains subversive material or information'[40] and Nevada's requirement, imposed through its regulation of courses of study using approved texts, that lessons must 'emphasize the benefits of free enterprise as compared to other economic systems; . . . teach the principles of the profit motive and competition and the way in which investments generate progress and growth in the economy.'[41]

Pursuant to its powers to review and select textbooks for use in the state's local school district, the typical state textbook committee adopts regulations which specify the content of texts for which it is soliciting bids from publishers. These regulations, along with any statutory requirements, become templates for publishers and authors. In some states, such as California and Texas, these specifications of content can be voluminous and extraordinarily detailed, so that text writing can become an exercise in complying with preordained and politically approved specifications rather than an expression of the subject-matter and pedagogical expertise of independent authors and scholars. Georgia's 'General Criteria for Use by the Textbook Advisory Committee', for example, prohibits the adoption of any text which includes '(1) any theme or statement that is derogatory to the democratic process . . . or (2) social unrest promoted as a tool for anarchistic goals and activity.'[42] In Texas a long public struggle in both political and legal arenas led the state to eliminate its requirement that Creationism be treated equally with evolution in biology texts. But numerous other content requirements remain, including such things as 'Textbooks shall not contain material which serves to undermine authority', or 'Textbook content shall not encourage life styles deviating from generally accepted standards of society.'[43]

In addition to statutory requirements and committee-created specifications, selections are influenced by the process of receiving and evaluating publishers' bids. For several years now the Texas state adoption hearings have provided a national spectacle in which the religious right has done battle with liberal supporters of established education over every conceivable item of textbook content.[44] It is in these hearings that publishers, editors and authors are sometimes grilled and shredded by committee members or by witnesses who are advocates of some particular orthodoxy.[45] These hearings, and the state-wide processes of text adoption which give rise to them in twenty-two states, have a major impact on the textbook publishing industry. Since nearly 20 per cent of the texts published each year are used in two of these states — Texas and California — these hearings and processes make it possible for special interest groups to magnify their pressure on publishers with a relatively small effort. Because text publishers must satisfy a market dominated by politically created specifications of knowledge, they are often compelled by business considerations to replace scholarship with politics as the basis for creating textbooks.

The First Amendment and Textbook Content

Because state-wide textbook selection processes heavily influence the 'spectrum of knowledge' which is made available to teachers and students, and which becomes the basis for testing, grade promotions and ultimately the conscience and consciousness of the rising generation, the First Amendment stakes could not be clearer.[46] Perhaps the most revealing way to force the contradiction between majority schooling and freedom of intellect and spirit into the public's consciousness would be a frontal attack on the very existence of state-wide textbook selection. A constitutional attack on state textbook selection would also be the most pragmatic and justifiable place to start, because state-wide processes are so categorically restrictive of teacher professionalism and so distant from the possibilities of negotiated or mediated settlements of value conflicts possible on the school level. Such an attack on the state-wide selection process would bottom on a basic understanding of schooling as value-socialization, the First Amendment as a protector of minority views and the importance of freedom of opinion and belief in a democratic society.

The principles of the First Amendment constitute the lynchpin of individual political sovereignty and of any democratic government whose legitimacy rests upon the just consent of the governed. These principles require that the government remain scrupulously content-neutral where the expression of beliefs, opinions and information are concerned, whether such expressions be secular or religious.[47] At the same time it would defy logic to prohibit the government from regulating the *expression* of beliefs and opinions, while permitting it to regulate the *formation* of these same beliefs and opinions. If the state were permitted such control of belief formation, First Amendment protections of expression would be meaningless and the government would become self-perpetuating, a kind of political perpetual-motion machine in which dissent becomes almost literally unthinkable.

Schooling is a primary mechanism, though certainly not the only one, by which beliefs and world views are formed and reinforced. Children, except those of the very wealthy, are generally not voluntarily in attendance at schools of their family's choice, but go instead to the local public school in which government-approved texts containing majority-approved and politically formulated content are uniformly in use. Negotiating and mediative processes by which value conflicts may become constructive of community consensus are rare. The potential for reorienting the disputants and redefining values tends to be converted into a win/lose struggle by the absence of school choice and by the effect of majoritarian ideology and school structure.

Were it possible to select texts which met professional standards and remained value-neutral, the government neutrality toward belief formation required by the First Amendment could be attained in the present structure of public schooling. But that is neither possible nor educationally desirable. As anyone who has ever taught or attended a class, read or written a book knows, education cannot be value-neutral. Efforts to avoid value controversy in schools by 'dumbing down' texts have succeeded only in creating a bland and homogenized education. In this sanitized world children are taught a managerial mentality which values nothing intrinsically and which fosters an uncritical mind and an unquestioned tendency either to accept authority or to rebel mindlessly against it.

Applying the First Amendment principle of government neutrality in matters of belief formation to schools which must inevitably be value-laden exposes the central contradiction in American schooling. Majority control of school content is inconsistent with individual freedom of intellect and spirit. Without a substantial shift of power in the schools from majority control to the value preferences of individual families[48] and the independent professional judgment of individual teachers[49] schooling will continue to undermine intellectual freedom and the constitutional system of individual political sovereignty.

Where textbooks are concerned, the First Amendment would seem to require that the state be stripped completely of any power to prescribe content, either by selection or removal of books. The government may not prescribe the content of communication[50] among adults, nor regulate their choices with regard to opinion, belief, or worship. By what theory may that same government control the content of school texts which children must read and be tested on as part of compulsory schooling? National unity, the preservation of majority values, and the need for a mechanism to perpetuate common culture have been the most frequent arguments for this government control. There may be some core values in the Constitution itself (such as protecting the equal rights of people of colour and women, or preserving First Amendment rights of all). But beyond such constitutionally recognized core values, it is as true of textbooks now as it was of compulsory flag salutes in 1943, that

> As governmental pressure toward unity becomes greater, so strife becomes more bitter as to whose unity it shall be. Probably no deeper division of our people could proceed from any provocation than from finding it necessary to choose what doctrine and whose program public officials shall compel youth to unite in embracing. Ultimate futility of such attempts to compel coherence is the lesson of every such effort. . . . Compulsory unification of opinion achieves only the unanimity of the graveyard.[51]

Dissolving the contradiction between majoritarian schooling and freedom of intellect and belief requires that the process of textbook selection and use be radically decentralized, empowering families and enhancing the professional status and responsibilities of teachers. A beneficial side-effect of such decentralization would be a substantial decrease in the level of conflict over textbook content. The same results can be achieved throughout the schools by creating a system of equal school choice among all families regardless of race, religion, language, or economic status.[52] Changes of this magnitude are not likely to come about in textbook selection, curriculum control, or school choice until the central contradiction of our present system of schooling is acknowledged to exist.

Notes

1 Especially since 1980 there has been an increasing number of instances of school boards bowing to local or national pressure groups and removing books from school libraries and curricula. For listings and accounts of these incidents consult the newsletter of the National Coalition Against Censorship, the library of People for the American Way in Washington, D.C. and the American Library Association. Some of these conflicts are reported and analysed in E. Jenkinson (1979) *Censorship*, Carbonale: Southern Illinois University Press; R. O'Neill (1981) *Classrooms in the Crossfire*. Bloomington: Indiana University Press; and S. Arons (1983) *Compelling Belief*, New York: McGraw-Hill.

2 One interpretation of the First Amendment's application to compulsory schooling concludes that maintaining the schools as 'marketplaces of ideas' is sufficient to protect the freedom of expression rights of all the participants. This conception is limited in its analytic usefulness, however, especially as concerns younger students, text selection and the need to choose single texts in subjects required of all students. See M. Yudof (1983) *When Government Speaks*, Berkeley: University of California Press, generally and at Chapter 12.

3 See *Pierce v. Society of Sisters*, 268 US 510 (1925), and D. Tyack (1968) 'The perils of pluralism: The background of the *Pierce* case,' *American Historical Review*, 74; S. Arons (1976) 'Separation of school and state: *Pierce* reconsidered', *Harvard Educational Review*, 46.

4 John Stuart Mill recognized this as early as 1859 when he described state-sponsored education as '... a mere contrivance for moulding people to be exactly like one another: and as the mould in which it casts them is that which pleases the predominant power in the government, whether this be a monarch, a priesthood, an aristocracy, or the majority of the existing generation, in proportion as it is efficient and successful, it establishes a despotism over the mind...' (J.S. Mill, 1859, *On Liberty*, London: Parker and Son, 9.190–1).

5 *West Virginia v. Barnette*, 319 US at 637 (1943).

6 See, e.g., *Everson v. Bd. of Education*, 330 US 1 (1947); *Abington v. Schempp*, 374 US 203 (1963); *Lemon v. Kurtzman*, 403 US 602 (1971), *Mueller v. Allen*, 463 US 388 (1983), and *Wallace v. Jaffree* 105 S. Ct. 2479 (1985). There are literally scores of law review articles and books analysing this complex area of law and public education.

7 By one account there are fewer than 5000 adherents of Secular Humanism in the US. See the discussions of Secular Humanism in *Grove v. Mead*, 753 F2d 1528 at 1535 (1985) and in Chapter 7, 'Secular Humanism' of Jenkinson, Note 1, *supra*. For a discussion of the New Right's legal campaign on this issue, see S. Arons (1985) 'The great Secular-Humanism debate reveals a truth about public schooling', *Education Week*, 16 Oct.

8 See also O. McGraw (1976) 'Secular Humanism and the schools: The issue whose time has come', *Heritage Foundation*, Washington, D.C.; D. Bollier (1983) 'The witch hunt against "Secular Humanism",' *People For The American Way*, Washington, D.C.; D. Krauthammer (1981) 'The "Humanist Phantom"', *New Republic*, 25 July; and Arons, Note 7, *supra*.

9 Two cases, *Mozert v. Hawkins* in Tennessee and *Smith v. Mobile* in Alabama, are dealt with in detail below. See text at Note 26.

10 A special case of the attack against secularism has been the attempt to replace the teaching of evolution by Genesis. As long ago as the famous *Scopes* trial, attempts were made to criminalize the teaching of evolution in government schools. Though these efforts were declared unconstitutional in 1968 in *Epperson v. Arkansas*, 393 US 97 (1968), the issue has emerged again in new form. For the past ten years legislative efforts have been made to characterize Genesis as a science (Creation Science) and evolution as a belief system. Equal time for the two science/belief systems was then demanded. The courts have routinely declared such efforts to require the teaching of Genesis alongside evolution to be prohibited by the Establishment Clause of the First Amendment. In June 1987 the Supreme Court agreed and seemed to close the issue again by declaring a Louisiana law providing equal time for Creationism to be a violation of the First Amendment Establishment Clause. See *Edwards v. Aquillard*, 55 USLW 4860 (1987). One of the best discussions of equal time issue is D. Nelkin (1977) *Science Textbook Controversies and the Politics of Equal Time*, Cambridge: MIT Press.

11 The First Amendment protects these rights of expression and belief alongside the two religious freedom clauses. The significance of the fact that all of these freedoms of expression and belief are contained in a single Constitutional Amendment is discussed in Meiklejohn (1953) 'What does the First Amendment mean?' 20 Chi. L.R. 461 and in Thomas Emerson's (1966) seminal *Toward a General Theory of the First Amendment* New York: Random House.

12 Compare *President's Council v. Community Board 25*, 457 F2d 289 (CA2 1972) and *Zykan v. Warsaw*, 631 F2d 1300 (CA7 1980) with *Right to Read v. Chelsea*, 454 F. Supp. 703 (1978) and *Parducci v. Rutland*, 316 F. Supp. 352 (1970). See also Note (1979) 'Challenging ideological exclusion of curriculum materials', 14 *Harv. CR/CL Law Rev.* 485 and Note (1978) 'First Amendment limitations on the power of school boards to select and remove high school texts and library books', 52 *St. Johns Law Review* 457.

13 Included among the banned books were Bernard Malamud's *The Fixer*, labelled 'anti-semitic'; Langston Hughes's edited collection *Best Short-Stories by Negro Writers* for being 'anti-Negro'; and *Go Ask Alice*, an anonymously written anti-drug diary of a ruined teenager.

14 102 S. Ct. 2799 (1982).

15 *Island Trees v. Pico*, 102 S. Ct. at 2810.

16 *Ibid* at p. 2806.

17 The case deals only with improperly motivated removals of books from school libraries and specifically avoids the question of student, teacher, or parent rights where curriculum, text and library selections are concerned. The restriction on the school board's power is therefore minimal.

18 See Note 16, *supra*.

19 'Court bars rejection of textbook for racial reasons', *New York Times*, 5 April 1980, p. 6.

20 'Challenging ideological exclusions of curriculum materials', Note 12, *supra*, p. 485.

21 *Loewen v. Turnispeed*, memorandum of decision dated 2 April 1980, p. 24. The case report can be found at 488 F. Supp. 1138 (DC Miss., 1980).

22 *Ibid.*, p. 33.

23 ORS 337.260(1). Presumably this statute meant that any text which mentioned that Washington was a slave holder, or which indicated that Lincoln would have refused to sign the Emancipation Proclamation if that would have preserved the Union, could not have been adopted.

24 Official Court Reporter's transcript of an opinion delivered from the bench, dated 21 July 1984, p. 4.

25 *Ibid.*

26 *Mozert v. Hawkins County Public Schools*, 647 F. Supp 1194 (D. Tenn. 1986). The Supreme Court has refused to grant a review of the Appeal Court's ruling for defendant school authorities.

27 *Smith v. Board of School Commissioners of Mobile County*, 655 F. Supp. 939 (S.D. Ala 1987).

28 Tennessee has a state-wide selection process which requires that public schools use only texts adopted by the state. Sometimes more than one series of readers may be approved, giving local schools a choice; but in *Mozert* there were no approved alternatives to the Holt series, and the Hawkins County School Board had to rescind its initial approval of alternative texts for the plaintiffs' children.

29 The plaintiffs claimed that the texts were based on and taught such values as religious tolerance, feminism, magic, humanism and pacifism; and the Judge agreed.

30 *Mozert*, 647 F. Supp. at 1200.

31 In addition to the constitutional problem which would have arisen if the state had adopted reading texts congenial to the fundamentalist world view (even if only used by plaintiff's children), the defendants and their allies pointed out that the flexibility of selective home education for dissenters would make the school chaotic. For a discussion of the pros and cons of such chaos, see S. Arons (1986) 'Public education vs. individual liberty', *Baltimore Sun*, 21 December 1986, p. 1–D.

32 The case began as a challenge to an Alabama statute authorizing a one-minute period of silent meditation or prayer in public schools. After Judge Hand's initial approval of the prayer statute was reversed by the Supreme Court as contrary to the Establishment Clause of the First Amendment, he restructured the case as a contest over the establishment of Secular Humanism in state-approved textbooks. See *Jaffree v. Board*, 554 F. Supp. 1104 (1983) and *Wallace v. Jaffree*, 105 S. Ct. 2479 (1985) on the prayer/meditation issue and Judge Hand's bizarre understanding of the First Amendment.

33 The plaintiffs adopted the establishment-of-Secular-Humanism theory for their suit because it was clear to them that the courts had been quick to eliminate religious teachings from the schools, but very reluctant to view secular text selection as a form of censorship or an infringement of non-religious freedom of belief. Plaintiffs were right in claiming that their freedom of belief was infringed by the state's selection of approved values in textbooks; but their legal theory is destined to fail because it twists the meaning of religious establishment and fails to attack ideological impositions directly.

34 The decision that no student could use the challenged texts was dictated by the Establishment Clause analysis Judge Hand used. According to that analysis, the state may take no action with the purpose or primary effect of aiding religion. Even if plaintiffs' free exercise rights had been protected by allowing them to use other books (as was the case in *Mozert*), the state would still be aiding a secular religion by allowing students who favoured the books to use them.

35 *Smith v. Mobile*, 827 F2 684 at 690.

36 The twenty-two states and their statutes are Alabama (sec. 16–36–1 to 39); California (for only some grades); Florida (Title 15, sec. 233.07 *et seq.*); Georgia (General Statutes 32–707 to 32–724); Hawaii (Title 6, sec. 61–2 (7); Idaho (sec. 33–118, 33–512, and 33–1603 to 1605); Illinois (Chapter 122, sec. 28–1 *et seq.*); Indiana (Ch. 9, sec. 20–10.1–9–1 *et seq.*); Kentucky (sec. 156.400 *et seq.*); Louisiana (Rev. Stat. 17:351 *et seq.*); Mississippi (Ch. 43, sec. 37–43–1 *et seq.*); Nevada (Ch. 390, sec. 390.005 *et seq.* and selected provisions of Ch. 389 regulating courses of study); New Mexico (Ch. 22, article 15, sec. 22–15–1 *et seq.*); North Carolina (Ch. 115C, sec. 115C–85 *et seq.*); Oklahoma (Title 70, sec. 16–101 *et seq.*); Oregon (Ch. 337, sec. 337.011 *et seq.*); South Carolina (Ch. 31, sec. 59–31–10 *et seq.*); Tennessee (Ch. 20, sec. 49–2001 *et seq.*); Texas (Ch. 12, sub. ch. A–C, sec. 12.01 *et seq.*); Utah (Ch. 13, sec. 53–13–1 *et seq.*); Virginia (Ch. 14, art. 6, sec. 22.1–238 *et seq.*); West Virginia (art. 2 A, sec. 18–2A–1 *et seq.*).

37 Together, Texas and California reportedly account for nearly 20 per cent of the annual textbook purchases in the US each year. Their policies, therefore, have a limiting effect on the textbooks published and available in other markets. The interrelationship between the political specification of knowledge through state-wide text adoptions and the way texts are written, edited and published is complex. See de Castell and Luke, Chapter 7 and Apple, Chapter 12, this volume.

38 For example, Tennessee provides a $50 fine for any teacher or principal who 'uses or

permits to be used' a text not approved by the state (Ch. 20, sec. 49–2020). Louisiana makes similar activities a misdemeanour punishable by a fine of up to $500 or six months in jail, or both (R.S. sec. 352 D.). In Nevada 'any school officer or teacher who . . . knowingly fails to follow the regulations of the state board relating to use of textbooks' is punishable by a fine of up to $250 (Ch. 390, sec. 390.230 (3)). It is not clear whether these punishments for deviating from state-prescribed orthodoxy are counted on a per year, per term, or per lesson basis.

39 See the *Johnson* case, Note *supra*.

40 Tenn. Code 49–6–2202 (b) (2).

41 Nev. Code 389.080 2. (a) and (b).

42 Georgia's 'General Criteria', p. 3.

43 Texas Administrative Code, Title 19, Chapter 81, Sub chapter D, Section 81.71.

44 The most significant work done in Texas was supported by People for the American Way, a counterweight to Jerry Falwell's Moral Majority. The story there will someday make a good book. For an introduction to the weird textbook wars of Texas see 'Texas drops curb on science books', *New York Times*, 15 April 1984.

45 A great deal of energy has been expended on trying to make these hearings fair and balanced; but virtually no one has asked whether even the ultimate in due process guarantees could make state control of textbook content consistent with a system of freedom of expression which is designed to protect minority views from just such majority control.

46 City or district-wide selection processes in other states create the same problems, but they do not appear in such bold relief.

47 The text of the First Amendment reads: 'Congress shall make no law respecting an establishment of religion, or prohibiting the free exercise thereof; or abridging the freedom of speech, or of the press; or the right of the people peaceably to assemble, and to petition the Government for a redress of grievances.' For materials helpful in integrating these seemingly disparate rights into one system of freedom of belief and expression see Note 11, *supra*.

48 See *Mozert*, Note 26, *supra*.

49 Although the *Johnson* case ignored the First Amendment claims of teachers, Judge Burus commented that, 'These decisions [among texts] must remain within the discretion of those best equipped to make them: the professional educators . . . .' If this line of reasoning were followed to its logical conclusion, teachers, their professional judgment and their relationships to students and families would replace state statutes and committee decisions as determinative of textbook selection. The result would be considerably less conflict among community groups over text content and considerably more freedom of intellect and belief for students and teachers.

50 Schooling may be regarded as a process of communication between the culture and the individual student. Texts are of primary importance in structuring the content of this communication; and so the government arguably has no more power under the First Amendment to regulate the content of textbooks than it has to regulate the content of any other communication.

51 *Barnette* 319 US at 641.

52 School choice has become an item of great interest in the past few years of the current reform movement in the US. See, for example, the Special Report, 'The call for choice' in *Education Week*, 24 June 1987. One of the most thoughtful arguments for school choice is J. Coons and S. Sugarman (1978) *Education by Choice*, Berkeley: University of California Press. For the argument that school choice has important constitutional dimensions from both First and Fourteenth Amendment perspectives see Arons, 'Separation of school and state', Note 3, *supra*; S. Arons and C. Lawrence (1980) 'Manipulation of consciousness: A First Amendment critique of schooling', 15 *Harv. CR/CL Law Rev.* 309, and Arons, *Compelling Belief: The Culture of American Schooling*, Part 4.

Part IV
Textbook Language, Authority and Criticism

Chapter 17

Instruction of Preliterate Cultures

Eric Havelock
Yale University

Human culture is not inherited but learned, and through language transmitted from generation to generation. The transmission does not occur spontaneously, though many anthropologists seem to assume that it does, at least in societies identi-fied as 'primitive'. It requires a mechanism, a social device, an institution of some kind, providing a method of instruction, which will pass on a knowledge of what is in storage, or at least some essential part of this knowledge from adults who have learned it to the young who have not yet learned it. 'Education' is the term which we now employ to identify this mechanism, considered both as a process and as an institution or set of institutions, schools, colleges and universities, devised to implement the process. These require their own apparatus, the services of specialists suitably skilled and economic support provided by the community.

Ever since the Greeks the frame of reference and court of appeals, the source of knowledge, the basis of faith and the guide to action have reposed in documents, whether textbooks or treatises, bibles, poetry or prose, works of fact or fiction — artifacts to be handled, read, taught and indoctrinated, digested, consulted, quoted and sometimes memorized.[1] It would appear that as a result our terminology for dealing with anything expressed in language reflects that condition under which language becomes an artifact, that is, becomes inscribed. Even such a fundamental word as 'literature' describes language as it is portrayed in letters, just as 'grammar' implies a rationale applied to signs and symbols graphically present on a surface.

How can such storage be managed in a culture which is non-literate, one in which language has not become a visible artifact? The conditions under which language exists and functions in preliteracy are strictly acoustic. It is the ear not the eye which universally confers acquaintance with linguistic information of any kind. It is the ear which is required to assist in storing it.

When we consider the time scale within which the social evolution of our species has occurred, it becomes evident that oral cultures have had in the remoter past a more protracted existence than literate ones, and appear moreover, to judge from the evidence of artifacts, to have continued to subsist successfully in some parts of the world — South America, for example — in later periods when writing was elsewhere in common use. It would appear that the means available for this purpose in preliterate societies must differ sharply from those used in literate ones.

A first step towards discerning the genius of oral preservation is taken when we examine the genius of the document: why is it 'informative' in a sense in which language as it is spoken in the vernacular is not? Why does it furnish a court of appeal and a source of reference? Surely because the statements contained therein, being as it were frozen in script, are stabilized and are, as we say, 'reliable'; they cannot be changed without changing or replacing the document, and this in effect means that a document preserves information because it preserves the words of the information. It is forbidden to alter the words, and it is also forbidden to alter the order in which the words are placed, their syntax in short, for the stability of the statement relies upon preserving this order and upon this stability in turn depends the viability of the document as a court of appeal.

All syntactical statements which purport to state a formula, a principle, a truth, or extended statements which compose a plot, a thesis or a theory, or a set of 'meanings' which are to achieve the status of permanent or preserved language, are submitted to the control of a written version which *qua* version remains invariable, not subject to the whim of arbitrary manipulation or faulty recollection. The 'original', as we say, is always there.

In the behaviour of language without benefit of documentation, where is the principle of fixed order first perceptible? Surely in the grammar of the language itself. This requires such conventions as are indicated in the distinctions between the various parts of speech and their interrelations and functions. But this kind of order is only formal and analytic. It deals solely with the abstract properties of words. There is a second level of grammar which we might call the grammar of linguistic propriety or 'anthropological grammar'. This requires that combinations of words make sense, as we say, in agreement with the common experience of the group using the language. So the linguistic convention excludes from the normative such statements as 'man bites dog' or that 'grapes are gathered from thorns' or 'figs from thistles'. It disallows the injunction that we should 'love enemies'. Such statements, if they are made, reflect deliberate paradox: they violate common sense, as we say, they imagine the culture which happens to use this language as being stood on its head.

Such proprieties in the arrangements of words may automatically identify not only various persons as types, but also the relationships in which they are normatively involved. The way the family is arranged, so that family behaviour is regulated from generation to generation, is laid out in words which when severally pronounced identify the relationships between the members, and tend to memorialize and conserve the usages which the relationships require.

A non-literate culture can in this way maintain a basic identity for itself simply by maintaining the stability of its vocabulary and syntax. The vernacular can do this. Using such a vocabulary one retains after acquisition the information whom to marry and whom not, whom to consort with and whom not, whom to love, whom to hate, what to eat, what to wear; one learns automatic responses to given situations; cultural expectations are supplied.

This kind of stored information works automatically; its directive power over behaviour is exercised below the level of conscious thought. Yet its location resides in the individual brains of members of the group. Can these individuals be relied on to respond automatically and always to the common signals of the language, to obey them with consistency? Will the signals be implemented by responses which are automatic reflexes? Will a man and a woman always mate according to the rules, whatever they are, of mating? Will they automatically treat their children according to prescribed modes of nurture and protection? Will they remain content with property duly inherited? Will they always perform the tasks allotted to them by group modes of division of labour? Or will they inter-mittently wish to behave eccentrically, in terms of the common code? Will they wish to trespass, secretly to steal or openly to rob by violence? Will they use hostility towards friends rather than their proper enemies? Will they simply with-draw into idleness and sloth?

These are random examples of the phenomenon of human individuation, per-ceptible in the behaviour of the human brain and extending to differentiation in the shapes of human bodies. While it is true that animals exhibit some individuation within a given species, its degree is limited; the social behaviour of an animal group in terms of mating habits, food gathering, rearing of offspring and the like proceeds according to programmes which seem self-fulfilling. In human society the component members can behave on the one hand as though they were members of a herd, and on the other as though they were living outside the herd. Man's behaviour in culture reflects the tension between these opposed tendencies, and the tension is reflected in the way language is used. For its role is paradoxical: on the one hand, the accepted mores, a stability of expected relationships, are woven into its syntax; on the other, it can be spoken in ways to justify the repudiation of what is expected; it can be spoken as it were defiantly as well as conventionally; it can be used to express the arrogance of the individual over against the claims of the common consensus. Human societies, unlike animal ones, contain inherently the seeds of their own instability. The individuation which renders this possible is itself a function of language. What is needed is language applied to the purpose of warning against this possibility and suggesting means of correction when it occurs. Society will need some form of managed language beyond the vernacular. The linguistic signals governing behaviour will have to be made more explicit.

It will be thought that these conclusions coincide with the emergence of a body of law, oral or written, promulgated by chiefs, judges, courts, kings, oligarchs, to which obedience is required from members of the group and enforced by penalty. But this way of looking at it oversimplifies the historical process by accelerating it. Literacy has made modern societies familiar with the notion of laws in the plural existing as a corpus of institutions, procedures and penalties for violation. These, however, are only the end product of a need experienced in developing societies to formulate special statements of many kinds which are framed to guide, control and correct. Let us call these directives, varying in influence and importance, but framed as explicit statements of what ought to be done.

There remains one body of cultural knowledge which, whatever the form of government, must in an oral society become communal. This can be described as a general awareness of custom-law, apprehended not in the shape of specific edicts but as a body of maxims or sayings which describe the proprieties of behaviour both personal and social. These proprieties constitute the 'mores' of the society, to use a Latin term; in the Greek they are conveniently identified in the words 'nomos' and 'ethos' in the singular, or 'nomoi' and 'ethe' in the plural: the custom-laws, the folkways, the habits of a people. It is of interest to note that by etymology both these terms, which when literalized can be rendered as 'law' and 'ethics', signify in their original usage not principles or beliefs but localized human activities, that of distributing or managing land in the case of 'nomos', and that of living in a place or a haunt in the case of 'ethos'. Their inspiration is behaviouristic, not philosophic, legal, or moralist. This body of maxims (as they become when incorporated in contrived statements) represents the common consciousness of the group, its sense of what is fitting, decorous and seemly. It corresponds somewhat to the literate notion of equity, whether legal or moral.

Overall, the knowledge that has been stored in the form of wisdom or of history in this manner will wear the appearance to literate eyes of being 'religious'. The whole secular body of knowledge and skills has to be preserved in linguistic formulas which are ritualistically memorized, and in reenactments which are ritualistically performed. The gods standing at the apex of group history preside over the whole body of knowledge. They authenticate it. They represent not so much an article of faith as a means of identity.

The rules for preservation, which alone will make storage effective as a control over behaviour, will continue to require stability in the statements made, so that they survive not subject to arbitrary alteration or faulty memorization. But this rule has to go beyond what is found in the general proprieties of word connection; it must in the case of explicit statements require that the words composing them and their syntactical relations both remain unchanged. Specific statements are now required which per se can survive without modification.

We are asking of an oral culture this question: do you have any device, the equivalent of documentation in a literate culture, which is available to guarantee that a series of words shall be preserved in the oral memory in an order of relationship which does not change as this series is transmitted from mouth to mouth and memory to memory? One which preserves a unique syntax between uniquely chosen words and not just a general syntax of the language? Yes, comes the answer, there is one way to do this: the words have to be arranged in a rhythmic sequence which is independent of the words themselves considered as words but to which they have to respond acoustically. The mouth, which has learned to arrange speech sounds to conform to the grammar of the linguistic code, must now learn the further trick of so selecting these sounds that they not only 'make sense' but set up a kind of music in the ear both for speaker and listener which is governed by rhythmic periods which repeat themselves. The recall of this kind of 'music' itself makes some demand on the memory, but the act of recall is relatively easy because rhythms are repetitive; that is their essence; they can provide a spell, a standardized incantation to which the words of a required statement can be fitted so that as pronounced they reproduce the rhythm. Once so placed, they remain relatively immune to arbitrary change or imperfect recollection, for their order cannot be shifted (Havelock, 1982, pp. 115–19).

Preservation after this rhythmic fashion will involve a new order of memorization, lying outside the ability to learn a language code. Whether this secondary ability is genetically encoded as language, or whether it is only a learned ability, part of the programme which our species has devised for itself, is an unsolved question.

The saying or the parable can furnish clues to the consciousness of a people, but not the key to that consciousness. To achieve extension of statement required the invention of an extendible rhythm, converting it into a repetitive metre, which produces what may be described as a series of sayings of roughly equal acoustic length, following one another as a series of waves in extended duration. The oral memory by this method is led on to recall the sequences, and so master a whole programme of instruction. Such, it is suggested, is the genesis of the epic as it has subsisted in all oral cultures. It arises in response not to artistic impulse but to functional need. It constitutes a massive attempt at oral storage of cultural information for re-use.

Within a strictly non-literate culture storage will range in coverage from the closed saying through the ritual hymn to the longer myth and the extended epic. An oral culture will found itself on a compendious body of stored information, directive or descriptive, which is expressed in rhythmic language apart from the vernacular and which can be thought of as an enclave of contrived speech existing within the vernacular. Its vocabulary is likely to be specialized to some extent when compared with vernacular converse but such specialization, whether a result of archaic survival or invented contrivance, will be such as to increase the rhythmic capacity of the statements. To this enclave the oral society will entrust the overt expression of its 'nomos' and 'ethos', its 'mores', its 'values', to use a literate and rather misleading term. While the syntax of the vernacular tongue will betray the proprieties of behaviour practised by the group, the enclave will memorialize their importance; it will describe what happens when they are contravened; it will admonish and alert; above all, it will energize in language the sense of identity of the group.

In modern parlance priest, bard, prophet and sage define separate types of specialist. Originally, they can be thought of as representing divergent aspects of a common craft, the exercise of which gave such specialists their power in oral society. It is to be noted that with the onset of craft literacy the rituals of cult become incorporated in documented formulas, that is, in liturgies, incantations and the like, which are likely to be hoarded in varying degrees of sanctity, which means secrecy. Hence the power of the priest in craft literate societies, as for instance in Jewish society after the reign of Solomon, tends to increase at the expense of the minstrel and the prophet. He has acquired the functions of a scribe.

The common office and honour of such specialists in the community rested upon their control of the information contained in their poetry, and which their art rendered transmissible between the generations. They were the 'authorities', but equally, the acceptance of this authority in the absence of documentation rested upon the degree to which their songs, hymns, incantations, epics and dances were communicated to the populace at large and held in the memories of the individuals thereof. This would require constant participation of audiences at oral performance to guarantee the safe transmission of the whole verbal enclave of contrived speech. It became far otherwise when a craft literate monopoly over documentation allowed its practitioners to control an interpretation of sacred writings not otherwise available. In the linguistic sense all oral societies had to be functionally 'democratic', if that much misused term is allowable.

If it is a mistake to seek to separate the bard from the priest and prophet in oral society, it is equally mistaken to view him as a mere entertainer. Entertainment was one of the objectives of performance, but this was subordinate to the performer's functional role as the reciter of preserved statements. A festival of recitation, of song and epic accompanied by dancing, was no more or less sacred, and so protected, than a ritual sung before a shrine, nor was it any more or less entertaining. The notion of poetry as the expression of purely aesthetic values in the modern literate sense must be given up as we approach the poetry of preliteracy. The explorer Captain James Cook encountered in Tahiti in 1769 a preliterate society wholly free at that time from literate contact or contamination. His report has the advantage of naivete. He was not an anthropologist seeking to organize and interpret what he saw or heard. Though ignorant of the language, he was able to become aware of the existence of a speech specially contrived. He noted the activities of the Tahitian specialist who managed the songs, recitations, the dances and the rituals. His biographer also describes how he encountered the 'marae', family structures made of coral stone containing courtyard and altar surrounded by sacred trees, which are 'ministered to by a priesthood the very language of whose invocations was an esoteric thing.' But was it? Was the rhythmic structure and functional purpose of this language any different in essence from the performance in mime, dance, recitation and song which were managed by the 'arivi', who, it is said, celebrated 'the seasonal festivals and those that marked the great events of communal life.' Such reports describe a functioning apparatus of oral education. The explorer, equipped with the presuppositions of a literacy in which such performances had become only entertainment, could view the 'arivi' only as 'strolling players'. Their true social function eluded him (Havelock, 1978, pp. 20–2).

Did oral society make any provision for teaching any part of the code as contained in rhythmic speech to children and adolescents? We should distinguish here between specialized information transmissible within families of specialists, and that which could be viewed as constituting a programme of general education for the society as a whole. The practices observed in Tahiti seem to reveal a degree of partnership between the populace and the specialists who performed and recited constantly before audiences who listened and may have participated. The effect of constant performance would be to diffuse a memory of the contrived language among the populace as a whole; the oral wisdom became thus transmissible between the generations simply by its reiterated recital.

There is a Homeric passage which may reflect a more structured method of guaranteeing the continuity of the tradition. Andromache, lamenting the fate of her son after his father Hector has fallen in battle, commemorates the lot of the male orphan in the following words (*Iliad*, 22.490–499):

> The loss of a father isolates a child from other children
> He hangs his head his cheeks streaked with tears
> In his destitution the child resorts to his father's associates
> Tugging one by his cloak and another by his tunic
> They may take compassion on him and one will hold out a cup to him for just a sip
> The taste will touch his lips but will not touch his palate
> But another boy with living parents will beat the boy out of the banquet
> Hammering him with fists and harrying him with insults
> 'Beat it! Your father is not a member of our banquet. You have not got a father.'
> And in tears the child resorts to his widowed mother.

In a later age when the institution described had fallen into disuse, the passage was felt to be an inappropriate digression and was obelized. It can be suggested, however, that it lifts for a brief moment the veil which normally shrouds those proceedings which were adopted in an oral society for educating children. The male child attended the common mess table of his elders (the Greek word rendered 'associates' also means 'mess-mates'), the one to which his father was assigned; his father's presence guaranteed his own right to attend. Why was attendance important to him? The passage celebrates only the consumption of food and drink, but he could get these from his mother. Such symposia, however, were also the occasion for musical performance accompanying the recital of encomia, songs and epic narratives. The practice continued throughout Greek history, though in later and literate conditions its character changed; musical recital from memory was replaced by bookish quotations, as in *The Professors at Dinner*, a work by an author of the late second century after Christ which purports to describe the learned conversation at one of these occasions. Literacy had banished any need for the presence of the younger generation, who now learnt to read in schools. But in an oral culture, the boys, listening to their parents celebrate, learnt themselves to some degree to master the skills of contrived speech. In such a social context, assisted by private tuition, a hero like Achilles would himself learn the art of singing the deeds of heroes. Learning these, he would learn also to be 'a speaker of words' as well as a 'doer of deeds' (*Iliad*, 9. 442–443). In the last third of the fifth century BC Aristophanes produced a comedy called 'The Banqueters' which featured fathers and sons at mess-tables. The institution was still in being aty that time or it could not have been exploited by the dramatist for comic purposes.

child, 'Please be quiet', they frequently adopt such indirect forms as 'I hear talking.' As they point out, given conventions of the classroom, these indirect directives are polite forms of speech. However, we may note in addition that by simply commenting upon the violation of a norm, teachers attribute the norm not to themselves but to a transcendental source, and the norm thereby carries greater authority by being above criticism.

The speaker/speech distinction may also help to explain Feldman and Wertsch's (1975) finding that teachers in classrooms rarely used modal auxiliaries (such as may, might, or could) or expressions of uncertainty (such as I think, believe, hope, or feel). If teachers take themselves to be the exponents of someone else's views, those of the textbook writer, that absence is quite understandable. As the views they express are not their own but those of the textbooks, their personal feelings, perceptions and so on are irrelevant.

The description offered of the authority of textbooks may appear too Victorian to be a valid description of the attitude of students to textbooks in modern, liberalized schools; nor does it seem to characterize the uses of textbooks by the more highly educated or especially the members of a professional group or academic peer group. As we well know, we (the readers of this volume) disagree with much of what we read even if it does often appear to come from a transcendental source; and even if it does appear to come from a transcendental source we attribute it to a writer who, we assume, is much like ourselves. This suggests the operation of an addititation factor, a factor which may underlie the development of critical reading as opposed to the study, memorization and assimilation of texts we discussed earlier. This point takes on additional significance when we consider the fact that educational authorities have more recently called not only for learning but also for critical thinking.

As Goody (1978), Lakoff (1977), Brown and Levinson (1978) and many others have shown, to ask a question, to make an assertion, to issue a command, or to make a pronouncement, you must have the right within some relevant social group. The same is true, I suggest, for the right to criticism and to dissent. The social relations required for the free offering of requests and assertions and their equally free criticism/rejection may be called peer relations. Thus children with their peers freely make assertions and deny others (cf. Klein and Miller, 1979; McTear, 1979), and academics with their colleagues freely advance ideas and criticize the ideas of others because they act as a peer group; they have the right to speak and to be heard as equals. Once admitted to a peer group, the written work of peers is again taken as an expression of the views of the individual who wrote them; the author and his text are reunited, so to speak. Anything that could now be said directly to the author as an equal (perhaps even more) can also be said/written against his text. That is, a peer group both invites the possibility of criticism and reunites the author with his writings. Membership in that peer group comes at least in part from being a participant in that particular form of discourse, that is, through becoming a writer. It is this peer relationship, I suggest, which invites critical reading and critical thought.

The situation, however, is very different for the author's subordinates, namely, students and audiences, and especially the author's exponents, namely teachers, who, because the words are neither their own nor originate with a known member of their own peer group, lack the right to criticism. It is interesting to note that Rousseau (1966), in his *Essay on the Origin of Languages*, pointed out that he distrusted script for this very reason; writing and especially print removed the accent and signature of the speaker from his utterance which therefore took on a spurious life and authority of its own (Derrida, 1976). This divorce, as suggested above, is a source of authority of the written word.

There are, therefore, two obvious ways of enhancing the prestige and authority of assertions and thereby of assuring the perlocutionary effect of assent. One is to make the claims true and valid and thereby 'above' suspicion; the other is to originate from a superior source and therefore be 'above' suspicion. These two are ordinarily conflated. Even true ideas come under heavy criticism, as Kuhn (1962) and others have shown, from peers and superiors — Roentgen from Lord Kelvin, or Galileo from Pope Urban VIII and so on. But even partial truths originating from authorities, elders, or some more transcendental source, tend to minimize criticism. And criticism is least likely when ideas have both some validity and a transcendental source. Textbooks, like religious ritual, have both some validity and a transcendental source. Textbooks, like religious ritual, are devices for putting ideas and beliefs above criticism.

When viewed in terms of their function, then, ritualized speech in a traditional society and written texts in a literate society turn out to have much in common. Both ritualized speech and written texts serve an important archival function in preserving what the society takes to be 'true' and 'valid' knowledge, knowledge from which rules of thought and action may be derived. They both help to preserve the social order by minimizing dispute. This task is achieved, however, in quite different ways, depending upon, as Havelock(Chapter 17, this volume) has pointed out, the form in which knowledge is stored for re-use. If stored in oral form, it appears as memorable, clear exemplars, pithy sayings, ritualized speech and condensed symbols. If stored in written form, it appears as lists and tables and in the detailed, explicit, expository prose of essays, encyclopedias and textbooks. But in both cases the knowledge so stored carries great authority because it appears to originate in a transcendental source, at least in a source other than the present speaker or a member of his or her peer group. Textbooks, thus, constitute a distinctive linguistic register involving a particular form of language (archival written prose), a particular social situation (schools) and social relations (author-reader) and a particular form of linguistic interaction (reading and study).

Any archival form, being traditionally or historically grounded, calls for comprehension and production strategies somewhat different from those employed in everyday speech, skills which may in fact require sustained 'education' for their acquisition. Basic to those strategies is the displacement of that speech from the speaker and the context of its production. That separation, I have suggested, produces an alteration in the illocutionary force and in preparatory conditions of utterance, with the result that the child's role is changed from that of participant to that of a recipient of language. The development of competence as a writer may again win for her or him the social role of equal participant and critic, but this time in the community of writers (see van Peer, Chapter 10, this volume). The child's growing competence with this somewhat specialized and distinctive register of language may contribute to the similarly specialized and distinctive mode of thought we usually associate with formal education.

Notes

1 An early form of this paper was presented as a seminar to the Department of Social Anthropology, Cambridge University, April 1979 and published in *Journal of Communication*, Winter 1980.
2 The propositional structure is more important than the semantic structure of such texts as indicated by the fact that meanings are supposed to be invariant across paraphrase; the same is not true, of course, for ritualized speech in which the 'very words' are critical.

References

BEGG, I. (1971) 'Recognition memory for sentence meaning and wording,' *Journal of Verbal Learning and Verbal Behavior*, 10, 176–81.
BELLACK, A. A., KLIEBARD, H.M., HYMAN, R.T. and SMITH, F.L. (1966) *The Language of the Classroom*. New York: Teachers College Press.
BLACK, H. (1967) *The American Schoolbook*. New York: William Morrow.
BLOCH, M. (1974) 'Symbols, song, dance and features of articulation,' *Archives Européennes de Sociologie*, 15, 55–81.
BLOCH, M. (Ed.) (1975) *Political Language and Oratory in Traditional Society*. London: Academic Press.
BROWN, P. and LEVINSON, S. (1978) 'Universals in language usage: Politeness phenomena,' in GOODY, E. (Ed.), *Questions and Politeness*. Cambridge: Cambridge University Press.
BROWN, R. (1977) 'Introduction,' in SNOW, C. and FERGUSON, C. (Eds), *Talking to Children: Language Input and Acquisition*. Cambridge: Cambridge University Press.
DERRIDA, J. (1976) *Of Grammatology*. Trans. G. SPIVAK, Baltimore, Md.: Johns Hopkins University Press.
EISENSTEIN, E.L. (1980) *The Printing Press an Agent of Change: Communications and Cultural Transformations in Early-Modern Europe*. Cambridge: Cambridge University Press.
FELDMAN, C. and WERTSCH, J. (1975) *Context Dependent Properties of Teachers' Speech*. Unpublished manuscript, Harvard University School of Education.
FERGUSON, C. (1977) 'Baby talk as a simplified register,' in SNOW, C. and FERGUSON, C. (Eds), *Talking to Children: Language Input and Acquisition*. Cambridge: Cambridge University Press.
FINNEGAN, R. (1977) *Oral Poetry: Its Nature, Significance, and Social Context*. Cambridge: Cambridge University Press.
GOODY, E.N. (1978) 'Towards a theory of questions,' in GOODY, E.N. (Ed.), *Questions and Politeness: Strategies in Social Interaction*. Cambridge: Cambridge University Press.
GOODY, J. and WATT, I. (1968/1963) 'The consequences of literacy,' in GOODY, J. (Ed.), *Literacy in Traditional Societies*. Cambridge: Cambridge University Press.
GREENFIELD, P. (1972) 'Oral and written language: The consequences for cognitive development in Africa, the United States, and England,' *Language and Speech*, 15, 169–78.
GREGORY, M. and CARROLL, S. (1978) *Language and Situation*. London: Routledge and Kegan Paul.

HALLIDAY, M.A.K. and HASAN, R. (1976) *Cohesion in English*. London: Longman.

HAVELOCK, E. (1973) 'Prologue to Greek literacy,' *Lectures in Memory of Louise Taft Semple* (second series, 1966–1971). Cincinatti, Ohio: University of Oklahoma Press for the University of Cincinatti Press.

HILDYARD, A. and OLSON, D.R. (1978) 'Memory and inference in the comprehension of oral and written discourse,' *Discourse Processes*, 1, 91–117.

HILDYARD, A. and OLSON, D.R. (1981) 'On the bias of oral and written language,' in TANNEN, D. (Ed.), *Advances in Discourse Processes*. Norwood, N.J: Ablex.

HYMES, D. (1962) 'The ethnography of speaking,' in GLADWIN, T. and STURTEVANT, W.C. (Eds), *Anthropology and Human Behavior*. Washington, D.C.: Anthropological Society of Washington.

INNIS, H. (1951) *The Bias of Communication*. Toronto: University of Toronto Press.

KLEIN, W. and MILLER, M. (1979) *Argumentation*. Paper presented at the conference 'Beyond Description in Child Language'. Nijmegen, The Netherlands, June.

KUHN, T. (1962) *The Structure of Scientific Revolutions*. Chicago, Ill.: University of Chicago Press.

LAKOFF, R. (1977) 'Language and society,' in WARDAUGH, R. and BROWN, H. (Eds), *A Survey of Applied Linguistics*. Ann Arbor, Mich.: University of Michigan Press.

LUKES, S. (1973) *Emile Durkheim*. Markham, Ontario: Penguin Books.

LURIA, A.R. (1976) *Cognitive Development: Its Cultural and Social Foundations*. Cambridge, Mass.: Harvard University Press.

McLUHAN, M. (1962) *The Gutenberg Galaxy*. Toronto: University of Toronto Press.

McTEAR, M. (1979) *Getting It Done*. Paper presented at the conference 'Beyond Description in Child Language'. Nijmegen, The Netherlands, June.

MALINOWSKI, B. (1923) 'The problem of meaning in primitive languages,' in OGDEN, C.K. and RICHARDS, I.A. (Eds), *The Meaning of Meaning*. New York: Harcourt, Brace and World.

MESSARIS, P. and CROSS, L. (1977) 'Interpretations of a photographic narrative by viewers in four age groups,' *Studies in the Anthropology of Visual Communication*, 4, 2, 99–111.

OLSON, D.R. (1977) 'From utterance to text: The bias of language in speech and writing,' *Harvard Educational Review*, 47, 257–81.

OLSON, D.R. and TORRANCE, N. (1983) 'Literacy and cognitive development: A conceptual transformation in the early school years,' in MEADOWS, S. (Ed.), *Developing Thinking: Approaches to Children's Cognitive Development*. London: Methuen.

PARRY, M. (1971) 'The making of homeric verse,' in PARRY, A. (Ed.), *The Collected Papers of Milman Parry*. Oxford: Clarendon Press.

ROUSSEAU, J. (1966) 'Essay on the origin of language,' in MORAN, J.H. and CODE, A. (Eds), *On the Origin of Language*. New York: Ungar.

RUBIN, A. (1978) 'A framework for comparing language experiences,' in WALTZ, D.L. (Ed.), *Theoretical Issues in Natural Language Processing*. (TINLAP-2). Urbana-Champaign, Ill.: Association for Computing Machinery and the Association for Computational Linguistics.

SACHS, J. (1974) 'Memory in reading and listening to discourse,' *Memory and Cognition*, 2, 95–100.

SAUSSURE, F. DE (1916/1974) *Course in General Linguistics*. Glasgow: Collins.

SCRIBNER, S. (1968) *The Cognitive Consequences of Literacy*. Unpublished manuscript, Yeshiva University, Albert Einstein College of Medicine, New York.

SCRIBNER, S. and COLE, M. (1978) 'Literacy without schooling: Testing for intellectual effects,' *Harvard Educational Review*, 48, 448–61.

SCRIBNER, S. and COLE, M. (1981) *The Psychology of Literacy*. Cambridge, Mass.: Harvard University Press.

SINCLAIR, J. and COULTHARD, R.M. (1975) *Towards an Analysis of Discourse: The English Used by Teachers and Pupils*. Oxford: Oxford University Press.

TORRANCE, N. and OLSON, D.R. (1987) 'Development of the metalanguage and the acquisition of literacy: A progress report,' *Interchange*, 18, 1/2, 136–46.

WATSON, R. and OLSON, D.R. (1987) 'From meaning to definition: A literate bias on the structures of word meaning,' in HOROWITZ, R. and SAMUELS, S.J. (Eds), *Comprehending Oral and Written Language*. San Diego, Calif.: Academic Press.

Chapter 19

Beyond Criticism: The Authority of the School Textbook

Carmen Luke
James Cook University of North Queensland
Suzanne de Castell
Simon Fraser University
and
Allan Luke
James Cook University of North Queensland

Orientation: Olson on Texts and Schooling

'On the Language and Authority of Textbooks' (Chapter 18, this volume) develops Olson's general discussion of the cognitive and cultural 'bias' of print to explain the force and meaning of a specific genre of text, the school textbook. Our purpose in this chapter is to explore Olson's view of the school text, focusing on the distinctive communicational constraints of both the school text and the classroom context. To this end we will examine the textbook's mode of discourse, the techniques of text construction, its material quality and the institutional practices which circumscribe it. We take note of Foucault's (1972) explanation, which we share, that 'the statement', textual or spoken, embodies an authority and meaning only insofar as it exists in a 'discursive field' — a field of use and exchange.

> To say that statements are residual . . . is not to say that they remain in the field of memory, or that it is possible to rediscover what they meant; but it means that they are preserved by virtue of a number of supports and *material techniques* (of which the book is, of course, only one example), in accordance with certain types of *institutions* (which are not the same in the case of a religious text, a law, or a scientific truth). This also means that they are invested in techniques that put them into operation, in *practices* that derive from them, in the social relations that they form, or, through those relations, modify. (emphasis added; Foucault, 1972, p. 123)

Since the advent of typography and the subsequent rise of mass schooling, society's valid statements have been encoded in and transmitted through books (Eisenstein, 1980; Innis, 1951; Ivins, 1953; Luke, 1988). When we refer to 'curricular knowledge', that which is intentionally transmitted in the classroom, we generally refer to knowledge within the school textbook. Despite historically differing educational aims and instructional approaches, the school text continues to embody the 'authorized version of society's valid knowledge' (Olson, Chapter 18, this volume). In accordance with changing epistemology, ideology and disciplinary knowledge, textbooks are the products of changing techniques which lead to periodic revision, re-editing, obsolescence and replacement of texts (see Apple, Chapter 12, this volume; de Castell and Luke, Chapter 7, this volume). Yet the text qua text has remained constant — a fixed locus within the schooling system from which the means and ends of instruction are derived.

It is claimed that the reason for the enduring centrality of texts to education resides in the distinctive intellectual processing required to extract information from textual language, information which can be preserved because of the permanence of print. Olson draws attention to similarities between ritualized speech in traditional oral societies and written texts in literate societies, showing that both are ways of 'putting ideas and beliefs above criticism', and that both 'serve an important archival function in preserving what the society takes to be "true" and "valid" knowledge . . . from which rules of thought and action may be derived' (p. 241). Olson argues that 'any archival form, being traditionally or historically grounded, calls for comprehension and production strategies somewhat different from those employed in everyday speech, skills that may require sustained "education" for their acquisition' (p. 241). Access to textual knowledge requires an educated sensitivity to the differences between 'what is said', literally, as in print, and 'what is meant', figuratively, as in speech (p. 237).

The significant role of textbooks in education, then, is a function of their ability to 'make meanings more explicit' in a manner which places those meanings 'above criticism'. Olson explains that 'Although never completely successful, these texts are an attempt to construct statements in which the literal meaning is an adequate reflection of the speaker's intentions, and which, as a result, preserve their meanings across speakers and situations' (p. 237). Since schooling aims to transmit to each new generation 'culturally significant knowledge', then, textbooks are an ideal format. Olson suggests this is so for reasons *intrinsic* to texts: 'their linguistic forms per se' (p. 237). The distinctive linguistic register of textbooks involves, according to Olson, 'an emphasis on definitions of terms . . . on meanings formal-ized through a specification of criterial features and strict word boundaries.' Secondly, he notes 'an emphasis on complete and unmarked grammatical forms, typically well-formed declarative sentences', and thirdly, an emphasis on 'explicit logical structure relating clauses and sentences' (p. 237). These structural elements enable textbooks to model 'the bias of writing towards explicit, autonomous meanings.'

Because texts are explicit, and because they preserve 'the very words', they maintain historically grounded, culturally significant information in a durable and objectified form across time and space (Innis, 1951). In this sense, then, the information to be acquired is 'in the text' (Olson, Chapter 18, this volume, p. 239). Olson then specifies the 'social relations expressed and maintained by written text' as 'authorized' valid knowledge which the student must master. Having already shown how the language of texts is different from the oral language of the child, so that a new and difficult set of cognitive and linguistic skills must be mastered before the student can criticize the text, Olson draws attention to the disjunction between the reader and the text author as an additional source of authority. Written texts separate the speech from the speaker, and thereby give texts a kind of 'transcendental' status (p. 239). Olson explains, 'Recall that as long as the speech originates with the current speaker, his listeners know that it is just *his* assertion, and that as a result it is apt to reflect *his* knowledge, *his* interests. . . . Hence his utterances are open to criticism' (p. 239). Intrinsic to textual language, then, is what Olson views as 'a device for managing authority'. The separation of the speech from the speaker/author, which is an intrinsic feature of the written text, tends to make the words 'impersonal, objective and above criticism'.

The centrality of textbooks to schooling, then, derives from the authority of texts, and, for Olson, text authority has two main sources. First, particular linguistic structures make texts explicit, albeit inaccessible, until those structures have been mastered by the student. Second, texts appear 'above criticism' because of the separation of the speaker from the speech, and the corresponding dis-sociation of the speaker from the reader, so providing an impression of textual objectivity and neutral validity.

Olson's is a valuable contribution to understanding the discursive power of the school text. However, his primarily linguistic analysis of school texts needs to be supplemented by a description of the social situations specific to schooling. Hence we may see how textual form and institutional context together constitute text authority. To this end a critical stance will be taken towards each of Olson's major claims prior to elaborating those social relations which, we argue, more fully account for text authority. First, then, we ask whether it is indeed the case that texts are (ideally) explicit, and that knowledge is (ideally) 'in the text'. Second, we question whether it is primarily from the separation of the speaker/author and the speech/text that school texts derive their authority.

Is the Meaning in the Text?

The form and content of school texts do indeed frame school knowledge in a form associated with neutral objectivity (see Crismore, Chapter 11, this volume). The pedagogical danger of the scientific 'framing' of educational knowledge is that it will undermine, rather than enhance, the student reader's capacity to criticize; that, once in the classroom, textual authority will become textual authoritarianism precluding criticism. Authors of disciplinary texts (e.g., maths and science books) strive for clarity of meaning, for explicit and unambiguous presentation of factual data; authors of basal readers strive for unambiguous narratives and tightly controlled syntactic and semantic structures, less likely to be misunderstood by readers and, as Olson notes, to 'delimit possible interpretations'.

Olson sees the school text as an extension of the tradition of the empirical scientific essay (see Heath, Chapter 9, this volume). Royal Society prose style, epitomized in the philosophic treatises of Locke and Hume, set as its goal a 'return back to the primitive purity and shortness, when man delivered so many things, almost in an equal number of words' (Sprat, 1667/1966, pp. 391–2; see also van Peer's discussion, Chapter 10, this volume, of Montaigne as the originator of the 'essai'). Foucault (1977) offers a description of this movement:

> In the 17th and 18th centuries, a totally new conception was developed when scientific texts were accepted on their own merits and positioned within an autonomous and coherent conceptual system of established truths and methods of verification. Authentification no longer required reference to the individual who had produced them; the role of the author disappeared as an index of truthfulness (p. 126).

How successful was this scientific tradition in influencing English prose style? The authors of seventeenth and eighteenth century scientific essays aspired to a completeness within the text itself, such that all salient information, all relevant premises, as well as the logical structure by which they were interrelated, were so clearly explicit that no outside, extra textual reference was required for full comprehension of the text. But whatever the aspirations and pretensions of empirical philosophers and scientists, historical reflection and conceptual analysis tell us that the ideal of a self-contained, totally explicit text is naive and impossible.

Arguing for this neutral, logically explicit character of modern textbooks, Olson notes that the prose style of Locke's *Essay Concerning Human Understanding* (1689/1969) 'well represents the intellectual bias that originated at that time and to a large extent characterizes our present use of language' (Olson, 1977a, p. 268). Yet several historians (Willey, 1934; Purvner, 1967) have argued that this tradition had less impact on the form of modern prose than commonly thought. Purvner notes that

> Though the English language may have derived something more from this idiom of science than Sprat predicted, it is not from this source that modern English has taken its character. The prose form which did emerge triumphantly during the second half of the seventeenth century, the style of which Dryden was the great exponent, was not characterized by scientific starkness. Its outstanding quality was not plainness but flexibility. (1967, p. 99)

Thus, seventeenth century scientific prose spawned a parallel tradition of allusive and satirical prose, exemplified in the essays and broadsides of Swift, Addison and Steele, and Johnson, arguably as rich and historically significant (Kenner, 1962). To claim that the school text, either disciplinary or literary, is a descendant of Royal Society style is to ignore the continuing place of non-scientific literary prose in the education of children. Many intermediate and secondary language arts and reading texts, for instance, still attempt to capture a richness, flexibility and allusiveness of textual language, as reflected in the selection of a wide range of literary and journalistic prose styles.

It is possible as well to critique the notion of a totally explicit and logically entailed text on conceptual grounds. Every disciplinary text necessarily pre-supposes reference to the discipline which makes up its historical and contemporary context. In the absence of such context the text itself cannot possibly 'say what it means'. The premises of an argument may be clearly stated, yet what counts as a relevant premise varies from one discipline to the next. We rely on background disciplinary knowledge in order to know why this premise counts as a premise in every generic case. The logical structure of an argument may be explicitly stated, yet what counts as an argument varies across disciplines — similarly with concepts and their interrelations, discipline-specific lexical usage and so on. In most cases we do not fully understand any particular text until we have some concept of the discipline into which it fits, and in which it has its sense and significance. Conversely, we do not understand the discipline adequately until we are familiar with the historical works which make it up. In the case of the educational text students are reliant on previous courses, readings and teacher explanation: the cumulative background knowledge which makes pursuit of the text's propositional and linguistic features possible in the first place.

Similarly, many literary critics express an increasing scepticism about the possibility of determining a fixed and correct meaning based on the formal 'intrinsic' properties of the text. Fish (1980), for instance, argues that the reader's experience of the text is contingent on strategies learned from an 'interpretive community'. The claim here is that no text is unsituated: that the text is 'rewritten' with each reading. This reader-driven theory of the acquisition of textual knowledge is perhaps extreme, implying as it does that interpretations and interpretive communities wholly determine the meaning of the written text. However, developments in speech act (Searle, 1975), reader response (Fish, 1980), rhetorical (Burke, 1957) and semiotic (Scholes, 1977) theories of literature compel a reconsideration of the belief shared by advocates of scientific prose and the New Criticism alike: that the meaning is in the text, and can be determined solely by reference to the text. Thus, post-New Criticism literary theory draws our attention to the background knowledge of the reader and the social situation of the act of reading as determinants of meaning, interpretation and criticism.

These observations regarding the historical evolution of modern prose, the disciplinary background knowledge of the reader and the situation or context of interpretation all indicate that knowledge is not, nor could it be, 'in the text' *solus*. Arguing against the concept of self-contained and self-justifying curricular knowledge, Esland (1971) notes that 'the problems which are thought to reside *in* a body of knowledge ... are themselves socially constructed' (emphasis added, p. 77). Moreover, the claim to 'autonomous' explicitness is ideological in its attempt to render controversial epistemic assumptions about the institutional selection, framing, distribution and control of curricular knowledge as taken for granted (Young, 1971; see Taxel, Chapter 3, this volume; Wald, Chapter 1, this volume).

With this in mind, we must look critically at Olson's concept of the nature of school texts. Unlike literary works and disciplinary texts, textbooks have a technical structure which punctuates the text, and thereby constrains what can count as authorized textual content (see Crismore, Chapter 11, this volume). As a result, 'what is true in a school book may not be true', for example, 'in a work of historical research' (Austin, 1962, p. 143). Today, as in the recent past, the techniques of curriculum development are evaluation driven so that what counts as curricular knowledge is largely a function of how and by what criteria the acquisition of text knowledge is evaluated. To facilitate instruction and assessment, it is common for school textbooks, and this includes literary works, to frame ideational and skill components into sections that are familiar to us all. Recall, for instance, finding at the end of chapters pages entitled 'concepts and ideas', 'important words', 'things to do', 'fact quizzes', chapter summaries and, most commonly, 'comprehension questions' which guide and delimit our experience of the text. This editorial compartmentalization, aided by graphics and layout formats, reflects a very different discourse structure than that described in Olson's analysis. The intentional sectioning and punctuating of information reinforce the apparently 'neutral' character of the information, and serve distinct instructional ends. But it is not at all the same information as it would be, were it in a linguistic form which derived its authority from the words themselves rather than the various discourse markers inserted by authors and editors for instructional purposes. That is to say, it is this controlled and coded structure of school texts which constrains what is to count as 'being in the text'. Very different information is rendered explicit, with the textbook's editorial and graphic format modifying as it does the reader's response to the prose itself. How, then, can we say, as a generalization, that, like other texts, school texts preserve 'the very words' of the author/speaker 'across generations and cultures'? The notion of the school text as an idealized (explicit) prose does not account for the discourse structure of many basal readers and prescribed course books currently in use.

Similarly, Olson's analysis requires a further specification of the crucial difference between the 'text *per se*' and the text *in use*: more specifically, the text in use in the rule-bound classroom. For the student reader is constrained by a variety of contextual factors *extrinsic* to the text, but *intrinsic* to the social structure of schools. These are very different from the contextual constraints on the reader of popular novels, the literary critic and the scientist.

The Text in Use

Undoubtedly, the school text must be examined for its intrinsic linguistic features. Techniques for assessing readability, lexical cohesion, propositional coherence and discourse structure are necessary hermeneutics to determine the relative accessibility of textual knowledge. However, if we are concerned with the actual sources of text authority, we must consider the extratextual and interactional practices which mediate its educational use. As Watzlawick, Beavin and Jackson (1967) point out, 'Failure to realize the intricacies of the relationships between an event and the matrix in which it takes place . . . either confronts the observer with something "mysterious" or induces him to attribute to his object of study certain properties which the object may not possess' (1967, p. 21).

There is little 'mystery' about what happens to the text once in classroom use. The student's apprehension of textual content and form is controlled by curricular, instructional and administrative guidelines and objectives which have at least as much to do with institutional considerations as cultural and linguistic ones. How and what the student learns from the text is highly dependent on the specific manner in which the text is taught; instructional practices delimit the pragmatic context within which the text is read and interpreted.

Teaching of the text has taken very different forms in different educational epochs. For instance, in late nineteenth and early twentieth century classicist and 3Rs instruction, school texts were primarily literary works and it was assumed that learning the text was best assured through rote memorization and oral recitation of the printed word. Educational progressivism de-emphasized text-centred learning and called for silent reading and 'learning by doing' instruction; texts featured 'interesting' stories about local situations. The text was not abandoned, but was to be interpreted and 'experienced' through interactive projects and discussions (de Castell and Luke, 1986). Hence much of what would yet be seen as textbook knowledge was acquired in largely oral dialogical settings, rather than through a monological confrontation with the text, as under classicist methods. Today's paradigm text is the programmed instructional manual; students learn 'skills' rather than coherent bodies of literature and disciplinary knowledge. The text is taught through the guise of multimedia approaches; lesson packages channel learning of the printed word through games, films, skill-level workbooks and prepared activity worksheets (Lorimer, 1986; see Lorimer and Keeney, Chapter 13, this volume; de Castell and Luke, Chapter 7, this volume). This remains, indeed, teaching the text — yet the media of instruction are now so diverse that, in effect, different sets of discourse structures, both within and outside the text, are conveyed to students.

Teaching of the text, moreover, takes various forms within the same historical period. Anyon's (1981) comparison of the curriculum and the 'curriculum in use' indicates that the same text may yield different meanings and themes according to variations in social context. As a result, 'students of different social class backgrounds are likely to be exposed to qualitatively different types of educational knowledge' (p. 3).

By contrast, Olson's analysis is framed in terms of the student reader's unmediated confrontation with the text. We need to recognize, however, that the student's relationship with the text is by no means personal and unmediated. Historically, teaching of the text has always been the teacher's primary function. This presumes that the text necessitates skilled interpretation, so that a mediator is required between textual knowledge and the preliterate, unschooled student. This mediated relationship is analogous to that of the lay and deity in the Middle Ages, which required authoritative scriptural exegesis (Eisenstein, 1980; Graff, 1987a, 1987b). The Medieval Great Chain of Being involved a hierarchical structure of mediation between the biblical text and the common person, and called upon the talents of élite literati (Chaytor, 1966).

Similarly, teachers are the modern-day arbiters of textual knowledge. They are the elders, the 'clerics' who initiate children not only into the prescribed knowledge of an era, but also into the literate processes requisite to the acquisition and application of that knowledge. Moreover, it is from teachers that students acquire not only a corpus of knowledge and skills, but also an attitude towards learning — in literary terms, a 'sensibility' towards the text. In this respect the teacher is like the literary critic, an arbiter of questions of style, aesthetic taste, propositional validity and rhetorical force, who provides student readers with a running metatextual commentary with which to process the text (see Baker and Freebody, Chapter 21, this volume).

Thus, the school text is always the object of teacher mediation. One instructs with and through the text; a student confronts textual knowledge via teacher mediation. In the classroom situation the text is the locus of information exchange. Inasmuch as the text for a particular subject, theme, or topic constrains the content of classroom information exchange, so does the teacher mediate the exchange between student and text. And within this communicational system of the classroom, a system supporting a particular structure of information exchange (Wells, 1981; Stubbs, 1983), the student assumes an acquiescent, *non-authoritative status* in relation to both the text and teacher.

Conventional classroom discourse is about the text, based on the text, or directed by it. Teachers introduce, explain, discuss the text and assess comprehension of both form and content. Although more commonly, instructional methods and objectives are externally directed by teachers' guides and curricular guidelines, teachers individually interpret both mode of instruction and textual knowledge. Probably much to the dismay of curriculum developers who seek to 'teacher-proof' instructional systems, when teachers read to children they cannot help but intonate, pause and discuss in an individually selective manner. As Elbaz (1981) has noted, teachers are not 'passive transmitters of knowledge' (cf. McNeil, 1987). Tacitly and intentionally, teachers will emphasize and de-emphasize, select and exclude. This teacher interpretation of what is to be learned from the text helps define for the student what must be acquired as text knowledge. Partly, this is because students soon learn that what a teacher selects and emphasizes in a text will most likely be tested. Tests, examinations and daily reinforcement of 'correct' student response reflect a particular 'reading' of the text, a distinct and often idiosyncratic interpretation of what is important and valuable within it. In this *context of use*, then, the text is necessarily reconstituted in an operational sense by a prior pedagogical reading, which may or may not 'preserve the very words' of the authored text.

Author, Authority and Authorization

Ideally, textual discourse, print, is more open to criticism than speech, utterance (Goody, 1977; Olson, 1977 a). The permanence of written language allows it to be reread and more closely scrutinized than language used in speech. Textual information can be assimilated and compared within and between texts; the permanent character of writing enables the reader to comment critically upon the text. In dialogue, however, the hearer cannot catalogue in memory with any reliable precision the linear sequencing of data, the logical argumentation of the speaker. Hence, it is more difficult to detect inconsistencies or contradictions in speech.

Goody (1977), Olson (1977 a) and McLuhan (1962), furthermore, argue that exposure to textual media biases the reader's cognitive processing in favour of the linear representation of logical, analytical thought. It would appear, then, that the school text should lend itself to critical analysis and scepticism on the part of student readers, particularly in the absence of direct speaker/author immediacy. In most school situations, however, neither text nor teacher utterance is criticized forcefully, much less critically analyzed. We may explain the latter phenomenon by reference to the institutional authority relations which place the student in subordinate status to the teacher. And in part, we accept Olson's explanation that the views teachers express may be seen not as their own (and hence open to criticism) but as those of the text, the text transformed into utterance.

How may we explain this failure to criticize the text, particularly in the light of the arguments supporting the inherently criticizable character of textual knowledge? Olson draws our attention to the 'more highly educated or especially the members of a professional group or academic peer group' (p. 240) who, of course, typically criticize texts. But, he explains, 'To ask a question, to make an assertion, to issue a command, or to make a pronouncement, you must have the right within some relevant social group. The same is true, we suggest, for the right to criticism and dissent. . . .' (Chapter 18, this volume, p. 240) Students are not within the appropriate and sanctioned social group to be entitled to criticize the school text. In classroom discourse students' claims to an equally authoritative 'reading' of the text as that of the teacher can lack legitimate status, becoming 'mis-invocations' (Austin, 1962): speech acts undermined by the speakers' lack of legal status. So it would seem that what situates texts 'above criticism' has less to do with authorial absence. The explanation lies, rather, in the social relations governing the production and use of texts. Olson explains that 'students and audiences, and especially . . . teachers . . . because the words are neither their own nor originate with a known member of their peer group, lack the right to criticism' (p. 240–241).

The conditions of exclusion from 'rightful' criticism imply a correlative condition of inclusion, granting the 'right' to criticize the school text. Olson writes:

> Once admitted to a peer group, the written work of peers is again taken as an expression of the views of the individual who wrote them; the author and the text are reunited, so to speak. And anything that could now be said directly to the author as an equal (and perhaps even more) can now be said/written against his text. That is, a peer group both invites the possibility of criticism and reunites the author with his writing. Member-ship in that peer group comes at least in part from being a participant in that particular form of discourse, that is, through becoming a writer. (Chapter 18, this volume, p. 240)

This condition of inclusion in the 'peer group' whose right it is to criticize the text is, however, a limited explanation of the criticism of the *school* text, because it idealizes the relation of author, text and reader which occurs in the context of the school. Author, text and reader stand in different relation where texts derive their authority from being 'authorized' rather than 'authored' (see also Apple and Lorimer and Keeney, Chapters 12 and 13, this volume).

Let us examine this claim further. Olson parallels the relationship of speaker/utterance/hearer with that of author/text/reader. Within this schema, to accept or criticize the utterance, the hearer consults or questions the speaker. To accept or criticize the text, on the other hand, the reader consults or questions the author necessarily on the basis of the authored text. Both situations presuppose that the authority to adjudicate questions of meaning rests with the originator of the text or utterance. Utterance gives us access to the speaker as, in the sense explained by Olson, 'one among equals'. We have 'rightful' access to the author if, according to Olson, we have gained admission to the relevant interpretive community, part of that condition involving the ability to write a (critical) text of the relevant quality and kind. However, what counts as the relevant kind or level of critical 'rewriting' in the case of school textbooks is different from that of other generic types of texts. With the separation of reading and writing as distinct areas of class-room instruction, admission to a peer group (i.e., grade level, reading group, or stream) is more often granted on the basis of an achievement test score than the student's capacity to write 'against the text'. Furthermore, the authority of the textbook comes, not in virtue of its authorial origin, but in virtue of its having been *authorized* by an administrative source, whose authority in turn is insti-tutionally bound and not solely based on authorial peer group membership.

The school text, unlike most other print information, such as scholarly journals, mass paperbacks, magazines and newspapers, is unique in its culturally stipulated role of authority. The legal enforcement and sanction of public schooling not only ensures a universal right to education, but also enforces partici-pation. Thus, the textbook has a legally assured captive audience. Government prescribed and authorized texts constitute a common experiential and linguistic basis upon which each generation's fundamental literacy and knowledge are based. Indeed, while a given textbook may not be as widely circulated as, say, *Time* or *Educational Sesearcher*, it is universally (i.e., regionally) taught and experienced. Almost all children who attended North American schools between 1950 and 1960, for example, read about Dick and Jane, Spot and Puff. In contrast, the adult's out-of-school acquisition of knowledge from print is an individually selective process which is not guided by the institutional rules and teacher interpretation which mediate knowledge acquired from prescribed print in schools. Foucault argues that even the *same* text, or statement, is transformed when used in a particular insti-tutional context:

> Similarly, between the text of a Constitution, or a will, or a religious revelation, and all the manuscripts or printed copies that reproduce them exactly, with the same writing, in the same characters, and on similar substances, one cannot say that there is an equivalence: on the one hand

... [their] identity varies with a complex set of material institutions. ...
(1972, p. 103)

If the identity of a textual statement, its meaning and authority, are dependent upon an epistemic 'ground' and institutional support, then the conditions for criticism are likewise derivative. As Anyon's (1981) study shows, class-differentiated treatments of the text result in extreme variations in students' (learned) conceptions of the nature, validity and criticizability of 'school knowledge'.

Through what literate and epistemic achievement, then, could the 'right' to criticize, or to gain entry into the 'peer group' be had? In fact, neither literate ability nor scholarly achievement could be sufficient conditions for this right. The 'authorization' which is the actual ground of the authority of the school text is completely contingent in relation to those conditions identified by Olson's analysis. That is to say, the conditions specified by Olson as reasons for the text being 'above criticism' do not fully explain or justify that status; they function instead to legitimate as 'above criticism' institutional mechanisms which are in fact *beyond criticism*.

The Textbook as Icon

In his explication of 'the social relations expressed and maintained by written texts', Olson suggests that '... it may be because children assume that textbooks have greater authority that they are willing to devote serious and prolonged study to books, rather than simply reading them' (p. 239). He is referring to the communicational devices, structurally inherent in written language, which 'may make the words impersonal, objective and above criticism' — specifically, the separation of speech from the speaker. Olson additionally notes that 'it is the role of books in our culture that makes them an ultimate authority in matters of dispute.'

Why should we presuppose that 'children *assume* that textbooks have greater authority' [emphasis added], when we know with certainty that this is what children are taught to believe? Olson's claim for the authority of texts is largely based on differences between oral and written codes such that the absence of the speaker renders the text immune from criticism. But as he points out, the institutional authority relation between student and teacher parallels the status difference between reader and writer. And why should we suppose that the student's belief in the authority of texts derives from the intrinsic structural features of written language or from cultural tradition, rather than from the nature of school authority relations? The point is, of course, that we cannot explain text authority exclusive from school authorization. Our inquiry into textbooks must be, advise Watzlawick, Beavin and Jackson (1967), 'extended to include the effects ... on others, their reactions to it, and the context in which this all takes place' (p. 21). We must extend our focus from 'the artificially isolated monad to the relationship between the parts of a wider system.' Surely, it is within the context of the classroom that a *systemic*, rather than a structural analysis of authority must be sought. By taking the classroom situation into account, then, that context can be

than to their actual authors. Thus, for students authorship is more often irrelevant than a distinctive source of textual authority, and that irrelevance gives rise to yet another level of institutional misnomers which detach the text even further from the author (e.g., 'the blue reader', 'your skilpak'). The school text is thus more closely associated with a corpus of 'indisputable' disciplinary or lesson content than with a potentially fallible author.

It is even more tightly associated with the teacher in charge of that subject-matter. For it is the teacher/mediator who explains text material, who directs dialogue about a text, who indicates closure of a lesson and who, in this sense, embodies and reconstitutes the text in use. Finally, it is the teacher who tests student performance in modes of textual exegesis, be they decoding, recall, comprehension, or formal criticism. Thus teachers are in fact, and by status, in command of textual knowledge. As such, text and teacher can be seen to co-constitute a domain of knowledge, and to co-constitute one authoritative identity.

The Curriculum Is Not in the Text

It is our contention that the effectiveness of the textbook is, above all, dependent on its status as part of a comprehensive and rule-bound institutional order. The student responds to the text as but another element of the larger institution as much as she/he responds to the actual language and content of the textbook per se. Over the last decade reading researchers have maintained that the student's responses to the text are conditioned by prior knowledge, coded into ideational schemata (Anderson and Pearson, 1984). One implication of schema theories is that the student's cultural and class background, as well as commonsense knowledge and linguistic competence developed outside the school (Olson, 1977b), affect his/her ability to apprehend and assimilate textual knowledge. Consistently overlooked, however, is the student's schematic knowledge of the school, classroom and teacher, which mediates reactions to all aspects of the schooling process, a principal one of which is the school text.

It seems clear, however, that in order to take into account 'the context in which the phenomenon occurs', we must also focus on both the de jure (legitimated) and de facto (actual) status of teacher and textbook in the classroom. The power of the word of the textbook is premised on the social rules governing the environment of the reader, as much as on the intrinsic structural and linguistic features of the text. We have argued for a more interactive and pragmatic explanation of text apprehension whereby meaning is contingent on the inter-action between the reader's prior knowledge, the institutional setting within which the reading task is situated, the teacher who teaches the text and the distinctive features of the textbook per se. This relationship, we have noted, is delimited and constrained by the rules of schooling which position teacher, text and student in hierarchical levels of power and authority.

The school textbook is currently the object of exhaustive research, development, marketing and implementation. Curriculum designers and reading psychologists are continually altering, adjusting and redesigning texts in search of more effective ways of conveying textual knowledge. In light of this relatively recent enthusiasm, it is instructive to recognize that the curriculum — its form and content, its validity and authority — is *not* 'in the text'.

References

ANDERSON, R.C. and PEARSON, P.D. (1984) 'A schema-theoretic view of reading,' in PEARSON, P.D. (Ed.), *Handbook of Reading Research*. New York: Longman.

ANYON, J. (1981) 'Social class and school knowledge,' *Curriculum Inquiry*, 11, 1, 3–42.

APPLE, M. (1979) *Ideology and Curriculum*. London: Routledge and Kegan Paul.

AUSTIN, J. (1962) *How to Do Things with Words*. Cambridge, Mass.: Harvard University Press.

BARTHES, R. (1977) *Image — Music — Text*. New York: Hill and Wang.

BURKE, K. (1957) *The Philosophy of Literary Form*. 2nd ed. New York: Vintage.

CASTELL, S. DE and LUKE, A. (1986) 'Models of literacy in North American schools: Social and historical conditions and consequences,' in CASTELL, S. DE, LUKE, A. and EGAN, K. (Eds), *Literacy, Society and Schooling*. Cambridge: Cambridge University Press.

CHAYTOR, H.J. (1966) *From Script to Print: An Introduction to Modern Vernacular Literature* (2nd ed.) London: Sidgwick and Jackson.

EISENSTEIN, E. (1980) *The Printing Press as an Agent of Change: Communications and Cultural Transformations in Early Modern Europe*. Cambridge: Cambridge University Press.

ELBAZ, F. (1981) 'The teacher's practical knowledge: Report of a case study,' *Curriculum Inquiry*, 11, 1, 43–71.

ESLAND, G. (1971) 'Teaching and learning as the organization of knowledge,' in YOUNG, M.F.D. (Ed.), *Knowledge and Control: New Directions in the Sociology of Education*. London: Collier Macmillan.

FISH, S.E. (1976) 'Interpreting the variorum,' *Critical Inquiry*, 3, 3, 465–79.

FISH, S.E. (1980) *Is There a Text in This Class? The Authority of Interpretive Communities*. Cambridge, Mass.: Harvard University Press.

FITZGERALD, F. (1980) *America Revised: History Schoolbooks in the Twentieth Century*. New York: Vintage.

FOUCAULT, M. (1972) *The Archeology of Knowledge*. New York: Harper.

FOUCAULT, M. (1977) *Language, Counter Memory and Practice: Selected Essays and Interviews*, Edited by D. Bouchard. Ithaca, N.Y.: Cornell University Press.

GOODY, J. (1977) *The Domestication of the Savage Mind*. Cambridge: Cambridge University Press.

GRAFF, H.J. (1987a) *The Labryinths of Literacy: Reflections on Literacy Past and Present*. Lewes: Falmer Press.

GRAFF, H.J. (1987b) *The Legacies of Literacy: Continuities and Contradictions in Western Culture and Society*. Bloomington, Ind.: Indiana University Press.

INNIS, H.A. (1951) *The Bias of Communication*. Toronto: University of Toronto Press.

IVINS, W.M. Jr. (1953) *Prints and Visual Communication*. Cambridge, Mass.: Harvard University Press.

KEDDIE, N. (1971) 'Classroom knowledge,' in YOUNG, M.F.D. (Ed.), *Knowledge and Control: New Directions for the Sociology of Education*. London: Collier Macmillan.

KENNER, H. (1962) *The Counterfeiters*. Bloomington, Ind.: Indiana University Press.

LOCKE, J. (1969) *An Essay Concerning Human Understanding*. New York: Meridian Press.

LORIMER, R. (1986) 'The business of literacy: The making of the educational text,' in CASTELL, S. DE, LUKE, A. and EGAN, K. (Eds), *Literacy, Society and Schooling*. Cambridge: Cambridge University Press.

LUKE, C. (1989) *Pedagogy, Printing and Protestantism: The Discourse on Childhood*. Albany, N.Y.: State University of New York Press.

McLUHAN, M. (1962) *The Gutenberg Galaxy*. Toronto: University of Toronto Press.

McNEIL, L.M. (1987) *Contradictions of Control: School Structure and School Knowledge*. London: Routledge and Kegan Paul.

OLSON, D.R. (1977a) 'From utterance to text: The bias of language in speech and writing,' *Harvard Educational Review*, 47, 3, 257–81.

OLSON, D.R. (1977b) 'Oral and written language and the cognitive processes of children,' *Journal of Communications*, 27, 3, 10–26.

PURVNER, M. (1967) *The Royal Society: Concept and Creation*. Cambridge, Mass.: MIT Press.

SCHOLES, R. (1977) 'Towards a semiotics of literature,' *Critical Inquiry*, 5, 2, 105–20.

SEARLE, J. (1975) 'The logical status of narrative fiction,' *New Literary History*, 1, 2, 319–32.

SPRAT, T. (1966) *The History of the Royal Society of London* (1667). London: Routledge and Kegan Paul.

STUBBS, M. (1983) *Discourse Analysis*. Oxford: Blackwell.

WATZLAWICK, P., BEAVIN, J.H. and JACKSON, D.D. (1967) *The Pragmatics of Human Communication. A Study of Interactional Patterns, Pathologies, and Paradoxes*. New York: Norton.

WELLS, G. (1981) *Learning through Interaction*. Cambridge: Cambridge University Press.

WILLEY, B. (1934) *The Seventeenth Century Background. Studies in the Thought of an Age in Relation to Poetry and Religion*. London: Chatto and Windus.

YOUNG, M.F.D. (1971) 'An approach to the study of curricula as socially organized knowledge,' in YOUNG, M.F.D. (Ed.), *Knowledge and Control: New Directions for the Sociology of Education*. London: Collier Macmillan.

Chapter 20

Sources of Authority in the Language of the School: A Response to 'Beyond Criticism'

David R. Olson
Ontario Institute for Studies in Education

Luke, de Castell and Luke (Chapter 19, this volume) do a considerable service in their attempt to show that the authority of written texts, school textbooks in particular, derives not only from the particular linguistic properties of the texts themselves — their explicitness and impersonality, for example — but also from the social or institutional contexts in which those texts are owned, taught and studied. Texts, they say, are 'above criticism' primarily because the social institutions — governments and schools — 'authorize' them. Moreover, the properties of texts that I identified as being the source of their authority are, in fact, they say, primarily to justify the authority of social institutions — forms of schools, forms of government, forms of religion and the like — which they say are indeed 'beyond criticism'. So that the meaning and authority of textbooks that I describe are, in fact, meaning and authority of the institutions that mediate those texts.

To oversimplify, I discuss the internal or intrinsic structure of the texts that are taught, studied and consulted, while they discuss the external social structures that teachers, texts and children are inserted into. I think that they would, if pressed, agree that the authority of teachers and schools could not exist without a 'text' of some form — a body of knowledge or procedures, a sacred tradition, or a fixed oral or written text which would provide the basis for instruction in the first place. I also think they would agree that those texts are refined or specialized to serve their social functions. Prayers, for example, differ from encyclopedias. On my side, if pressed, I would have to admit that an obsolete textbook, even if it had all the requirements of explicitness and impersonality, would not have the authority if it was not adopted by some school, teacher, writer, or student. We can see that both a certain kind of text and a certain social organization are important to the ceding of authority to a teacher or a text. But just what is the relation between the internal and the external, the text and the context?

Luke, de Castell and Luke's chapter is important, I think, because it keeps the focus on the relation between the internal and the external sources of authority. I agree that theories of 'text' that ignore the social, institutional context are inadequate, while theories of social structure and authority, which simply talk about the exercise of power without seeing how that authority is created and exercised in particular social contexts such as reading and study, are banal. So their push is just in the right place. However, their view of this interaction is somewhat different from mine. I would look for the relations between the intrinsic and the extrinsic in terms of an identity; the pattern of authority in the larger society is reflected in the pattern of authority in the text. My view is that the matter of who is permitted to have opinions, of how opinions are validated or rejected in the texts, and of how those texts are used is a reflection of the social structures built around those texts. Furthermore, it is not so much a matter of text and context as it is of finding two parallel structures. To me the structure of language and texts is neither subordinate nor superordinate to the social structure. A change in one is as likely to change the other and vice versa. Hence, it is not unlikely, indeed it seems extremely likely to me, that changes in the technologies of communication and the resulting changes in language, texts and discourse could affect the social order just as readily as the social order could impose structure of interpretation on language and texts. Their view, on the other hand, is that the social order is the most important factor, and that it transforms and reconstitutes the language and texts.

We all agree that texts are not only taken as true but also as having authority. Just how that truth and authority are conceived, I suggest, can be seen in the structure of the texts themselves. Hence, the writing of texts is not a trivial matter. The task facing writers is not only to make texts assimilable; it is to make clear both the grounds for accepting claims as true and the grounds for granting persons, texts and institutions authority. However, the teacher's role is equally important. The teacher's authority derives not simply from his or her institutional authority but rather from his or her own knowledge or competence, from his or her own right to hold opinions rather than merely express the opinions of others. That is the kind of authority that teachers may pass along to children. Even if they hold a low status position in the social order of most schools, children, too, have the right to hold their opinions, to express them and to have them taken seriously if they are honest, informed, considered, or significant.

Chapter 21

Talk around Text: Constructions of Textual and Teacher Authority in Classroom Discourse

Carolyn D. Baker and Peter Freebody
University of New England

Textbooks have a central place in the organization and practice of teaching and learning in schools. It is one of the major tasks of contemporary schooling to acquaint children with literacy. Understanding, learning from and later producing written texts are activities which have a privileged place within school culture. Both the formal curriculum and the assessment of students are weighted heavily towards competence with written text.

Given that school textbooks present school knowledge (content) within a school technology (literacy), it is not surprising that textbooks are treated as 'authoritative' sources of content and method. One aspect of the ongoing interest in the character and function of school textbooks — the question of the source of the 'authority' of the school text — has been the topic of recent debate. This debate can be formulated as whether the authority of school texts lies 'in' the structure of the text, or whether this authority derives from the broader institutional context in which such texts are used.

Olson (1977, and Chapters 18 and 20 this volume) has argued that the authority of school textbooks is lodged to a considerable extent in their 'particular linguistic properties', 'in the structure of the texts themselves' (Olson, Chapter 20, this volume, p. 262). He has advanced the view that the prose styles adopted in textbooks, as distinct from those in oral communications, are characterized by impersonality: the writer and reader are separated, the 'knowledge' is detached from identifiable human sources, and assertions appear to have truth value independent of any particular expositor of the knowledge. This manner of writing assigns an objectivity and an 'autonomy' to the text, visible partly in the explicitness and highly conventionalized nature of the language used to serve the specialist logical functions of scientific discourse (Olson, 1977).

Luke, de Castell and Luke (Chapter 19, this volume) have countered Olson's position that such authority is intrinsic to texts by emphasizing the importance of factors which are extrinsic to texts but 'intrinsic to the social structure of schools'.

They have pointed to the nature of authority relations in schools and classrooms as the crucial context for the status assigned to texts. In contrast to Olson's analysis, which presupposes a reader's 'unmediated confrontation with the text', their own position casts teachers as the mediators of textual knowledge who provide students with 'a running metatextual commentary with which to process the text'. Thus in reading lessons, as well as in other classroom uses of written texts, there are for students two parallel texts to be managed and integrated: the written text itself and the teacher's oral commentary on it via questions and responses to answers. It is the teacher who 'reconstitutes the text in use'. They further suggested that it is teacher authority to which textual authority is effectively subordinated (Luke *et al.*, Chapter 19, pp. 258). Olson (Chapter 20, this volume, p. 262) rejected the view that 'text' is subordinated to 'context', maintaining that textual structure and social structure are parallel and equally influential structures, one the mirror of the other.

Our response to the question of whether texts are self-authorizing or whether they are authorized in the course of specific instructional practices begins with the proposition that the 'authority' of texts cannot be separated from the 'authority' of the teacher or the school, an assumption which would be shared by both sides of this debate. We begin with the further assumption that the authority of texts, of teachers and of the school should be seen as accomplishments of pedagogy rather than as preconditions for pedagogy. Thus we do not view 'authority' as an intrinsic property of texts or of social structure. Our interest is in text-authorizing practices which may be observed in the course of classroom instruction, and in the relation of these to the authority of teachers.

Neither Olson nor Luke *et al.* provide illustration of classroom practices through which 'authority' comes to be found in or attached to texts, although Luke *et al.* provide an outline of teachers' management between the relations of teacher, text and students. In this analysis they have introduced a vital link between 'the text itself' and teacher utterances about text. It is this linkage which is the focus of this chapter.

Through our analysis of some reading lessons in the early years of schooling, we will show how the relation between 'text' and 'context' is displayed in the activities of teaching and learning to read. We focus on the early years of schooling, and on reading lessons to illustrate ways in which 'authority' is assigned to texts and to teachers.

Instructional Practices

Our concern in this chapter is with how the 'authority' of texts and of teachers is accomplished in actual instances of reading instruction. In the beginning years of school children are assumed not to know how to read, even in the most technical sense, while the teacher's expertise in the ways of text is unproblematic. However, we would argue that teachers authorize themselves as teachers in demonstrations of competence with text: that is, that teacher authority and textual authority are reciprocally made resource and complement.

In this chapter we take particular interest in teachers' questions and reception of student answers, since much teaching of reading seems to be organized through question-answer sequences. This is a pervasive and virtually a defining form of teacher-student talk generally, which itself carries and displays presumptions about ownership of knowledge, power relations and the nature of 'learning' (see Edwards, 1980, 1981; Young, 1984).

We draw from Heap's (1982, 1985, 1986) research on the organization of talk in reading lessons, and particularly the 'comprehension' phases of reading lessons, for the essentials of our analysis. Heap has advanced an ethnomethodological view of how reading lessons can be studied. The most salient elements of this approach for our concern with the reciprocal construction of textual and teacher authority can be outlined briefly. Firstly, this position is concerned not with what reading is taken to be theoretically but rather with what counts as reading procedurally. This question requires the analysis of practices within reading lessons to examine how teacher-endorsed readings of a text are made available to students. Secondly, this research has shown that the comprehension phases of reading lessons are 'game-like' in that the task for students appears to be to answer teacher questions. Thirdly, Heap has concluded that while reading lessons may contain the production of propositional knowledge, the point of the comprehension phase of reading lessons is not 'the transmission of a propositional corpus', but 'comprehension of culture and the logic of its organization and possibilities. The text is simply the site for launching that comprehension' (1985, p. 265).

Heap's analysis of reading lessons contains some observations on how the status of the text is described through teacher questioning. Essentially, teachers orient students to text either as a source of information or as a basis for inference. Thus the text needs to be consulted or 'remembered'. Consultation and remembering are activities occasioned by and retrospectively acknowledged by the teacher. Certainly in the early years of school reading lessons are a public group activity and contain the same implicit enculturation into the rules of classroom participation which are found in other formal lessons (cf. Mehan, 1979).

In order to participate in reading lessons, the student must bring 'cultural logic' to an interpretation of a text, particularly in response to teacher elicitations where the text is used as a basis for inference. We take this logic to be cultural logic as the teacher understands it, for it is only when the student's logic, as displayed in answers to questions, appears to model the teacher's logic, that an answer might stand as an adequate answer and thus 'count' as reading. The game, as we see it, is for the student to guess what the teacher's logic is. In this chapter we treat teacher questions as corrigible descriptions of culture, and the text as a resource for describing preferred teacher-student relations.

We therefore view the text as more than 'the site for launching ... comprehension of culture.' We see it, practically, as the site for constructing a basis for teacher authority and as a basis for organizing and describing the social relation between teacher, student and school knowledge. The construction of teacher questions and teacher responses to student answers includes a psychological as well as a social constitution of the child as reader and the child as student, which we will elaborate below. It is in this way that Heap's work on the social organization of reading activities provides a route to describing a relation between text and context which is also a description of the relation between teacher and student.

Our main point is to describe the intimate connection between talk around text and the social organization of authority relations between teachers and students. Teachers may be shown to use various practices to assign authority to the text and simultaneously to themselves. Such embedded descriptions of teacher-student relations may be seen in the social organization of reading lessons. 'Learning to read' in school involves learning to adapt to a particular context of teacher-student relations within which text is studied. In the very early years of school this may involve talk about pictures rather than print. This talk may be seen to describe the teacher-student relation as much as the book or the picture being consulted.

We shall provide a number of examples of teacher questioning and student answering, from oral reading and 'comprehension' phases of reading lessons in the early years of school, to illustrate these points. In particular, we shall attend to how teachers refer to text, either as source of information or basis for inference, and treat these referrals as displays of teacher knowledge and teacher authority, and as containing constitutions of the child-reader in relation to teacher and to text.

The Running Metatextual Commentary

Luke *et al* (Chapter 19, this volume) have pointed to the 'running metatextual commentary' which teachers provide as mediators of the relation between children and text. Some general features of this metatextual commentary are outlined and illustrated in this section. Our first example is drawn from a teacher-made audio-tape which is designed to guide an individual kindergarten child's reading of a book. We can observe in this example a repertoire of practice which will also be observed in our transcripts of group reading lessons.

Example 1
Carefully turn over the page from the outside edge. Here's Mrs. Wishy-Washy. She doesn't really look very happy, does she? You can tell because her hands are on her hips. And she isn't smiling.
Let's read page number 8.
Point to the number 8.
That's right.
The first word is ALONG. Point to it. Read it with me now.
ALONG CAME MRS. WISHY WASHY. Dear she has a funny look on her face now.
JUST LOOK AT YOU SHE SCREAMED.
She's definitely not very happy. But I wonder what she's going to do about it. Let's find out. Turn over the page.

This tape-recorded reading lessons contains illustrations of the teacher's direction of observation and of internal response to the pictures and the text. The teacher's running commentary provides for exactly what the student is to attend to and how the student is to respond. It provides interpretations to be used in elaborating the story (e.g., 'hands on hips' indicates 'not happy') — an illustration of Heap's point that teaching reading looks much like teaching culture. The teacher's directives and comments comprise a particular construction of the story in these ways. The teacher is effectively announcing what there is of interest and note in the text.

The running metatextual commentary builds an emotional component into the reading of the story, particularly anticipation ('I wonder what. . . . Let's find out'). It also builds in an imagined discourse between teacher and child reader, in which the child is assumed to be following directions and in which the teacher asks the questions and leads the 'wondering'. The questioning and wondering serve as descriptions of the text. This commentary also offers a description of how the child could be responding to the story — in this sense, the teacher's construction of the child's 'mind'.

In this example we can see how the teacher assumes an interpretive position between the story and the child, inserting comments into the reading of the story, and fragmenting the story at selected points with calls for internal responses from the child reader. These insertions comprise the teacher's metacommentary which will be a feature of reading instruction throughout school life. Such meta-commentary does not appear merely to parallel the text, but at this very early point in reading instruction to penetrate and shape the text. Thus it is a meta-commentary not only on the text itself but on the social relations in which school learning from text will occur.

The Teacher-Text Partnership

A teacher-text 'partnership' is built up through various teacher practices which can be observed in beginning reading lessons. Luke *et al.* (Chapter 19, this volume, p. 258) have proposed a similar idea in their point that 'text and teacher can be seen to co-constitute a domain of knowledge, and to co-constitute one authoritative identity.' This is not in our view 'intrinsic to the social structure of schools', but is a product of instructional practices. First, we can observe some practices which demonstrate to students the teacher's privileged knowledge of the text.

Example 2: reading lesson, Year 1: *The Little Red Kaboose*
1. t [commences reading] What sort of train is that? [points to text]
2. p Big?
3. p Little?
4. p Steam?
5. t How do we know it's steam Jody?
6. p 'Cause of the smoke.
7. t Yes. The smoke here [points to picture].

The teacher's first question and the students' attempts to produce a correct answer in this segment illustrate the teacher's use of implicit frames of reference for creating and ordering experience, in this case experience apparently of the text.

The problem for the students here appears to be to grasp the occasioned meaning of 'sort' and to display that understanding through the production of a word which the teacher can then hear as satisfying the tacit presumption of the question — in this case, apparently, that the question was not about size but about how the train is powered. In some respects this problem is similar to the categorization problem identified in MacLure and French (1981), a problem for students which is not confined to questioning about text.

The students' answers in this segment stand as evidence of the absence of any principled way of determining the meaning the teacher attaches to 'sort' on this occasion. The teacher's eventual concurrence with 'steam' does not resolve this problem, for there is no way to determine that 'steam' is the only possible 'correct' answer. We do not know that Jody located 'steam' in any principled way, although the teacher's responses in lines (5) and (7) suggest that Jody could have found it in a principled way: that is, that the smoke in the picture is an obvious and sufficient clue to describing the train 'correctly' as 'steam'. Just what the students are to have attended to in the picture to arrive at this answer is only retrospectively made available to them by the teacher. This may apply to Jody as well as any other correct answerer. Jody might have noticed the smoke only after the second question was put, and might have tried 'steam' on other grounds. (Also, the teacher might have 'found' the smoke only after Jody's answer.) Jody is here not only being told that her answer is correct, but that she must have found it correctly. That is, correct answers are retrievable from the text using correct procedures. The teacher is offering a reading of the text which will stand as the correct reading not only for all practical purposes, but because it is shown to be constructed using the correct sense-assembly procedures. The teacher indicates that this way of reading the text is provided by the text itself, retrievable through correct attention to detail such as that implicitly attributed to Jody in this instance, and presumably eventually available to all students. This is a construction of the text and of Jody's competence which are further linked to the teacher's competence to ask about and pronounce on the content and methods of the text.

Also significant for our present interests is that in this instance we have an illustration of how a teacher takes a proposition (the train is a steam train), produced through the question-answer format, and locates the proposition 'in' the text. ('Yes. The smoke here.') The teacher has used an answer to support and legitimize the text as a source of knowledge. The correctness of the answer via reference to the text also legitimizes the question itself: the question is shown to have been a competent one by having an answer to it available in the text. It is a form of self-authorization using the text as resource. The teacher has connected her pronouncement of an answer as 'correct' to the text, evidencing her prior and privileged knowledge of the text.

The question-answer-evaluation format of reading comprehension lessons presumes that the teacher can know or does know the answer. More fundamentally, it is presumed that the teacher does know or can know the appropriate question. The pragmatics of classroom participation by students involves minimally an appearance of trust in these presumptions.

Example 2a: same lesson, shortly after the preceding segment
1. t Why is it [the train] getting slower and slower and slower?
2. p Because it's a real steep hill and the carriages might fall off?
3. t It's a very, very steep hill, yes. [resumes reading]
4. p He must be strong.
5. t Yes, he must be! [resumes reading] Who knows why they have tunnels for trains to go through?
6. p To keep them out of the rain.
7. t Does rain hurt trains? Jack?
8. p To go through big hills.
9. t Yes, that's right. If you have a big hill like that. . . . [continues to explain]

In this further segment, the teacher extends questioning beyond inference from the text (line 1) to extra-textual considerations (line 5). Discussion of and about the text shades into discussion about the world outside the text. The question in line 5 comes to count as part of the lesson about the text, as shown in lines 7 and 9 where the teacher comments on the acceptability of the students' attempts to explain the presence of tunnels, but drawing here not on the text as source, but on her own cultural knowledge as source. This method of relating the text to everyday life through consult-the-text questions alongside consult-your-commonsense-knowledge questions also displays the teacher as arbiter in both realms of knowledge, able to cross the boundaries with ease. This travelling also imbues the text with a real-life context. However, whether a question is to be answered from the text or from outside it is to be decided on each occasion of a question being put.

In line 7 the teacher supplies an interpretation of how one student must have arrived at a wrong answer. Both teacher and students are heard as speaking primarily in glosses of their respective reasoning procedures. It is the teacher who provides formulations of what the students' reasoning procedures must have been ('Does rain hurt trains?'), of whether their method and the cultural logic attributed to it were right or wrong. Heap (1985, p. 264) has pointed out that students need to 'sort out what kind of possible world the . . . story is to be taken to represent.' The world that is held to be the relevant world for a particular question is the one made public and sanctioned by the teacher. The student's use of that relevant world in producing an answer is part of what will come to count as a competent reading. In the Kaboose lesson the train has human-like qualities but the notion of 'hurt' is disqualified: the student is shown to have selected what is announced to be the wrong frame of reference for this question. Another child's comment, 'He must be strong!', is, however, endorsed by the teacher. This potential for shifting frames of reference may apply more to the kinds of fictional texts used in early reading instruction than to expository text. It appears to be the teacher who cues students to one or the other frame of reference, who can alternate between invoking the world of fiction or the world of fact from the same text. This problem for children, to decide which frame of reference is in play on some occasion of adult questioning (see also Mehan, 1976), is in part produced through the provision of textual material which blends 'fantasy' with 'reality'.

The construction of teacher questions is a construction of the nature of the text itself. Teacher questions may indicate that the answer lies 'in the text'. Alternatively, teacher questions may carry the implication that the answer lies in bringing the student's knowledge or experience to the text. We suggest that this is not strictly inference from the text, but inference to the text, where it is the text, and not the student's knowledge, which is to be made coherent and plausible (cf. McHoul, 1982). We suggest further that it is describable also as inference to the teacher's discourse, where it is the teacher's questions which are to be made coherent and plausible. This will be addressed in more detail below.

Where the answer lies 'in' the text, or can be inferred from the text, the teacher is presumed to know the text in a privileged way, in order to pronounce on the adequacy of the answer. Where the answer lies in conjoining some extra-textual knowledge to the textual clues, the teacher is presumed to know how to accomplish such a connection between 'everyday' knowledge and textual knowledge. Thus, teacher authority and textual authority are deeply interpenetrated. The text in this sense is a support for teacher claims to and demonstrations of authority. At the same time the teacher pronounces from an assumed professional 'knowledge about knowledge' what the text will provide for and accommodate as correct interpretation, and what it means to ask questions about and thus to describe a text.

This theory of reading text (the text contains the answer, one has to learn how to look), concretized through the questioning and answering routine, places the teacher in a position of mediation between student and text. It is the teacher who describes the text in her questions, correct answers to which constitute student competence. The text is given a particular shape by the nature of the teacher's questioning. While students may discover that not all teacher clues are equally salient, these subtleties do not discount students' reliance on teachers' utterances as the foundation for their sense of 'knowing' the text and for their sense of 'knowing' how to read.

The partnership of teacher and text is indicated also in the teacher practice of answering from within the text:

Example 3: Year 1

t.   . . . if you look at this picture you can see something else with the alligator
p.   hippopotamus [whispered]
t.   What other animals are (they? A bit hard to tell when
p.   (hippopotamus
t.   they're dressed up in clothes, isn't it. Andrew?
p.   (   ) see umm there's a hippopotamus there?
t.   Umhm. And what do you think the other one is? Daniel?
p.   (   )
t.   Bill?
p.   a hippopotamus?
t.   Possibly, we'll find out when we open the story. Let's start now. [twelve
     seconds whispering, giggling] SMALL HIPPO AND BIG RHINO, you
     were right, LIVED DEEP IN THE FOREST. . . .

The children who offered 'hippopotamus' are praised from within the teacher's reading of the text ('you were right'). The teacher is apparently deferring to the text as the source of the answer, but also evaluating the answer from within the text. The partnership is demonstrated through such devices.

The Construction of the Child-Teacher/Text Relation

Wait and See. Example 3 (above) contains illustrations of the wait-and-see practice, in which the teacher introduces puzzles to be solved. In the next segment (taken from the same lesson) the teacher twice suspends discussion of a puzzle and refers the students to the text as the source of the knowledge:

Example 3a: Year 1
t. Who is the stranger? Andrew?
p. Crocodile
t. Think about the name of the story, it is an
p.   alligator
t. and ps. All-i-ga-tor
t.   Yes alligators and crocodiles look a lot alike, don't they Daniel?
p. (Yeah my, my sister's got an alligator
p. (Yeah
p. (Only   only   only some have got small beaks and some have got long beaks
p. (But there's a diff-
t. (We'll have to have a look and see what the difference is later.
p. There's a difference in 'em.
t. Mmmhmm. Do you know the difference?
p. Umm one can swim and one can't.
t. We'll have to find out, won't we? THE ALLIGATOR DIDN'T ANSWER. . . .

Further, what students are 'allowed to know' about the text at some point in the reading of the story (cf. Heap, 1982, p. 44–5) is established by the teacher. In our next example the teacher controls the public reading in a way that disqualifies a student who already 'knows' the story from answering. The formal lesson is conducted as a demonstration that students do not know until taught.

Example 4: Year 1
t. The story's about Arthur. Let's have a look at the picture
p. (   ) my brother has this
t. What do you think this story's going to be about? Mike?
p. Um I was just going to s
t. You've read the story, have you ('cause your brother's got it
p.   (Yeah
t. Well, if you *haven't* read it, Now if you keep making that noise I think

primarily as a resource for describing the differential statuses of teacher and student, but also for linking these differential statuses to the public activity of 'reading'. It is a demonstration of the reliance students must place on the teacher's pronouncements of the adequacy of their guesses, while the text does not deal in guesses but in assertions. These procedures also work to turn fiction into fact: to reconstitute a 'story', anticipated through children's imaginations, into factual events — what really did happen: 'What else might a rabbit do . . . ? . . . Right, and that's exactly what he did.' Here we see the 'authority' of the text conveyed to children.

Although the medium of early reading instruction appears to be largely fictional material, and although there appears to be a great deal of use made of the imaginative capacities of children, a positivist epistemology permeates early reading instruction as it does other teaching settings (cf. Young, 1984). Children are cast as inhabitants of the world of possible knowledge until they are taught. Texts are made to contain actual knowledge — 'facts' of occasion, of sequence, of personality and so on. These 'facts' are conversationally produced after and as evaluations of students' guesses, imaginings and inferences in 'fictional' realms. These instructional practices may underwrite those attitudes to text which Olson has described. We view those attitudes as products of pedagogy, not as preconditions for it. The use of fictional materials and the apparent use of children's imaginative capacities in teaching reading may be a central resource in the social production of such attitudes.

Culture, Logic and 'Reading Comprehension'

In these early reading lessons it often appears that teachers constitute students, for purposes of classroom discussion, essentially as sources of ideas and guesses. We have found that some lessons involve a great deal of this imaginative guessing practice, to the extent that students may come to assume that good guessers are treated by the teacher as good readers. There is considerable evidence that students' 'thinking' in this context is assessed as good or not good against the implicit criteria underlying the teachers' questions, such that these guessing routines take the form of attempts to read the teacher's mind.

Heap (1986) has concluded that these sequences are lessons in culture. Our interpretation of this point is that the culture being transmitted is that version of culture which can be assembled by a student out of the sequential and thematic dimensions of a particular teacher's particular questions. Luke *et al.* (Chapter 19, this volume, p. 252) pointed out that teachers describe texts in an 'individually selective manner'. Their utterances must be heard or treated by students as a competent description of culture. The student's task in learning culture then becomes the task of accomplishing a coherence across the teacher's utterances (cf. McHoul, 1982).

In Example 5 below another Year 1 teacher has completed an oral reading of the story and is questioning students about one of the pictures in the book.

Example 5: Year 1

t.   What else has he got on to keep him wet, uh dry.

ps. hh wet

p.   wet hh

t.   Robert

p.   Boots?

t.   Yes big, boots what-do-we-call those big boots?

p.   Gumboots!

t.   Two names that I know of, don't call out hands up, Nicolas did you have one? Yes Nicolas?

p.   Gumboots

t.   Call them gumboots and there's another name too.

ps. (   )

p.   Galoshes

t.   Or galoshes that's three names 'cause I (could only) I didn't think of galoshes.

p.   rubber boots?

t.   I didn't think of — that's four 'cause I didn't think of (hh) rubber boots either the one I'm thinking of starts with whuh (4.0)

p.   (   )

p.   Wet boots

t.   Not wet boots

p.   (   ) boots

p.   Wellington //boots

t.   //Good try though Tim, wellington boots yes wellington boots. And what's the other thing he's got on (3.0) for cold and wet.

p.   (   )

p.   (   ) coat

t.   a big, big coat a big raincoat

p.   (   ) //

t.   //Cold wet and how do you know it's night.

p.   Because it's//

t.   //Apart from the fact it tells you in the story.

p.   Uh!

t.   Chris, I wonder if you can tell us. How do you know it's night from this picture?

p.   Uh! 'cause he's, ahh!

p.   Lamp

t.   Yeah he's got big lamp, hasn't he. Can you see what he's got on underneath his

p.   pyjamas

t.   wet weather clothes?

p.   hh

p.   Pyjamas

t.   Do you think he sort of took a lot of time getting out of bed?

```
ps.   (no
ps.   (yes
t.    Getting dressed rather?
ps.   (yes
ps.   (no
t.    Did he take a lot of time getting dressed?
ps.   (no
ps.   (yes
t.    Have a look here what, what does this tell you
p.    pj's
p.    p-
t.    He's still got his pj's on hasn't he so, he (might
ps.   ((    )
      have had to?
ps.   (     )
p.    Pyjamas
p.    (     )
t.    He might have had to?
p.    they're pyjamas
p.    Get out in a hurry
t.    In a hurry so perhaps it was some sort of an emergency.
```

This lengthy exchange concerning the farmer's apparel exemplifies a number of points. First, the teacher signals explicitly that some of the intended answers are located not in the text but rather in the teacher's mind ('Two names that I know of . . . the one I'm thinking of. . . . Apart from the fact that it tells you in the story . . . he might have had to. . . ?'). This is an implicit lesson that school knowledge is located with the teacher. A second observation is that the farmer's apparel plays no part in the subsequent story line: the teacher appears (to us) to be elaborating on a detail of the illustration without linking this elaboration to the text as a story. This is an implicit lesson in the absence of boundaries around the territory a teacher could choose to survey inside the context of 'teaching reading'.

The teacher is displaying how to do a reading of the illustration, what to 'wonder' about, what counts as a resolution of the puzzle the teacher poses. Reading lessons in the early years of school characteristically contain considerable material which gives students access to how the teacher thinks. Such lessons confirm the importance of competence in answering teachers' questions about text as evidence of 'reading ability'. The teacher's metatextual commentary here is a display not of knowledge of the text or of the story directly, but of sanctioned observational and reasoning procedures. The 'reading' and 'comprehension' of texts may be viewed essentially as the 'reading' and 'comprehension' of the teacher. While the teacher does a reading of the text, students do a reading of the teacher. We see here that the technical aspects of reading become subordinated to the cultural resources necessary to answer a teacher's question (cf. Hammersley, 1977). This practice in following a teacher's line of commentary on a text is practice for answering questions in reading tests (cf. Heap, 1986).

In this particular lesson, lasting about seventeen minutes, the teacher asked a total of seventy-nine questions, twenty-three of which were stated explicitly to indicate that the location of the answer is in the teacher's mind. It should also be pointed out that of the thirty-two questions drawing apparently on the pupils' 'background knowledge' (e.g., 'What do we call these big boots?' in the excerpt above), many were reformulated to indicate that the teacher had particular answers in mind (e.g., 'Did he take a lot of time getting dressed?' in the excerpt above). In other instances students' answers were followed by evaluative comments signalling the specific frame of reference which should have been conveyed in a student's answer, as in the following example:

Example 5 a: Year 1

    t. If you had a chance to be one of the things in our story which, or — someone in the story which would you like to be?

    p. hh!

    t. Carl?

    p. The cricket. I mean the big weta.

    t. (The big weta

    p. (Oh so would I

    t. Why would you like to be the big weta

    p. 'Cause he comes last

    t. He comes last, but what's what happens to him that's so uh so good do you think

    p. 'Cause he, he gets to stay in the bed

    t. He gets to stay in the bed.

This example is instructive in that the teacher is requesting personal opinions from the students which, it might be thought, are entirely within the discretion of the answerer (cf. Heap, 1985, pp. 262–3). A 'correct' answer to such a question would appear to reside neither in the text nor in the teacher's mind. The teacher nonetheless indicates that there is a proper rationale and frame of reference even for a personal preference. Prior to that specification, no guidance is given as to what grounds students should use to decide their preference.

Thus, while the apparent source of an answer lies in the student's background knowledge, in personal preferences, or in the illustrations in the book (as in fifteen of the questions in this lesson), the reformulative and evaluative utterances of the teacher can be seen to reveal that virtually all of the retrospectively correct or adequate answers are so found in relation to the teacher's ongoing construction of a reading of the story. It is the teacher's 'reading' and the teacher's 'thinking' which are the targets of the students' guesses.

It is in this important sense that 'reading' as an organized activity cannot be separated from the relation of teacher and student. The teacher invades and imbues the text with his or her own interpretation during the course of reading instruction. That interpretation is effected within a particular constitution of the student and the student's status in relation to both text and teacher.

In these kinds of sequences it is far more than the child's 'technical' skill in extracting some information from the text that is involved. In the lesson sampled above there is only one question (of a total of seventy-nine) asked by the teacher which explicitly calls on memory for an event in the text. It is rather the child's understanding of the teacher's culture, as it is made available in the teacher's commentary on the text and the teacher's description of what counts as a reading of the text, that is being called upon.

It would appear more important in these kinds of lesson sequences for students to be in tune, culturally and intellectually, with the teacher, and to be able and willing to search for a 'cultural logic' underlying the teacher's 'individually selective' attention to the detail of the text, than to be able to read the words. It could be seen to be irrelevant for this kind of lesson that any child could read the words. It does not appear to be assumed that any child or all children can or cannot read the words. We may ask, 'What appears to be taught here? What is this a lesson in?' We would conclude that this is essentially a lesson in school culture and, more particularly, a lesson in the politics of school knowledge.

In the very early years of school, where reading is construed as an activity whose procedures have yet to be taught, it can be sustained that only the teacher has privileged access to the knowledge and the methods of a text. This presumption is built through the partnership teachers establish between themselves and the texts as complementary sources of authority, 'to co-constitute one authoritative identity' (Luke *et al.*, Chapter 19, this edition, p. 258). With the child constituted essentially as a non-reader, as non-expert in the content and methods of the text, the scope for the demonstration of teacher know-how is exceptionally broad. Teachers' questions are demonstrated to be competent questions and thus documents of a competent reading. Students' answers, as we have illustrated, are treated as defeasible attempts to access the implicit cultural logic behind the public reading which the teacher is leading.

Later in the school years, when it is presumed that students can already read in the technical sense, the written text may be consulted more closely, and there may be fewer pre-reading imaginative practices than we have observed in beginning reading lessons. For comparative purposes we will present a segment from a fourth-grade lesson:

Example 6: Year 4
(a) t. Alright. What was he doing when the explosion happened?
    p. [inaudible]
    t. No he wasn't. What was he doing when the *explosion* happened?
    p. He was in the radio place.
    t. Yes. Why would he be using the radio, Paul?
(b) t. Right. So why was he lucky when he got onto the raft, Jenny?
    p. [No response]
    t. Go back and read it. Come on! You're not following the reading.
(c) t. What did he do with the raft, Donna?
    p. [No response]
    t. Read it and find out. [waits]

p. He tied them together.
t. Right, he tied them together. What did he use to put them together?

In these segments we hear the teacher's questions as designed to draw out details of the sequence and concurrence of events, with most attention given to establishing (what will be taken to be) the facts of the story. The students are pointed explicitly to the text as source or basis for inference, and to 'following the reading' as a pre-condition for answering. The teacher's questioning leads a post-reading reconstruction of events, a reversal of the pre-reading 'wait and see' practice observed with beginning reading lessons. While the students may now be constituted differently with respect to their technical skill in extracting information from the written text, we do not see that the political relation has changed from that displayed in our earlier examples. The social context of the reading instruction remains the same: the teacher's privileged access to the text is continually marked through the teacher's use of an institutionally-given prerogative to ask the questions and to announce the correctness of answers — to describe what will count as an understanding of the story. The text is treated as a factual domain and an authoritative source, but it is the teacher's questions and reception of answers which assign that status to the text. The teacher is in control of the 'reading' of the text.

Teacher questions are not conventionally treated as defeasible descriptions of the text, while student answers are continually so treated. At even more advanced levels of schooling, and with a variety of more specialized texts, this distinction between the status of teacher readings and student readings is maintained and is a political reality of school life. Students may be able to challenge teacher readings through their independent readings of a text, but they may do so at their peril if evaluations of 'correct' or 'skilled' readings continue to be assessed against some cultural standard. And there is no other way that they can be assessed.

Coda: Theories and Practices

We have advanced in this chapter an ethnomethodological view of the process of early reading instruction. This is not a view we would consider would be known or shared by teachers of reading, whose practices and strategies are shaped by various theories of reading and of reading instruction.

Bereiter (1986) has acknowledged that the ethnomethodological study of reading instruction is significant for psychologically-based theories of reading. These theories are premised on the idea that the pedagogically salient aspect of reading resides in its being an individual, internal process; Heap's analyses, in contrast, are concerned with the description of reading lessons as public, group activity. Within the psychological tradition, teacher questions are presumably designed to organize and facilitate students' thinking about and 'processing' of the text. The text, in turn, is taken to be a combination of ideas, propositions and inferences which can be properly or improperly understood, retrieved or made.

We have adopted an ethnomethodological view of reading lessons in this chapter, treating the text as a resource for the discursive construction of many possible readings, and teacher questions as documents of a possible logic underlying one of those possible readings.

The phenomena we have observed within question sequences in comprehension phases of reading lessons may derive from teachers' access to and familiarity with certain psychologically-based theories of reading. We will comment on the possible logic and on some of the features of the teachers' practices in the examples we have presented and attempt to account for them with reference to these theories. We will also comment on some possible disjunctions between the theory (as provided by some psychological theories) and the application (as illustrated in this chapter). We conclude with some concerns we have about the apparent application of psychological theories of reading in classrooms.

The persistent involvement of students' 'background experience', is, on face value, compatible with some cognitive theories of reading comprehension (e.g., Schallert, 1982). Such theories have stressed the need to locate material to be comprehended in the prior knowledge of the learner, a need which is encapsulated in the maxim: 'Comprehension is building bridges between the new and the known' (Pearson and Johnson, 1972, p. 24). From this viewpoint comprehension is an internal psychological process by which an incoming message is structured and made concrete by the relevant organized knowledge of the reader. 'The meaning is not in the message. A message is a cryptic recipe that can guide a person in constructing a representation' (Anderson, 1977, p. 422). Thus, a useful activity associated with reading might be seen to be the teacher's calling into play those aspects of the background knowledge of the students which will facilitate comprehension of the story.

It is possible to account for the questioning practices of the teacher, particularly in Examples 5 and 5 a, in terms of such an account of the comprehension process. However, two critical issues are raised about the way in which this theory of reading is effected in the lesson: first, the teacher's 'backgrounding' questions seem rarely to draw the students further into the text, but rather can be seen as episodic diversions into details which the teacher sees as interesting, instructive or worth discussing. While such discussion may serve various instructional purposes, the point remains that the effect may well be to draw students away from the text.

A second consideration concerns the relation of questions to the story line. Developing recommendations from theories of reading comprehension for teacher questioning, Beck (1984, p. 15) suggested that, 'First, questions should proceed in a sequence that matches the progression of ideas or events in the story. Second, questions should be framed to highlight the interrelationships of story ideas.' Such a prescription assumes that there is, independent of a particular reading of a text and in some a priori way, a 'progression of ideas . . .' and a (set of) 'interrelationships of ideas . . .', an assumption shared by reading comprehension tests. From within this construction of 'reading comprehension', the persistent use of episodic diversions into 'background knowledge' could interfere with learning to read, partly by presenting to students a picture of the school's version of the public activity of 'reading' which dislocates the talk from the text.

In Example 6, taken from a fourth-grade reading lesson, we observe a far closer connection of talk to text. In this example the teacher appears to be questioning to 'match the progression of ideas or events' in the story. It may appear that 'the text' is generating the sequence of events to be elicited from students far more than is the case with picture-books. Olson's (1977, p. 86) comment that 'knowledge comes to be defined as that picture of reality appropriate to the requirements of a particular technology, explicit written text' may apply more to the questioning routine observed in the fourth grade lessons than to our kindergarten and first grade examples. The structure of the 'text itself' might be seen to occasion teachers' uses of 'what happened next', questions, although beginning school reading books also rely heavily on the story form. There may be features of the textual organization which provide more readily for questioning about particular aspects of a text, especially where the narrative practice itself is not made a topic (see Baker and Freebody, 1987; see also Baker and Freebody, forthcoming, for a more complete analysis of the texts themselves). We would, however, maintain that how a teacher designs questioning is always a product of the teacher's own reading of the story, to which the organization of the text would certainly contribute. This reading might also be informed by a professional literature about procedures and concepts in reading instruction. As any text provides for multiple readings, the teacher's running commentary cannot be seen to reflect the text's structure, but to construct it for all practical purposes.

The 'wait and see' and 'imagine and consult' practices we have described in beginning reading lessons have interested us as descriptions of the relation of child, text and teacher. We presume these practices are employed with the intention of interesting and involving the students in the possibles of a story, informed by theories of reading. These practices could be taken as illustrations of what Heap (1985, pp. 265–6) has called taking the text 'off the page and into the culture', to turn 'boring maps' into meaningful texts. The construction of possible texts would appear to be a fruitful educative experience. Our concern with our examples of how this might be done rests on the extent to which these practices appear to include a subordination of the child's knowledge to textual knowledge and to the teacher-text partnership: the teacher questions the children, the text contains the answer to the teacher's question. This appears to be consistent with 'the dominant epistemic practices in our schools' (Young, 1984). We are not unaware that the construction and maintenance of textual and teacher authority might be viewed as desirable outcomes of reading instruction or of schooling, but we do not share that view of what reading is for.

Another equally notable effect of forays into students' background knowledge and preferences can be seen when such questions are placed within the pattern of evaluative utterances used by teachers. Not only are the students' abilities to demonstrate knowledge of words or memory for events in a story assessed by teachers, but teachers also pronounce upon the acceptability of students' contributions from their background knowledge and preferences. Teachers thereby exercise the prerogative of the school to pronounce upon the acceptability of students' apparently personal feelings and aspects of their lives out-of-school.

The exhortations to teachers to call upon and employ students' knowledge and feelings about various topics appear to 'personalize' learning and render instruction more child-centred. However, the location of such techniques in a teacher-centred, evaluative organization of talk in the classroom may serve to expand the legislative boundaries of schooling into personal and social areas of the child's life which may bear no apparent relevance to the child's acquisition of skills such as reading.

In this chapter, we have suggested that the latitude teachers display in questioning sequences is part of the demonstration to students of the breadth of the teacher's authority. The more episodic the diversions, the harder students must work to access the logic underlying the discussion, and how it relates to the words or the story. The more expansive the discussion, the more difficult is the task of making coherent the teacher's running metatextual commentary. The broader the range of background knowledge, imagining, inferencing and guessing children must produce in order to take part successfully in the public activity of reading lessons, the less 'reading lessons' appear to be about the text at all. Talk around a text, in the beginning years of school, may thus be viewed essentially as a description of the political relations between teacher and students. The 'authority' of the text is both a resource in and a product of that description.

Acknowledgment

We wish to thank the teachers who provided the opportunity to audio-tape reading lessons in infants' classrooms. We also wish to thank Christine Perrott for providing us with further examples of reading lessons in infants' and primary classrooms. All of our examples are taken from reading lessons conducted in New South Wales schools in 1982–1985.

References

ANDERSON, R.C. (1977) 'The notion of schemata and the educational enterprise,' in ANDERSON, R.C., SPIRO, R.J. and MONTAGUE, W.E. (Eds), *Schooling and the Acquisition of Knowledge*, Hillsdale, N.J.: Lawrence Erlbaum.
BAKER, C.D. and FREEBODY, P. (1987) '"Constituting the child" in beginning school reading books,' *British Journal of Sociology of Education*, 8, 1, 55–76.
BAKER, C.D. and FREEBODY, P. (forthcoming) *Children's First Schoolbooks: Introductions to the Culture of Literacy*. Oxford: Blackwell.
BECK, I. (1984) 'Developing comprehension: The impact of the directed reading lesson,' in ANDERSON, R.C., OSBORN, J. and TIERNEY, R.J. (Eds), *Learning to Read in American Schools: Basal Readers and Content Texts*. Hillsdale, N.J.: Lawrence Erlbaum.
BEREITER, C. (1986) 'The reading comprehension lesson: A commentary on Heap's ethnomethodological analysis,' *Curriculum Inquiry*, 16, 1, 66–72.
CAZDEN, C.B. (1981) 'Social context of learning to read,' in GUTHRIE, J.T. (Ed.), *Comprehension and Teaching: Research Reviews*. Newark, Del.: International Reading Association.

EDWARDS, A.D. (1980) 'Patterns of power and authority in classroom talk,' in WOODS, P. (Ed.), *Teacher Strategies: Explorations in the Sociology of the School*. London: Croom Helm.

EDWARDS, A.D. (1981) 'Analysing classroom talk,' in FRENCH, P. and MACLURE, M. (Eds), *Adult-Child Conversation*. London: Croom Helm.

HAMMERSLEY, M. (1977) 'School learning: The cultural resources required by pupils to answer a teacher's question,' in WOODS, P. and HAMMERSLEY, M. (Eds), *School Experience: Explorations in the Sociology of Education*. London: Croom Helm.

HEAP, J.L. (1982) 'The social organisation of reading assessment: Reasons for eclecticism,' in PAYNE, G.C.F. and CUFF, E.C. (Eds), *Doing Teaching: The Practical Management of Classrooms*. London: Batsford.

HEAP, J.L. (1985) 'Discourse in the production of classroom knowledge: Reading lessons,' *Curriculum Inquiry*, 15, 3, 245–79.

HEAP, J.L. (1986) 'Cultural logic and schema theory: A reply to Bereiter,' *Curriculum Inquiry*, 16, 1, 73–86.

MCHOUL, A.W. (1982) *Telling How Texts Talk: Essays on Reading and Ethnomethodology*. London: Routledge and Kegan Paul.

MACLURE, M. and FRENCH, P. (1981) 'Routes to right answers: On pupils' strategies for answering teachers' questions,' in WOODS, P. (Ed.), *Pupil Strategies: Explorations in the Sociology of the School*. London: Croom Helm.

MEHAN, H. (1976) 'Assessing children's school performance,' in HAMMERSLEY, M. and WOODS, P. (Eds), *The Process of Schooling*. London: Routledge and Kegan Paul.

MEHAN, H. (1979) *Learning Lessons: Social Organisation in the Classroom*. Cambridge, Mass.: Harvard University Press.

OLSON, D.R. (1977) 'The language of instruction: The literate bias of schooling,' in ANDERSON, R.C., SPIRO, R.J. and MONTAGUE, W. (Eds), *Schooling and the Acquisition of Knowledge*. Hillsdale, N.J.: Lawrence Erlbaum.

PEARSON, P.D. and JOHNSON, D.D. (1972) *Teaching Reading Comprehension*. New York: Holt, Rinehart and Winston.

SCHALLERT, D.L. (1982) 'The significance of knowledge: A synthesis of research related to schema theory,' in OTTO, W. and WHITE, S. (Eds), *Reading Expository Material*. New York: Academic Press.

YOUNG, R.E. (1984) 'Teaching equals indoctrination: The dominant epistemic practices of our schools,' *British Journal of Educational Studies*, 32, 3, 220–38.

Chapter 22

Texts and Contexts: A Response

Courtney B. Cazden
Harvard Graduate School of Education

In the spring of 1958, just thirty years ago, the (US) Social Science Research Council sponsored an interdisciplinary conference at which linguists, psychologists and literary critics explored the characteristics of style in language. In his concluding remarks on 'linguistics and poetics', Jakobson proposed a framework for investigating the 'constitutive factors in any speech event, in any act of verbal communication' (1960, p. 353). He schematized them as follows:

CONTEXT

ADDRESSER..........MESSAGE..........ADDRESSEE

CONTACT

CODE

and explained:

> Each of these six factors determines a different function of language. Although we distinguish six basic aspects of language, we could, however, hardly find verbal messages that would fulfill only one function. The diversity lies not in a monopoly of some one of these several functions, but in a different hierarchical order of functions. The verbal structure of a message depends primarily on the predominant function. (p. 353)

Since these ideas were developed at a conference that brought together linguists and literary critics, and since Jakobson himself worked in both fields, it is not surprising that his scheme has proven useful in both. In many programmatic statements for the developing field of sociolinguistics, Hymes (1962) has discussed the importance of such a framework for research. More recently, Scholes, calling Jakobson's article 'the place where much later work in the semiotics of literary discourse begins' (1982, p. 184), has returned to Jakobson's diagram as a way of mapping the various schools of critical theory and interpretation.

Some examples of these conversions may be useful as a perspective for the important issues raised by the set of papers in this section. *Addresser* and *addressee* in Jakobson's scheme are combined (along with any other audience members) as *Participants* in Hymes's mnemonic acronym, SPEAKING. In Scholes's adaptation to critical theory, a focus on addresser characterizes *author-oriented* theory that 'seeks to recover the authorial intention as the key to a text's meaning' (p. 9), while a focus on the addressee characterizes *reader-oriented* (or reader-response) theory. *Text* (both form and content) becomes the *Act* component of Hymes's acronym, and in Scholes's map the focus of New Criticism, 'which has been at the center of American critical thought until the past decade' (p. 10). Finally, Jakobson's *context* becomes Hymes's *Situation* (both physical setting and culturally-defined scene), and the focus of historical scholars and 'Marxists and other sociocritics' in Scholes's map.

In thinking about any of these category sets it is important to remember Jakobson's statement, quoted above, that a single function (or feature or focus) is rarely the whole story. It becomes a question for research, ideally ethnographic (Radway, in press, n.d.), just which members of the set are influential in any given sociohistorical situation, and how that influence happens. In short, either in the past or in the present, we have to look and see. The justification for one interpretive ground or another is a matter for analysis in particular cases. Any more general assertion can only emerge from, and be grounded in, multiple sociohistorically situated analyses.

The importance of such an ethnographic approach has been consistently urged by Hymes and others in sociolinguistics. It seems to me just as important in research on response to and attitudes toward any written texts — literature and textbooks alike. While some division of labour may be an understandable result of academic specialization, there is special value in research that looks at multiple features. Radway's *Reading the Romance* (1984), referred to in several chapters here, is a notable example of a rich account.

Thus the importance of the research by Baker and Freebody (see Chapter 21, this volume). They examine how actual teachers and students discuss specific texts in a particular institutional setting: elementary school reading-group lessons. But their conclusions are necessarily limited, and do not fully address the issues raised about text structure by Olson. As Baker and Freebody point out, the texts being read in the reading lessons they observed (in kindergarten, first and fourth grades) are narratives, whereas Olson is discussing expository textbooks, presumably in subject-matter areas like science and social studies. In the latter it is not just beliefs about and the attitudes toward the nature of reading that are at stake, but beliefs about and attitudes toward the nature of our knowledge of the world.

Elsewhere (Cazden, in press) I have argued against the 'myth of autonomous texts', but I agree with Olson that some texts, especially textbooks, are written as if they were explicit and autonomous statements of how some piece of the world actually is. My unease with ethnomethodological work (with which Baker and Freebody identify themselves) is that in contrast to ethnography that assumes variation, it frequently implies that the practices uncovered are non-contingent and universal (Cazden, 1976; Tuman, 1987, pp. 130–5). Eventually, we will have to develop a model of text interpretation that includes both universal and socially contingent processes, perhaps along the lines begun by Schauber and Spolsky (1986) for literature.

In his note of response to Luke, de Castell and Luke, Olson holds out the possibility of variation and change (see Chapter 20, this volume). I want to agree with Olson on this possibility while acknowledging that alternative 'sources of authority in the language of the school' (the title of Olson's response) are hard to find. But no matter how pervasive the kinds of texts he describes, and the kind of discourse described by Baker and Freebody (and also by Lemke, 1982, 1986, in press, in high school science lessons), we have to keep looking for variation, and even help to create it (Cazden, 1987).

Consider one possible place to look. In his chapter on textbook adoption and censorship Arons (Chapter 16, this volume) discusses one unusual court case where the plaintiffs argued, in the end successfully, for the *inclusion* of a text, *Mississippi: Conflict and Change*, in the list of textbooks certified for purchase by public funds for state history courses. What was at stake in this case is exactly what Williams (Chapter 5, this volume, p. 59) describes as 'the recovery of discarded areas, or the redress of selective and reductive interpretation.' And the work of the interracial group of writers of the new Mississippi history, and of the coalition of parents, lay activists and clergy who sued for its adoption, also fits Williams's comment that 'much of the most accessible and influential work of the counter-hegemony is historical.'

Does *Mississippi: Conflict and Change* differ in style as well as content from its racist predecessor, *Your Mississippi*? And what has changed in classrooms where the new text is used? Is there change only in the set of meanings about Mississippi past and present that are taught as 'fact', or is there also a discernible shift to classroom discourse that can 'nurture within students a critical, imaginative, creative attitude about their condition in the world' (Tuman, 1987, p. 161)? Significant differences between texts may be accompanied by differences in discourse, either as cause or effect. But 'two parallel structures' (suggested by Olson in his response) are not the only possibility. Lewis and Simon (1986) provide a feminist critique of a university class discussion of Radway's feminist *Reading the Romance*.

Studying variation is important for two quite different reasons. First, it is important theoretically. We need to see variation and/or attempted change in a system in order to understand its workings more fully. Rich as *Reading the Romance* is, Radway reflects critically on its limitations:

> We [who conduct ethnographic studies of the media] have often either reified or ignored totally other cultural determinants beside the one specifically highlighted. Thus in my own analysis of a small group of romance readers there is no discussion whatsoever of the ways in which the practice of romance reading might vary with respect to race or class (n.d., p. 11).

Second, because in the present book we are concerned with a living institution of public schooling that requires restructuring but not abolition (as some of us would argue about other structures in society), we have a responsibility to try — with our analyses, not just our hopes — to help the actors in that system change their script.

Before closing, I want to call attention to one kind of text not mentioned in the other chapters that may become increasingly important in schools: computer programs and databases. I am personally knowledgeable only about computer use for the value-free skill of word processing, and so have to rely more on the views of others. Some experts express concerns about the new media (*Instrumentalities*, in Hymes's scheme) that are relevant for this book.

In the case of textbooks authors' names are provided, even if those names are usually not sufficient to provide clues to their referential perspective and point of view. The intent of the publishers, concerned as they are with obtaining as large a share as possible of a very diverse market, is to seem to have no perspective or to have an all-inclusive one. But however honest the intent, the attempt will fail. The selectivity that is entailed by the authors' referential perspective cannot be avoided; it can only be made harder to discover.

In comparison with textbooks, the perspective that controls the selection and presentation of information in computer programs and databases may be even more hidden. One critic of computer science, Joseph Weizenbaum, describes the problem in his book, *Computer Power and Human Reason*:

> Our society's growing reliance on computer systems that were initially intended to 'help' people make analyses and decisions, but which have long since both surpassed the understanding of their users and become indispensable to them, is a very serious development. It has two important consequences. First, decisions are made with the aid of, and sometimes entirely by, computers whose programs no one any longer knows explicitly or understands. Hence no one can know the criteria or the rules on which such decisions are based. Second, the system of rules and criteria that are embodied in such computer systems become immune to change, because, in the absence of a detailed understanding of the inner workings of a computer system, any substantial modification of it is likely to render the whole system inoperative and possibly unrestorable. Such computer systems can therefore only grow. And their growth and the increasing reliance placed on them is then accompanied by an increasing legiti-mation of their 'knowledge base'. (1976, pp. 236–7)

Weizenbaum continues:

> Not only have policy makers abdicated their decision-making responsi-bility to a technology they do not understand . . . but responsibility has altogether evaporated. . . . The enormous computer systems . . . in our culture have, in a very real sense, no authors. They thus do not admit of any questions of right or wrong, of justice, or of any theory with which one can agree or disagree. They provide no basis on which 'what the machine says' can be challenged. My father used to invoke the ultimate authority by saying to me 'It stands written!' But then I read what stood

written, imagine a human author, infer his values, and finally agree or disagree with him. Computer systems do not admit of exercises of imagination that may ultimately lead to authentic human judgment. (pp. 239–40)

Weizenbaum's is not the only expert voice expressing such concerns. More recently, Winograd and Flores (1986) write of possible dangers in the use of computerized decision-support systems — for example, in medical diagnosis. What I have called 'perspective' they call 'commitment':

> One immediate consequence of concealing commitment is an illusion of objectivity. . . . Computers neither consider nor generate facts. They manipulate symbolic representations that some person generated on the belief that they corresponded with facts. . . . The issue, though, is not just one of mistake or of conscious fabrication. It is in the nature of a 'fact' that it is an assertion by an invidivual in a context, based on a background of (implicit) pre-understanding. (p. 156)

In other words, to relate these concerns back to the topic of this book, while the perspectives (or 'commitments') underlying selection, organization and writing style are less publicly obvious in school textbooks than in other texts, they may be still more concealed, because of features of the medium, in computer programs.

But here, too, features of the programs themselves are only one part of a larger story. The concerns of people familiar with these features indicate an important site for research on interpretation. But we still have to look and see.

References

CAZDEN, C.B. (1976) 'If school is a performance, how do we change the script?' Review of A.V. Cicourel, *Language Use and School Performance. Contemporary Psychology*, 21, 125–6.

CAZDEN, C.B. (1987) *Classroom Discourse: The Language of Teaching and Learning.* Portsmouth, N.H.: Heinemann.

CAZDEN, C.B. (in press) 'The myth of autonomous text,' in TOPPING, D.M. (Ed.), *Third International Conference on Thinking.* Hillsdale, N.J.: Erlbaum.

HYMES, D. (1962) 'Models of the interaction of language and social life,' in GUMPERZ, J.J. and HYMES, D. (Eds), *Directions in Sociolinguistics: The Ethnography of Communication.* New York: Holt, Rinehart and Winston.

JAKOBSON, R. (1960) 'Concluding statement: Linguistics and poetics,' in SEBEOK, T.A. (Ed.), *Style in Language.* Cambridge, Mass.: MIT Press.

LEMKE, J.L. (1982) *Classroom and Communication of Science.* Final report to NSF/RISE, April. Ed 222 346.

LEMKE, J.L. (1986) *Using Language in Classrooms.* Waurn Ponds: Deakin University Press.

LEMKE, J.L. (in press) 'The language of classroom science,' in EMIHOVICH, C. (Ed.), *Locating Learning across the Curriculum.* Norwood, N.J.: Ablex.

LEWIS, M. and SIMON, R.I. (1986) 'A discourse not intended for her: Learning and teaching within patriarchy,' *Harvard Educational Review*, 56, 457–72.

LOEWEN, J.W. and SALLIS, C. (Eds) (1974) *Mississippi: Conflict and Change.* New York: Pantheon Books.

RADWAY, J.A. (1984) *Reading the Romance: Women, Patriarchy and Popular Literature*. Chapel Hill and London: University of North Carolina Press.

RADWAY, J.A. (in press) 'Reading', *Reading the Romance*. Introduction to the British edition.

RADWAY, J.A. (n.d.) *Where Is 'the Field'? Ethnography, Audiences and the Redesign of Research Practice*. Manuscript.

SCHAUBER, E. and SPOLSKY, E. (1986) *The Bounds of Interpretation: Linguistic Theory and Literary Text*. Stanford: Stanford University Press.

SCHOLES, R. (1982) *Semiotics and Interpretation*. New York and London: Yale University Press.

TUMAN, M.C. (1987) *A Preface to Literacy: An Inquiry into Pedagogy, Practice, and Progress*. Tuscaloosa and London: University of Alabama Press.

WEIZENBAUM, J. (1976) *Computer Power and Human Reason: From Judgment to Calculation*. San Francisco: W.H. Freeman.

WINOGRAD, T. and FLORES, F. (1986) *Understanding Computers and Cognition: A New Foundation for Design*. Norwood, N.J.: Ablex.

Author Index

Subject Index

sex education, 206
sexism
  in instructional materials, 34, 37
  stereotypes and, 37, 63
see also gender
sexual violence, 29n, 200
Shakespeare, W., 4, 6
'shared book experience', 84
Simon and Schuster, 18
Skinner, B.F., 79
Sleeping Beauty, 38–39
Smith, J., 6
Smith, O., 208
Smith v. Mobile, 209, 210, 211
Snow White, 39
Social and Environmental Studies
  (series), 172
social evolution, 223
Social Science Research Council
  (US), 284
Social Sciences and Humanities Research
  Council of Canada, 91n1
social studies, 104, 136t, 142, 143,
  173–175
  and Canadian history, 174–175
  creationism and evolutionism in, 164
  'division of labour' in, 66
  economics portrayed in, 66–69
  as 'facts', 143
  'indirect/inquiry' approach to, 134
  'market theory' portrayed in, 64–65
  pedagogy, 144
  textbooks, 51, 134–137, 146, 157,
  173–175
socialization, 39, 60, 131, 204, 212
sociolinguistics, 85, 284, 285
Sorority Girl, 25
Soviet Union, 46, 48–52
speech, 224, 226, 239, 246, 252, 283
  act, 72n3, 289, 245, 253
  context dependency of, 233, 234
  event, 141, 284
  interaction, 237, 238
  ritualized, 241, 242n2
speech departments, 111
spellers, 79, 113
spelling, 84, 130
Sprat, T., 248
Sprint (series), 18
SRA (series), 81
Starting Points in Language (series), 178
Starting Points in Mathematics
  (series), 178

Starting Points in Reading (series), 178
Steele, R., 248
Stepney Words, 188
stories, 192, 238
  affective meaning of, 101, 102
  form, 100, 103, 182n3, 281
  as linguistic units, 101
  listening and, 237
structuralism, 61–68, 72n2
students, 145t, 236, 255, 261
  criteria for textbooks, 135
  cultural differences, 87, 88
  as historians, 146
  linguistic differences, 87, 88
  as 'meaning makers', 197, 198
  nineteenth century, 114
  prior knowledge of, 272
  readings of textbooks, 68, 239,
  263–283
  rights, 205, 217n17
  social class of, 251, 258
  as textbook purchasers, 162
  use of textbooks, 135, 146, 150,
  263–283
  writing, 188–193, 195–201
Swift, J., 248
syllabic script, 234
syllabus, 66
syntax, 126, 224, 225, 226, 247
  of questions, 238

TAB book club, 18
Tahiti, 228
teachers, 165, 251
  authority over texts, 27–28, 86,
  238–239, 240–241, 242, 251, 257
  construction of, 28
  as consumers, 181–182
  education, 77, 127
  in-service training, 134, 138, 191
  as 'metadiscourser', 150
  publishers and, 27, 191
  rights, 205, 219n49
  'self-authorization', 273
  textbook selection, 54, 252
  work load, 27
teachers' guides, viii, 82–83, 86, 134,
  136, 138t, 163, 178, 252
teacher–student talk, 265–282
teen romances
  see romance novels
teletext, 89
television, 90, 155, 156, 178

Urban VIII, 241
unions, 110
  portrayal of, 34
university presses, 158
Up a Road Slowly, 21
Up in Seth's Room, 24
United States, 34, 79, 110, 167
  Civil Rights Movement, 36
  Constitution, 206
  culture, 6–9, 204–205
  'democratic socialist tradition' in, 47
  economic influence on
    Canada, 170–171
  First Amendment, 205, 208, 209,
    210, 211, 214–215, 216n2, 217n10,
    217n11, 217n12, 218n32, 219n49
  Fourteenth Amendment, 208
    'Gilded Age', 36
  immigrants, 6, 7, 11
  Judeo-Christian tradition in, 7,
    206–209
  literacy in, 77
  literary tradition, 32–15
  nineteenth century
    communities, 110–111
  Puritans, 6
  religious freedom in, 205–211
  Revolutionary War, 37, 48
  -Soviet relations, 46
  state textbook adoption
    statutes, 218n36, 286
  Supreme Court, 204, 206, 210, 211,
    212, 217n10, 218n32, 219n47,
    271n26
  Vietnam War, 38, 41, 49
Usherwood, V., 118
utterance, 193, 233–238, 252
  ritual, 234
  teacher, 274

Vai (Liberia), 234
Vivian Usherwood, 194n3
vocabulary, 62, 63, 172, 224, 227
Voltaire, 119, 122
'voluntarism', 69, 72n4
Vygotsky, L., 98, 196
  on higher psychological
    functions, 98

Wait for Marcy, 22
Waiting for Godot, 158
Washington, G., 6, 7
Weber, M., 54n

Webster, J., 12
Webster, N., 79
What Knowledge is of Most Worth?, vii
When the World's on Fire, 38
'whole language', 84
*Why Are They Lying to Our
  Children?,* 51
Wittgenstein, L., 127
women, 166, 201
  culture of, 4, 186, 187
  literacy and, 159
  middle class, 160
  portrayal of, 207
  in publishing, 161, 166, 167
  as readers, 110
  writers in literature anthologies, 4
  see also gender
Words by Heart, 38
'workbooks', 135, 136t, 137, 178, 251
Worker Writer movement (UK), 184
working-class
  culture, 4, 7, 184–187
  politics, 184, 185, 187
  writing, 184–187
workplace, 89, 99, 118–119
writing
  alphabetic, 233
  archival function of, 233, 241, 246,
    247
  autobiographical, 186, 190, 192, 193
  canonical forms of, 123–131
  collaborative, 118, 184
  communicative intent of, 124
  creative, 124, 125, 189, 196
  as cultural practice, 123–131
  discipline-specific, 143, 248–249
  expository, 149, 233, 236, 269
  as personal expression, 111
  pragmatic, 124, 125
  processes, 187
  register of, 236, 246, 247
  social functions of, 109–111,
    118–119, 124–125, 233–242
  students', 188–193, 195–201
  textbook, 111–120, 233–242, 263
  working class, 185
  see also essay
writing instruction, 83–84, 109–122,
    295–301
  'conferencing' in, 118
  as course of study, 116–117
  dictation in, 123, 129–130
  in European countries, 124–131
  handwriting in, 84, 131